WAFFEN-SS KNIGHTS AND THEIR BATTLES

Also by the Author
Dietrich's Warriors: The History of the 3. Kompanie 1st Panzergrenadier Regiment 1st SS Panzer Division Leibstandarte Adolf Hitler in World War II

Camouflage Uniforms of the German Wehrmacht: Manufacturers • Zeltbahnen • Headgear • Fallschirmjäger Smocks • Army Smocks • Padded Uniforms • Leibermuster • Tents • Non-Regulation Clothes • Post War *Werner Palinckx with Dr. J.F. Borsarello.* An indispensable guide for historians, collectors and military modelers, this book finally resolves the confusion surrounding many of the World War II Wehrmacht (both Army and Luftwaffe) patterns and garments and establishes a complete and concise system of identification and terminology. A comparative section with post-war fabrications is added as a tool for authentication. More than 10 different camouflage patterns are covered, including the super rare carbon overprint and Leibermuster. Authentic zeltbahns, helmet covers, caps, smocks, winter clothing, anti-gas outfits, body aprons, tents and more.
Size: 9"x12" • over 580 color & b/w photos • 288 pp. • ISBN: 0-7643-1623-0 • hard cover • $79.95

Afrikakorps:Tropical Uniforms, Insignia & Equipment of the German Soldier in World War II *Robert Kurtz.* The ultimate visual guide for collectors of World War II German tropical uniforms! Using actual items from top Afrikakorps collections – tunics, headgear, insignia, documents, field gear – as well as many World War II era photographs, this book covers it all in color. From mint issue items, to rare sun-bleached tunics and caps, the wide variety of tropical uniforms used by the Army, Luftwaffe, Kriegsmarine and Waffen-SS are illustrated in superb large format photography, including up-close detail.
Size: 9"x12" • over 730 color, b/w photographs • 300 pp. • ISBN: 0-7643-1920-5 • hard cover • $79.95

We are always interested in working with authors or collectors on wonderful book ideas. Contact us at **www.schifferbooks.com**, and page down to "For Authors – Submit a Book Proposal." Or call or write to us about your proposal.

...lk with your local bookseller. Their knowledge is one of the ...st tools in finding the correct book, and we all need to support ...m.

** Peter Schiffer and Team **
Designed & composed in America.
Printed in China.

WAFFEN-SS KNIGHTS AND THEIR BATTLES

The Waffen-SS Knight's Cross Holders Volume 1: 1939-1942

Peter Mooney

Schiffer Military History
Atglen, PA

Book design by Robert Biondi.

Library of Congress Catalog Number: 2008928022.

Printed in China.
ISBN: 978-0-7643-3088-9

Published by Schiffer Publishing Ltd.
4880 Lower Valley Road
Atglen, PA 19310
Phone: (610) 593-1777
FAX: (610) 593-2002
E-mail: Info@schifferbooks.com.
Visit our web site at: www.schifferbooks.com
Please write for a free catalog.
This book may be purchased from the publisher.
Please include $5.00 postage.
Try your bookstore first.

In Europe, Schiffer books are distributed by:
Bushwood Books
6 Marksbury Ave.
Kew Gardens, Surrey TW9 4JF
England
Phone: 44 (0)20 8392-8585
FAX: 44 (0)20 8392-9876
E-mail: info@bushwoodbooks.co.uk
www.bushwoodbooks.co.uk
Free postage in the UK. Europe: air mail at cost.
Try your bookstore first.

CONTENTS

Map List

SS-Obersturmführer Karl Nicolussi-Leck photographed in spring 1944 after the award of his own Knight's Cross (this award will be covered in detail in the relevant volume).

FOREWORD

In the first decades after the war, the public opinion was stamped by the victor powers. Nevertheless, not even in those days could it be denied that also on the German side brave soldiers and extraordinary achievements were to be found.

The latter, however, was traced back not to knightly values and virtues, but to Prussian obedience or similar influences which could also be explained by National-Socialist principles such as the '*Führerprinzip*' (leader principle). The opposite should mostly be the case, as the following example shows.

In March 1944, Kowel, an important railway junction with provision units and infirmaries was overrun and closed in. Supplied by air forces, the locked up ground troops were able to uphold the inner districts before I was ordered to open an aisle in the siege ring with the help of seventeen tanks in order to evacuate the nearly 2,000 wounded. In the evening, when we had eked out only half of the territory after having lost seven tanks, the *General Staff* declared the action to have failed and gave the order to abort the mission and move to defence positions in the northeast. Having heard radio messages from the surrounded troops, I was to conclude that already the next day the southern infirmary and the train station would be overrun. I knew that this would have resulted in the certain death of numerous wounded troops and medical staff – not by execution, but by cold, lack of food and lack of medical care. Therefore, I decided to refuse to obey this order and to continue the attack in the second half of the night instead. Also, expecting to be asked for confimation that I was following the halt order, I caused the Radio Operator to explain that the *Kompanie Commander* (myself), being urgently busy outside the tank, has so far been unable to confirm the halt order. After on direction of the tank leaders, whereby I concealed the halt command, in order to exclude their participation in the command denial, began the attack at four o'clock. After having lost another two tanks, I arrived in the surrounded area at dawn. Now we were locked in, too. However, with our help, the enemy was fought away from the southern infirmary and for seven days their raging attacks could be warded off until a powerful offensive broke the siege ring. Thus, after the bridges and rails had been repaired, the surrounded were able to leave the city.

So for disobeying orders I was awarded the Knight's Cross, i.e. I was given the Knighthood of the Iron Cross, even though I repeatedly disobeyed the order to abort the mission, which can be evidenced in written documents.

Actions lead by knightly ideals occurred far more often than the opposite, and after sixty years of peace this should be admitted in any publication.

Karl Nicolussi-Leck
Hochfrangart, 27 July 2006

INTRODUCTION

Bravery *n*. able to face and endure danger or pain
Courage *n*. readiness to face and capacity to endure danger
Valour *n*. courage, esp. in battle
Hero *n*. man admired for great or noble deeds
Heroism *n*. heroic conduct
Honour *n*. high respect, reputation; allegiance to what is right; thing conferred as distinction (esp. official award for bravery or achievement)
Loyalty *n*. faithful; true to allegiance; devoted to legitimate sovereign
— (Definitions taken from *The Oxford English Dictionary*)

The terms, *bravery*, *courage*, *valour* and *hero/heroism* are used extensively when describing the military actions of individuals throughout history. These words are not the sole possession of *any* particular country or even *any* particular period in history. These words are often used when describing military deeds that are considered above and beyond the normal call of duty when soldiers are executing the orders of their respective masters. I feel there are no better words to describe the military actions of the individuals that this work will focus on.

The words, *Honour* and *Loyalty* were carried upon the belt buckles of the individuals that this work will focus on. These are words that are used freely when describing various military formations throughout history. These terms are more easily used when the military campaign is going well or the military leader is seen to be performing well. These terms are found less often in situations where the odds are stacked against the campaign or leader in question. It takes a more robust individual or group of individuals to stand by the beliefs of these terms when they are certain that what they are fighting for is doomed to fail.

The following work will focus on a select group of individuals who number less than 500 people, but who, without any doubt, have left their mark upon the military history of our Human Race, that is, the Knight's Cross holders of the *Waffen-SS*. The purpose of this work is not just to list each person and their deeds, but to give an overall view of the situation from the start of the Second World War in September 1939 until its' end in May 1945 (viewed from the German perspective). Then within this overall global conflict, focus on the battles that they took part in. The main final focus will be upon the actions that resulted in the award of their country's highest award for bravery.

The award in question is that of the Knight's Cross to the Iron Cross and also the higher grades of this award including the Knight's Cross with Oakleaves, the Knight's Cross with Oakleaves and Swords and finally, the Knight's Cross with Oakleaves, Swords and Diamonds.

This first volume will cover from 1933 until 1942 and detail the awards of the first Knight's Crosses and the first handful of Knight's Crosses with Oakleaves, as no higher grades of this award were made by the end of 1942, to soldiers of the *Waffen-SS*.

This work has been compiled with the help of surviving holders of the awards listed above that include, Heinrich Springer, Johannes Goehler, Hans Siegel, Otto Kumm, Albert Frey, Remy Schrijnen, Ernst Barkmann, Karl-Heinz Boska, Karl Brommann, Karl Nicolussi-Leck, Paul Egger, Friederich Blond, Eberhard Heder, Karl-Heinz Euling, Siegfried Brosow, Heinrich Sonne, Harald Nugiseiks, Rudolf von Ribbentrop, Walter Girg, Karl-Heinz Lichte, Alois Schnaubelt, Heinz Jurgens, Oskar Schafer and Josef Rolleke. Unfortunately, since starting this project, some of these men have died. I am indebted to all of them, alive or dead and count myself as a lucky person to have met each of them or had correspondence with them.

In addition, the following *Waffen-SS* soldiers, who served alongside the holders of the Knight's Cross, also helped to compile this record, Erwin Bartmann, Robert Soulat, Jan Munk, Werner Volkner, Max Schmidt, Hans Maguscher, Adolf Schaafs and Helmut Hinze.

The photographs you will see in this volume have come from a variety of sources that include the Knight's Cross holders themselves and the *Kameraden* who served alongside them. Some of these are listed above, but equally, some of them have been handed to me at re-unions by *Kameraden* who did not provide their names, a few of these photographs were even posted to me by a *Kameraden* who did not provide any contact details at all! As they come from a variety of sources you will see that the quality of them does vary, please bear this in mind. One of the key sources was the extensive and impressive collection held by my long-time friend, Justin Horgan. Justin is a fellow enthusiast of the history of the *Waffen-SS* and someone who introduced me to my first *Waffen-SS* Knight's Cross holder. He has had the good fortune to have met, or had correspondence with, many of men that this project will focus on and I am indebted to him for his continued help and support. I would also like to thank Gary Woods for his permission to use the photograph of Sepp Dietrich dating from 1940. I have made every effort to obtain original photographic sources for this work.

Further help has come from Christoph Pan who liaised with Karl Nicolussi-Leck on my behalf and helped with the translation of the foreword. Also, Richard H. who took my map sketches and turned them into the maps you will see within these pages.

A special mention must go to John P. Moore who gave me his permission to use information contained within his *Führerliste Der Waffen-SS, Parts 1-4*. This excellent publication contains information on around 26,000 *Waffen-SS* officers and also the personal files of the Knight's Cross (and other high award) holders of the *Waffen-SS*. Without his permission, this work would not have been completed. I will take this opportunity to thank Mr. Moore and would advise anyone to invest in his publication as it provides a superb insight into the lives of the men who served in, and shaped, the reputation of the *Waffen-SS*.

I will finish this introduction by giving special mention to the most important people of all, that is my son Karl, daughter Alanna and of course, my wife Sandra. They provide continued and unyielding support to my hobby. They have joined me on some of my trips to the homes of the *Waffen-SS* Knight's Cross holders, have remained patient and understanding as I have slaved over notes for hours – after coming home from long days at work, thereby leaving little time to spend quality time with them. This work is dedicated to my children and my wife, without whose support this project would not have been completed.

The work on this project began ten years ago and the intervening years have seen the completion of my first book, *Dietrich's Warriors*. The work on this project continued throughout these ten years and I am pleased to see the end result. I hope you, the reader, will find this book interesting and informative.

Peter Mooney
Folkestone, Kent, June 2007

CHAPTER ONE

THE ORGANIZATION THAT BORE THE KNIGHTS

The Origins of the *Waffen-SS*

The origins of the *Waffen-SS* can be traced back to the *Stabswache* (Bodyguard). This unit was formed in March 1923 personally by Hitler to act as a personal protection squad, independent of the *S.A*. They were issued with black caps featuring the deaths head and a variation of the Nazi armband containing two black bands. In May 1923 their name was changed to *Stosstruppe Adolf Hitler* (Assault Troop Adolf Hitler). The *1. Kompanie* was commanded by *Lieutnant* Josef Berchtold, followed by *Captain* Julius Schreck. The first members of this unit included Josef 'Sepp' Dietrich.

The 9th of November 1923 saw the failed Putsch in Munich, which resulted in the crushing of Hitler's power at that stage. When Hitler got out of prison in 1925, he once again needed the help of a strong protection squad as he continued on his quest to be Germany's leader. The squad took the name of *Schutzstaffel* (Defence Squadron), which was officially abbreviated to '*SS*' on the 9th of November 1925. Entry into this organisation was restricted from the outset, creating an elite formation instantly. This was in contrast to the reconstructed *S.A*., which was a mass organisation. Julius Schreck was once again in command, but this would change a few times over the next few years until January 1929 when Heinrich Himmler was made the *Reichsführer-SS*. By 1926 there were 1000 men within the ranks of the *SS*, this had doubled by 1930. This growth of the *SS* lasted until the end of World War II. This unit based its' rank structure on the *S.A*., but due to growth, further ranks were added. An overview of the groups and ranks is below; the higher ranks would not appear until later during World War II:

Map 1 **Places of Origin: 1933 - 1942**

1	Leibstandarte Adolf Hitler	Berlin	March 1933
2	SS-Regiment Deutschland	Munich	October 1933
3	SS-Regiment Germania	Hamburg	August 1934
4	SS-Regiment Der Fuhrer	Vienna	March 1938
5	Heimwehr Danzig	Danzig City	January 1939
6	SS-Totenkopf Reiterstandarte	Berlin	September 1939
7	SS-Totenkopf Division	Dachau	September 1939
9	Polizei	Wandern	September 1939
9a	SS-Regiment Westland (Holland)	Vienna & Klagenfurt	September 1940
9b	SS-Rgt Nordland (Denmark & Norway)	Munich	September 1940
10	SS-Kampfgruppe Nord	Norway	February 1941
11	1. SS-Infantry-Brigade *(mot.)*	Cracow	April 1941
12	2. SS-Infantry-Brigade *(mot.)*	Cracow	May 1941
13	SS-Legion-Flandern *(Belgium)*	Radom	July 1941
14	SS-Legion-Niederlande *(Holland)*	Cracow	July 1941
15	SS-Freikorps-Denmark *(Denmark)*	Hamburg	July 1941
16	SS-Prinz Eugen *(Yugoslavia)*	Belgrade	April 1942

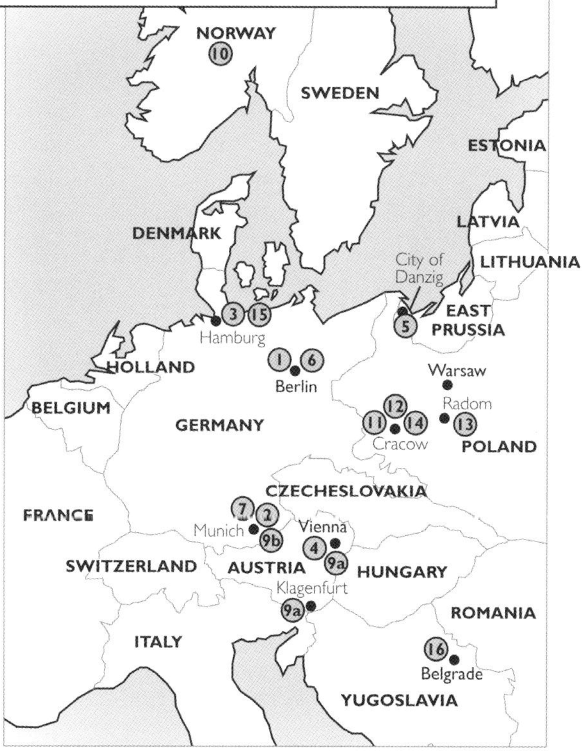

Rank Structure:

Schar (8 men)	*SS-Scharführer*
Trupp (3 *Scharen* – 30-40 men)	*SS-Truppführer*
Sturm (3 *Truppen* – up to 120 men)	*SS-Sturmführer*
Sturmbann (3 *Sturme* – up to 600 men)	*SS-Sturmbannführer*
Standarte (multi-*Sturmbanne* – up to 4000 men)	*SS-Standartenführer*
Brigade (multi-*Standarte*)	*SS-Brigadeführer*
Gruppe (multi-*Brigaden* – Division)	*SS-Gruppenführer*
Obergruppe (multi-*Gruppen* – Army Corps)	*SS-Obergruppenführer*
	SS-Oberstgruppenführer

The First Formation of the Future *Waffen-SS – LSSAH*

The next notable date for the *SS* was in 1933. Not long after Hitler assumed power as German Chancellor in January 1933, he once again focused on the need for a specific personal protection unit within the growing *SS*. He turned to one of his former protectors, that being Joseph 'Sepp' Dietrich, to command this new formation. The orders were for 117 hand picked men to arrive in Berlin on the 17th of March 1933. This new formation, under the command of one of Hitler's former protectors also initially took the name of the former protection squad, that of *Stabswache*, or to be precise *SS-Stabswache Berlin*. Within a few weeks they moved to their home for the rest of their time, the Lichterfelde Barracks in Berlin. Here they received a further name change to that of *SS-Sonderkommando Berlin*. This name stayed until the September 1933 Party Day when they received their new name, *Adolf Hitler Standarte*. They also were given new Cuff Titles and a banner bearing the Führer's name. A further name change occurred for this formation in April 1934 when they received the title *Leibstandarte SS Adolf Hitler*. Two months after this a small element of the *LSSAH* were involved in the Night of the Long Knives when the leadership of the *S.A.* was killed. After this day, the importance and power of the *SS* grew rapidly. The *LSSAH* continued to expand up to the outbreak of the Second World War. Prior to the outbreak of war, the *LSSAH* took part in the following actions, Saarland, Austria, Sudetenland and Czechoslovakia. By the outbreak of war it contained three *Battalions*. Within the ranks of these pre-war *Battalions* were people such as Kurt Meyer, Theodore Wisch, Martin Gross, Wilhelm Mohnke, Albert Frey and Hugo Kraas.

They were not the only unit to be formed and expanded during the pre-war period. Before examining the other formations in question and how they were expanded, it is worth examining how the rank structure was changed to cope with the growth between 1933 and 1934:

***SA* & *SS* Ranks**	***SA* & *SS* Ranks before 17/07/33:**	***SS* Ranks after 15/10/34: after 18/07/33:**
SS (SA)-Mann	*SS (SA)-Mann*	*SS-Schutze*
—	—	*SS-Obershutze*
—	*SS-Sturmmann*	*SS-Sturmmann*
—	*SS-Rottenführer*	*SS-Rottenführer*
SS-Scharführer	*SS-Scharführer*	*SS-Unterscharführer*
—	*SS-Oberscharführer*	*SS-Scharführer*
SS-Truppführer	*SS-Truppführer*	*SS-Oberscharführer*
—	*SS-Obertruppführer*	*SS-Hauptscharführer*
—	*SS-Haupttruppführer*	*SS-Sturmscharführer*
—	*SS-Sturmführer*	*SS-Untersturmführer*
—	*SS-Obersturmführer*	*SS-Obersturmführer*
SS-Sturmführer	*SS-Sturmhauptführer*	*SS-Hauptsturmführer*

The next major unit to be formed began life in October of 1933. It is worth pointing out that, unlike the *LAH*, who were trained in close proximity, the various *Battalions* and *Regiments* of what became *Das Reich* were not. As the formation of this overall unit is more complex, it is required to explain in more detail how this second formation came about.

The Second Formation of the Future *Waffen-SS – SS-Regiment Deutschland*

Like the *LAH*, this unit was formed when each *Allgemeine-SS Regiment* was ordered to send one member to the *Bavarian State Police's, Munich Regiment*. Enlisted ranks began a training course that lasted from October 1933 to June 1934. Whilst this was taking place the *Commanders* were put through a leader's course during March 1934 at the *SS* Cadet School in Tolz. On the 1st of July 1934 the unit received its' first official title, that of *Munich Political Readiness Unit*. This new formation had five *Kompanies* under the command of *SS-Obersturmbannführer* Ritter von Hengl, who was previously a member of the *Bavarian State Police*. Their first official public appearance was at the 1934 Party Day. On the 1st of October 1934 the *Munich Political Readiness Unit* was renamed as the, *I Battalion, SS-Regiment 1, SS-Verfugungstruppen*. They had also been recently moved to their new location in the Herzog-Wilhelm Barracks in Munich.

The second of the *Battalions* began life on the 6th of December 1933 in Prittlbach, near Dachau, northwest of Munich. The basis of this *Battalion* was Austrian *SS* and *SA* men who had voluntarily come to Germany to get away from strict controls imposed by the then Austrian Government. They were initially poorly led until the 1st of March 1934 when the *Bavarian State Police* took over and placed *SS-Sturmbannführer* Ranft in command. This formation had various names to start with that included, *Austrian Legion, Austrian Relief Organisation* and the *Schleissheim Relief Organisation*. All of the members of this formation were given German citizenship and then, in September 1934, they transferred to become the *II Battalion, SS Regiment 1*. At the start of April 1935, command of this *Battalion* was given to *SS-Sturmbannführer* Carl-Maria Demelhuber. His successor in September 1936 was *SS-Sturmbannführer* Wilhelm Bittrich.

The third element of this *Regiment* started life in May 1933 and contained volunteers from all over Germany. Their training area was in Ellwangen/Jagst, northeast of Stuttgart. They were under the command of *SS-Sturmbannführer* von Gottberg and at the start of October 1934 they were re-designated the *III Battalion, SS-Regiment 1*. In mid-1935 the command of this *Battalion* was given to *SS-Obersturmbannführer* Felix Steiner. This *Battalion* had a reputation for being athletic and competitive from the outset.

At the 1935 Party Day in September 1935 this entire formation was re-titled *SS-Regiment Deutschland,* or, *SS1 'D'*. Like their *LAH Kameraden* two years before, they also received a banner bearing this name. This day was the first time that the new *SS-VT* had appeared in public bearing weapons. In October 1935, von Hengl was replaced by *SS-Sturmbannführer* Georg Keppler as *Commander* of the *I Battalion*. On the 9th of November 1935 at the Feldherrenhalle monument *Deutschland* received their Cuff Titles bearing this name.

The first day of July 1936 was the next notable date for this *Regiment*. On this day Felix Steiner was promoted to *SS-Standartenführer* and given command of the entire *Regiment*. Also on this day, the *III Battalion* was re-designated the *IV Battalion* and a new *III Battalion* was raised. This new *Battalion* had *SS-Sturmbannführer* Kleinheisterkamp as its' *Commander* just prior to the outbreak of war. Pre-war actions of this *Regiment* included Austria, Sudetenland and Czechoslovakia. In March of 1938 Georg Keppler, Wilhelm Bittrich and other officers, together with the *II Battalion, SS-Regiment 1, Deutschland* were sent to Vienna and used to set up the *SS-Regiment 3, Der Führer*. However, before covering that *Regiment*, it is necessary to look at the next formation within the future *Waffen-SS*.

The Third Formation of the Future *Waffen-SS – SS-Regiment Germania*

This formation was started on the 25th August 1934 in Hamburg and had the initial title of the *Hamburg Political Readiness Unit*. Its' first *Commander* was *SS-Hauptsturmführer* Wilhelm Bittrich. This unit would become the *I Battalion, SS-Regiment 2, Germania*. *SS-Sturmbannführer* Wackerle took over command in April 1935. Also in April 1935, the *II Battalion* was raised under the command of *SS-Sturmbannführer* Walter Kruger and based in the area of Arolsen, east of Dortmund. At the same time the *III Battalion* was starting life in Niedersachsen, east of Bremen. The *Commander* of this unit was *SS-Sturmbannführer* Giebeler. On the 1st of October 1936 all three *Battalions* were placed under the overall command of *SS-Standartenführer* Demelhuber. The *Regimental* title of *Germania* was officially used for the first time at the Party Day in 1936. It was also here that they received their standards and Cuff Titles bearing that name. At that stage a few changes took place and the following people commanded the various *Battalions*, *I Battalion – SS-Obersturmbannführer* Wackerle, *II Battalion – SS-Obersturmbannführer* Walter Kruger, *III Battalion – SS-Obersturmbannführer* Giebeler. This *Regiment's* pre-war actions also included Austria, Sudetenland and Czechoslovakia. Pre-war members of this *Regiment* included Rudolf Lehmann, Fritz Langanke, Karl-Heinz Lichte, Wilhelm Weber, Heinrich Sonne and Eberhard Heder.

The Fourth Formation of the Future *Waffen-SS – SS-Regiment Der Führer*

Following closely after the successful action in Austria in March 1938, came the order to form a third *Regiment* for the *SS-VT*. That *Regiment* would be titled *SS-Regiment Der Führer,* later *SS-Regiment 3* and it would be commanded by *SS-Obersturmbannführer* Georg Keppler. The *I Battalion, Der Führer* was created by transferring the *II Battalion, Deutschland* to Vienna. If you recall, this *Battalion* consisted mainly of Austrian nationals. It was placed under the command of *SS-Sturmbannführer* Wilhelm Bittrich. The basis of the *II Battalion* came from *LSSAH* personnel and this unit was placed in Graz, under the command of *SS-Sturmbannführer* von Scholz. The *III Battalion*, under *SS-Sturmbannführer* Wackerle, was stationed in Klagenfurt and also had a foundation of *LSSAH* personnel. The rest of the personnel of these two *Battalions* came from Austrian volunteers. The *LSSAH* men transferred to *Der Führer* in 1938 included Albert Stendwedel. The *Regimental* title was officially given at the Party Day in 1938 and like its' three predecessors, they also received their named standard and Cuff Titles. Their pre-war actions included Sudetenland and Czechoslovakia.

These were the four main *SS* formations that existed prior to the outbreak of hostilities in September 1939. However, there is one further formation that was constructed from *SS* personnel prior to the war. It is worth noting their origins and purpose before covering the first campaign of World War II.

SS-Heimwehr Danzig

Alongside the *LSSAH, Deutschland, Germania* and *Der Führer SS-Regiments*, there were also the various elements of the *Totenkopfstandarten*. These later units were raised during the early 1930s and were responsible for running the concentration camps and performing other police and security-type duties. As the tension between Poland and Germany increased, it was felt that a protection unit was needed to cover the defense of the Free City of Danzig, within the borders of Poland. This city contained mainly German nationals and, until 1919, had been part of the German state of Prussia. That was changed as part of the Treaty of Versailles. The *SS-Heimwehr Danzig* was formed in the early part of 1939 with the sole purpose of providing protection for the inhabitants of Danzig. The basis of this unit came from the *III. Totenkopf Standarte 4*. To this was added around five hundred volunteers from the population of Danzig, bringing the numbers of this formation up to one-thousand-five-hundred men. The actual title of *SS-Heimwehr Danzig* was not officially used until mid-1939. On the 17th of August 1939, Cuff Titles bearing this name were issued along with the unit Colour Flags.

That covers all of the principle 'front-line' *SS* formations in place prior to the start of the conflict. So, what about the award and the first campaign?

CHAPTER TWO

A NEW AWARD, A NEW WAR, AND THE FIRST CAMPAIGN

The Knight's Cross to the Iron Cross

This work is not about the actual medal, its makers or how it was constructed. That is best left to medal experts or collectors, of which I am neither. As the work is about the individuals who were awarded this medal, I will only briefly cover the introduction of the award and then give an overview of the first campaign in Poland. This will lead straight onto the main focus, that of the battles and actions that resulted in the members of the *Waffen-SS* becoming holders of this award.

The Knight's Cross to the Iron Cross came into being on the 1st of September 1939 and is a true Third Reich period award. Its predecessors, the Second and First Class Iron Crosses first came into being in 1813, as did the higher grade Grand Cross to the Iron Cross. The first two grades can be considered fairly common with the following amounts being awarded from 1813 until 1945; Iron Cross Second Class (at least) 6.5 million, First Class Iron Cross (at least) 830,000. The Coveted Grand Cross to the Iron Cross has only been awarded to a total of twenty-one people in the period from 1813 to 1945. The Knight's Cross to the Iron Cross was intended to bridge the huge gap that existed between the First Class Iron Cross and the Grand Cross of the Iron Cross. In the region of 7,000 Knight's Crosses were awarded during the Second World War. The highest proportion went to members of the *Heer*. The total number of Knight's Crosses awarded to *Waffen-SS* personnel is disputed, but numbers at least 435. This work will detail each of these recipients.

As mentioned above, it was necessary for the potential recipient of the Knight's Cross to be a holder of the Second and First Class Iron Crosses. The award of this new medal was usually, but not always, made for a single act of bravery (although in the case of the *Luftwaffe*, was awarded for a number of confirmed 'kills'). The recommendation involved the potential recipient's *Commanding Officer* writing a report on specific actions and putting this forward for consideration. This recommendation was then forwarded to the Headquarters of the *Army High Command*. Adolf Hitler would personally read and approve each award. However, in the latter stages of the war, this was not always possible and there are instances where awards were authorized by high ranking officers.

Case White – The Campaign in Poland 1939: The Start of the Second World War

It is doubtful that all of the initiating powers in what became the Second World War were aware of what they were starting during those fateful September days of 1939 or the total final human, monetary and political cost to all involved. What is without doubt is that each one of us is still paying those high prices.

The act that started this conflict was Germany's invasion of Poland on the 1st of September 1939. Initially portrayed as an act of defence on the part of Germany, facts have since proved that this was not the case. Another fact is that France and then Britain declared war upon Germany on the 3rd of September for their invasion of Poland. This declaration started the process of a global conflict. Consistency of policy did not seem to concern France or Britain in those days, as on the 17th of September 1939, the U.S.S.R. also invaded Poland. This act on the part of the Russians did not bring about a similar declaration of war from France or Britain.

The German soldiers sent to conquest Poland did not have time to concern themselves with politics and went about their duty. The soldiers involved did contain elements of what would later become the *Waffen-SS*. These elements were the *Regiments, Leibstandarte Adolf Hitler, Deutschland, Germania,* and *SS-Heimwehr Danzig*. Although *SS-Regiment Der Führer* was mobilised, it spent the duration of the campaign in Poland on the Westwall defenses in anticipation of hostile actions from the western Allies. The elements of the *SS* that fought in Poland were placed within either Army Group North or Army Group South.

Poland: Army Group North

Army Group North consisted of the *3rd* and *4th Armies* under Feder von Bock and had the objective of moving from East Prussia and advancing south into Poland, also advancing through the northern Polish Corridor and onto Warsaw. They had to move to the rear area of the Vistula River, thereby making the right hand pincer.

The *SS-Regiment Deutschland* fought within the *3rd Army*. Their first seven days of action would see them fighting near the towns of Mlava and Chorzele, near the East Prussian border and then moving further south to Rozan near the Narew River. After a slight shift to the northeast they then continued south and by the end of week two *Deutschland* was fighting near Siedlce. The advance continued from that location during week three and went further southwest to Zelechow and Sobolew. However, on day sixteen, they were sent from these areas back to the northwest and the Modlin Forts complex. They would be involved in heavy fighting on the western part of this complex for the remainder of the campaign in Poland, the last of the fighting finished on the morning of the 29th of September 1939.

The first *Totenkopf* elements to see action during the Second World War were found in *SS-Heimwehr Danzig,* initially called *Gotze*. They also fought in the north, firstly in the city of Danzig, with a battle being fought around the main post office, which was over by day one. On the same day, south of Danzig, the first main battle for this unit was starting in Dirschau. This town is situated on the Vistula River and the objective was to take Dirschau and also the vital bridge over this river. This battle lasted from the 1st to the 5th of September. North of Danzig, on the coast, is an area known as Westerplatte. It was here that a simultaneous, second main battle was being fought by elements of *SS-Heimwehr Danzig* from the 1st to the 7th of September 1939. The third and final main battle for this unit was fought at Oxhofter Kampe, which is also on the coast, north of Zoppot. This is further north of Danzig and north west of Westerplatte. This battle lasted from the 8th to the 19th of September.

One part of the battle around Oxhofter Kampe involved fighting at Gdingen, slightly south of Oxhofter Kampe itself. One member of *SS-Heimwehr Danzig* at that time was Helmut Hinze. When I was discussing this fighting with him in 2007, he recalled that the fighting at Gdingen was the hardest for him during this campaign. He mentioned that the Polish soldiers in this area dressed in civilian clothes and lodged themselves in some of the houses. It took Helmut and his *Kameraden* three days to clear the handful of houses.

One of his other strongest memories is when, at only seventeen-and-a-half years old, his squad came across a town where the mayor and some other middle-aged men had been nailed by their hands and feet to a barn door. Their *Commander* gave the orders to take the men down, so they began to remove the nails. The *Commander* then told them to remove the barn doors first, with the people still attached. Then once the barn doors were on the ground, they could remove the nails and free the bodies for burial. Helmut recalled that it took them over an hour just to remove the doors, not helped by the extra weight of the bodies. Helmut went on to fight within the *SS-Totenkopf Division* and also the *Hitler Youth Division,* but this gruesome scene has stayed with him and left a very lasting and difficult memory.

When that battle at Oxhofter Kampe ended the *SS-Heimwehr Danzig's* campaign in Poland ended. It had cost them around seventy-five casualties, with thirty-eight of these being killed.

Poland: Army Group South

Army Group South consisted of the *8th* and *10th* Armies under Gerd von Rundstedt and was given the objective of moving to the large bend in the Vistula River, making up the left-hand pincer. The *LAH* fought within the *8th Army* and advanced eastwards from the German border on the first day of September and headed initially for Lodz. This city was surrendered on day eight, with this the *LAH* moved on towards the northern part of Warsaw, fighting close to the Polish capital for most of the second week. The third week of this first campaign would see the *LAH* fighting a little further north west, near the Bzura River. By week four they were fighting opposite Fort V, on the southern part of the Modlin Forts complex near the Narew River. It was whilst fighting there that the city of Warsaw surrendered. That brought the campaign to a close for the men of the *LAH* and what a costly campaign it had been, with casualties of 400 dead or wounded, out of around 3,700 men.

To follow the actions of the *SS-Regiment Germania,* we stay in the southern part of Poland. The *14th Army* were placed further to the east of the *10th Army* and had the objective of preventing the Poles from escaping eastwards behind the San River. The initial objective was the city of Cracow, *Germania* were to be found in this city on day seven of the campaign, after it had surrendered. Week two saw this *Regiment* being fragmented and elements were sent to various locations in this overall combat area. Javorov was one of the focal points along with the San River, their actions ending on the 19th of September 1939.

With that, we end the coverage of the front-line *SS* during this first campaign of what became the Second World War. Although specific numbers of casualties are listed for the *LAH,* none are listed for the other *SS* units. This first campaign allowed the *SS* to learn vital lessons that would serve them well in later campaigns. It also allowed the *SS* to expand, although staying small in number compared to their *Heer* counterparts, they did show early promise.

As discussed the overall plan had been to affect a pincer movement against the Poles, focused on the capital Warsaw. Army Group North moved eastwards and then southwards, with Army Group South moving eastwards and then north. Valuable assistance had been given by the *Luftwaffe,* who succeeded in destroying

Map 2 **Poland: 1st - 27th September 1939**

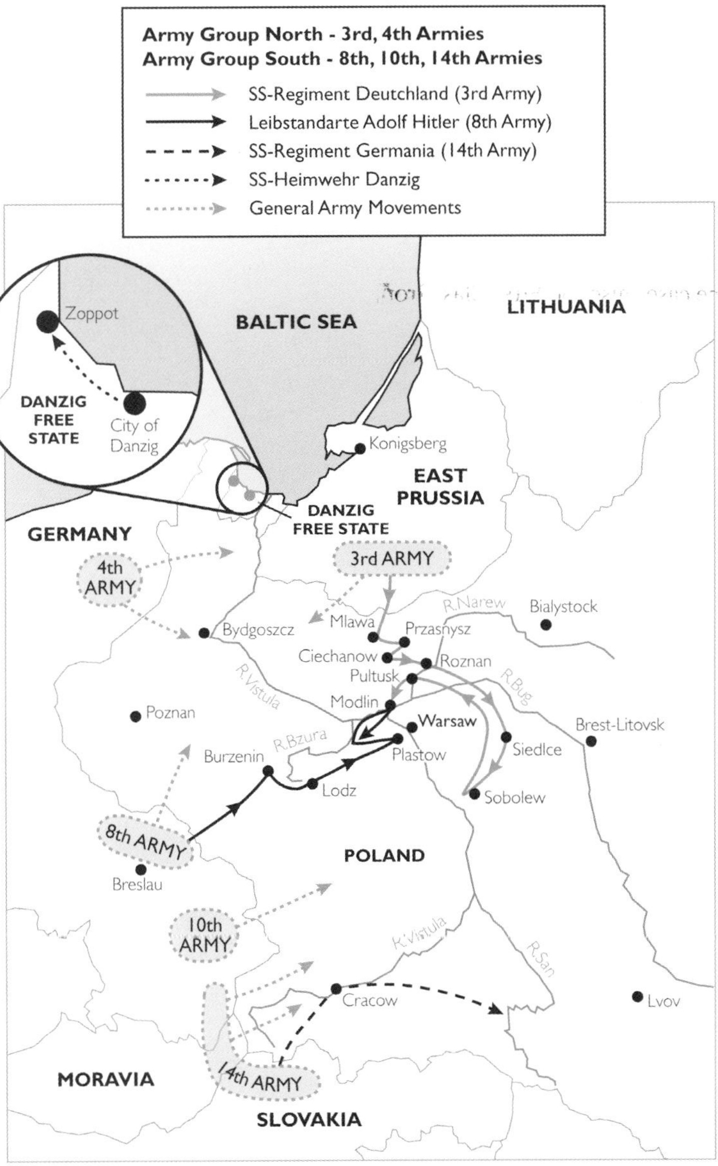

the majority of the Polish airforce on the ground. The Polish Corridor had been cut off by day three, by day seven the advance towards Warsaw was going exceptionally well, with the two jaws of the pincer being only sixty-five miles apart. Capitulation came on day twenty-seven and the last fighting finished on the 6th of October 1939.

In relation to the Knight's Cross, only high-ranking *Army* and *Luftwaffe* personnel were awarded this new medal for actions during the campaign in Poland. The *SS* would have to wait until the next campaign before some of their ranks became *Ritterkreuzträger,* or Knight's Cross Holders. However, what at least seventy of the future Knight's Cross holders of the future *Waffen-SS* did, was to earn the prerequisites for this award, that being the Second Class Iron Cross and in some cases also the First Class Iron Cross.

SS-Totenkopf-Reiterstandarte

Before concluding the overview of the campaign in Poland it is worth pointing out the forming of the first *SS* cavalry unit. This unit began life in mid-September 1939 and was formed from existing *SS* cavalry personnel. This new formation would eventually go on to become the *SS-Kavallerie Brigade* and later the *8th SS-Division 'Florian Geyer'*. However, for now their role would be to provide second line security, mopping up and other police-like duties, following behind the main body of advancing troops. Their first *Commander* was *SS-Standartenführer* Hermann Fegelein and at the outset his new unit numbered just under 500 men. They assisted the *German Army* in defeating the *Polish Army* during the remainder of this first campaign.

CHAPTER THREE

THE SS RECEIVE THEIR FIRST KNIGHT'S CROSSES

The First War-Time Expansion of the *Armed-SS*

In between the end of the battle for Poland and the start of the campaign in the west, the front-line *SS* underwent a period of expansion. The *LAH Regiment* had assault gun and artillery elements added to its' existing components. It was also renamed *Reinforced Leibstandarte Adolf Hitler.* The *Deutschland, Germania & Der Führer* Regiments were placed together in the *SS Verfugungstruppe Division*. Even before the campaign in Poland had finished, the third and fourth main units within the future *Waffen-SS* began their life.

The *SS Totenkopf & Polizei Divisions*

The forming of the *Totenkopf Division* started on the 18th September 1939. It was complete by the 16th of October, with official activation coming on the 27th of October. This new *Division* contained three infantry *Regiments* along with *Panzerjaeger, Artillery, Signals, Pioneer* and *Reconnaissance Battalions*. It was placed under the control of *SS-Gruppenführer* Theodore Eicke, who formed the *Division* in Dachau.

Also on the 18th of September, the fourth main unit within the future *Waffen-SS* began its' life. Elements of the normal police units were gathered together and formed into the *Polizei-Division*, in the area of Wandern. This unit would not officially receive the '*SS*' prefix until later in the war. In addition, the uniforms they wore resembled *Army* uniforms with police style insignia. One noted difference was the use of the *SS* style sleeve eagle, as opposed to the *Army* style eagle on the tunic breast. The *Polizei-Division* was placed under the control of *Generalleutnant* Karl Pfeffer-Wildenbruch; It also contained three *Regiments*.

Extensive training was conducted by all of the above *SS* units during the latter stages of 1939 and up to May 1940. The battle tested units focused on learning from the experiences gained in Poland, whereas the two new units focused on developing into *Divisional* formations within the short time frames allotted.

Case Yellow – The Campaign in the West 1940

The outline of the forthcoming plan was as follows: A diversionary attack would take place in the Low Countries, designed to draw the *Allies* to this region. When the *Allies* moved forwards against this attack, the main thrust would be launched. The position of this main thrust would be in the Ardennes region. This area was considered to be 'tank-proof' and it was not protected by the Maginot Line.

The German soldiers assembled for this campaign were divided into three Army Groups; Army Group B, under von Bock, contained the *18th Army* and the *6th Army*. They were in the north, opposite Holland and Belgium, and were given the objective of advancing quickly through the Low Countries, helping to draw the Allies to that region. Army Group A, under von Rundstedt, had the *4th Army, 12th Army* and the *16th Army*. They were in the middle, opposite the Ardennes region in southern Belgium and Luxembourg. They were the main thrust and had the objective of crossing the Meuse River at Sedan and advancing onto the coast, hopefully cutting off the bulk of the enemy in the Low Countires. Army Group C, under von Leeb, contained the *1st Army* and the *7th Army* and where in the south facing the formidable Maginot Line. Their objective was to attack this defensive line when the time was right.

The four principle *SS* units were contained within either Army Group B or Army Group A; There will therefore be no focus upon Army Group C within the framework of this book.

Army Group B and the *LAH*

The *Leibstandarte* were part of Army Group B and were attached to the *18th Army*. They were subordinated to the *227th Division*. Their advance began at 0600 on the 10th of May 1940. By the end of day one they had reached the Arnhem/Oosterbeek area, within the borders of Holland. They then advanced to the southwest towards Getruidenburg and then northwards towards Rotterdam and the Hague. They successfully achieved their objectives in this city by the 15th of May. After a short rest period they advanced through Belgium in a wide arc towards the southeast. After skirting the Dutch/German border near Aachen, they moved through central Belgium and on towards the Belgian/French border, passing through Dinant on the way. They crossed into France near Avesnes and then advanced to the northwest. By the 24th of May they had moved further to the northwest to assist in the battle developing around Dunkirk.

It was on this day that the order arrived to halt the advance, coming directly from Hitler himself. Max Schmidt, who was serving in the *LAH's 3. Kompanie* at that time, recalled his own and his *Kameraden's* astonishment at this order. They believed that the defeat of the enemy was close at hand. He also recalled that the briefing they received mentioned that Hitler considered the English to be 'Blood Brothers' and he preferred not to fight them. Max Schmidt and his *3. Kompanie Kameraden* were keen to finish the task they had started and it looks as though Sepp Dietrich agreed with them. He ignored Hitler's command and took it upon himself to order elements of the *LAH* across the Canal de l'Aa to capture the nearby Wattenberg heights. This was successfully achieved the same day (the actual attack resulted in the first award of the Knight's Cross and will be covered at the end of the chapter). The battle for the area around Dunkirk continued with vigour, and by the 4th of June 1940 the final resistance in this area ceased. The battle for France was not over and the troops had further work to do.

After the fall of Dunkirk the advance continued directly south. Within a week the Marne River had been reached and the Allier River was crossed less than a week after that. By the 20th of June, Clermont Ferrand had fallen to the men of the *LAH,* this amounted to an advance of over 350 miles in less than three weeks. They advanced to the southeast after that and reached St. Etienne on the 24th of June, the same day that the French signed the armistice. That ended the fighting in the west for the *LAH* and the rest of the *German Army.*

Army Group B and the *SS V Division*

In the early part of October 1939, the *Regiments Deutschland, Germania and Der Führer* were sent to Dresden, where they started the formation of the *SS V Division*, under the control of *SS-Gruppenführer* Paul Hausser. They began an intensive period of training during the remainder of 1939. They were moved further west to Munster in January 1940. The 10th of May 1940 would see this *Division* in Wesel, situated on the Dutch/German border.

One of the first actions and first successes for this overall *Division* and its' various components came in the form of the *SS V Division's, Reconnaissance Battalion.* They were initially placed with the *Heer's, 254th Infantry Division.* They started from Kranenberg, near the Dutch/German border, on the 10th of May 1940. The bulk of the *SS V Division* remained in Wesel and would not participate until day three – the 12th of May. The *Reconnaissance Battalion* divided into five attack groups and preceeded to attack the key bridges over the numerous rivers in the northeast section of Holland. Two of these attack groups found their objectives, the Nijmegen and Neerbosch bridges, destroyed and they returned to the *Battalion* the same day. Another attack group also found their Malden Bridge destroyed, but they moved southeast and joined the fourth group and assisted in the attack upon the Heumann Bridge. This attack was successfully completed later the same day. *Attack Group 2*, under *SS-Untersturmführer* Vogt, found their objective, the Hatert Bridge, damaged. Vogt led four men across this destroyed bridge, followed soon after by other groups. They attacked and overran the various bunkers near the bridge and established a small bridgehead (Knight's Cross action covered at the end of the chapter). The *Battalion* was not aware of his success at this point and they carried on pressing westwards through the Heumann Bridge as far as Niederasselt. The Grave Bridge was also destroyed, so they held their positions until the following day and then returned to the main *Division*.

The newest *Regiment* to the *SS V Division* was the *SS-Regiment 'Der Führer'* and, like the *Reconnaissance Battalion*, was sent into action on the first day, the 10th of May. They were attached to the *Heer's, 207th Infantry Division* and their first action went as follows:

They were under command of *SS-Oberführer* Keppler and they attacked across the Dutch border east of Arnhem with the objective of Issel River. They also found their bridges destroyed, but elements fighting near Doesburg discovered an undamaged bridge at Westervoort. An assault was started with the help of *Army* units, but the Dutch defenders blew the bridge. It was at this point that Keppler arrived and ordered the artillery and anti-tank guns to fire across the river and cover an attack by *SS-Oberscharfuher* Kepplinger of the *11. Kompanie, III Battalion*. This assault was made under heavy enemy fire from the nearby fort. *SS-Oberscharfuher* Kepplinger pushed on and over the damaged bridge with other men, he was the first man across. He and the men he led successfully captured the fort around midday (Knight's Cross action covered at the end of the chapter). This allowed the advance to continue and Wageningen was reached the same day. The next objective was known as the Grebbe Line and once again, *SS-Oberführer* Keppler would come to prominence.

On the 11th of May 1940, the assault on the Grebbe Line began. Wageningen was taken during the morning and the slow advance continued, by that evening the lead elements were within 600 metres of this main Dutch defensive position. Keppler once again used all available heavy guns to fire upon the Dutch, who in turn poured heavy fire on the positions of Keppler and his men. This Dutch weapons continued to fire upon Keppler and his men throughout the night aided by flares.

The 12th of May would see the addition of further heavy weapons and these joined the fight to attack the Grebbe Line. *SS-Regiment 'Der Führer'* moved forwards under the cover of artillery fire from *Heer* units. They successfully breeched the line and pushed forwards to take the many bunkers one by one, all the time under the concentrated enemy weapons fire. By the evening of this day the peak of the Grebbe Mountain was reached. The Dutch tried to re-take this vital high ground, but they failed. Some of the German units did get cut off for a time, but were later relieved. The Dutch were determined to re-take this area and they continued to rain everything they had upon the positions of *SS-Oberführer* Keppler and his men. This continued throughout the 12th and 13th of May. Elements of *Der Führer* were relieved on the 13th and the advance continued to Rhenen. The following day, the 14th of May, would see the official Dutch surrender. *SS-Oberführer* Keppler's determination successfully breeched the Grebbe Line (Knight's Cross action covered at the end of the chapter), but their actions did not end there. They continued their advance to the Dutch coast and reached Utrect, Amsterdam, Haarlem, Ijmuiden and Zandvoort two days later. They re-joined the *SS V Division* on the 17th of May 1940. They had a bloody and intensive start to their campaign in the west and recognition of this would come later, but for now, onto the actions of the main *SS V Division*.

The main *SS V Division*, as part of the *18th Army*, left the Wessel area in three main march groups. *SS-Regiment Deutschland* under the control of *SS-Standartenführer* Steiner (MGA), *SS-Regiment Germania* under the control of *SS-Standartenführer* Demelhuber (MGB) and then the rear echelon units (MGC). This was on the 11th of May 1940, and their initial advance was through the Reichswald Forest at Krenenburg and Gennep. The *Heer's, 9th Panzer Division* was also in this area and the roads could not cope with two *Divisions* trying to advance. Therefore, the actual advance did not make any headway until the following day. *SS-Regiment Deutschland* were the first to move forwards and they went through the southern part of Nijmegen and onto S'Hertogenbosch, their main target being Antwerp. At S'Hertogenbosch they got involved in a heavy firefight. This forced a detour southwest towards Lieshout. Here they met up with *SS-Regiment Germania,* who had moved through Uden. With *Deutschland* in the lead, the advance continued through St. Oedenrode, Best and Oirschot. This advance continued further southwest to Diessen, Hilvarenbeek and then northwest to Breda. *Deutschland* got as far as Goirle, south of Tilburg by the end of the 12th of May. The *Reconnaissance Battalion* where further south near Eindhoven, Son and Vessern, with *Germania* moving towards Antwerp itself.

The Dutch surrender was announced on the 14th of May 1940 and at this stage they had got as far as Ossendrecht. The main focus of the attack was the target of Antwerp, but this was stopped due to the surrender. The next objective was the Walcheren & Beveland Islands, which were not included in the main Dutch surrender. There was a mixed force of remaining Dutch, but mainly French troops positioned there. *SS-Regiment Deutschland* were given the task of taking this area. This advance began on the 15th of May 1940. The advance took them along the main road and also the northern edge into Beveland Island and by the evening the Beveland Canal was reached. There was no time to rest and the advance continued the following day. *SS-Sturmbannführer* Witt reached the south Beveland capital Goes in the afternoon and he and his *III Battalion* carried on up to the causeway that faced Walcheren Island. The enemy resistance grew stiffer as the advance continued, but despite this a small bridgehead was formed onto Walcheren on the 17th. This was expanded during the day, and by the end of that day, Middleburg and Vlissingen south are in the hands of *Deutschland*. The attack onto Walcheren, across the causeway, was made against strong enemy concrete emplacements. *SS-Standartenführer* Steiner led his men well and the successful conclusion of this part of the campaign was made the same day (Knight's Cross action covered at the end of the chapter).

With this fight over, the next objective lay ahead. *Deutschland* moved back through Breda, Tilburg and Eindhoven then turned south to Hasselt, where all of the *Divisional* elements were positioned. On the 19th of May, the advance westwards continued and moves were made to the southwest at Huy, on towards Dinant and south to Givet and then southeast to Hirson on the 20th of May 1940.

Further west, Erwin Rommel was having success in his advances towards the coast of France. The *SS V Division* was sent towards that area to help exploit Rommel's breakthrough. During the 21st of May, the towns of la Copelle, Guise, Bohain, Elincourt and Aubencheul witnessed their advance. *Der Führer* were in the lead and by the following day they had reached Aire, north west of Bethune. This *Regiment* dealt with a French tank attack on the 23rd, whilst also consolidating their control of this immediate area. They occupied Lilles and St. Hilaire and pushed onto the Lys Canal, between Merville and Estaires during the remainder of this day and the next. Further enemy tank attacks were launched against their positions.

On the 25th of May, Adolf Hitler issued his much debated halt order, which in fact gave the *Allies* vital breathing space and a chance to evacuate more troops. It is of interest to note that on this day, the three principle formations of the fighting *SS* were within thirty miles of each other on what was known as the Canal Line by the *Allies*. This was the main defensive line around Dunkirk. The *LAH* were near Watten, where Dietrich disobeyed the Führer Order – covered previously. *SS-Regiment Deutschland* were around six or seven miles south at St. Omer, attached to the *6th Panzer Division* for part of the day. The remainder of the *SS V Division* was southeast of St. Omer down as far as Aire. The *SS Totenkopf Division* were further southeast between Aire and Bethune. *Totenkopf's* actions will be covered later, but for now, back to the *SS V Division*.

The above mentioned halt order permitted the German troops to remain on the defensive only and they had to wait for two whole days to see what developed. Finally on the 27th of May 1940 the pursuit was allowed to continue. The remaining *Allied* troops and their *Commanders* were aware of the gravity of the rapidly changing situation and they were determined to provide as much resistance as possible. They had their backs to the sea and in front of them lay the massed ranks of the German armed forces. In the air, on the ground and out to sea, the *Allies* were being pounded and driven into an ever constricting area. They even ordered attacks to be launched to help buy a little time. At this stage, neither the *Allies* nor the Germans knew that this resistance around Dunkirk would be over in one weeks' time. Before that situation arrived, the Germans had further work to do and they were glad that the orders for the 27th allowed them to continue with their task.

The direction of this new attack would be eastwards towards the Belgian border. The idea was to close the noose and tighten the grip upon the area containing the enemy. The *SS V Division* shifted further south and closer to the *Totenkopf Division,* the only thing between these two *Divisions* was the *3rd Panzer Division*. The *SS V Division's* first hurdle was the Forest of Nieppe and an intensive battle raged there for two days.

Within the realms of this book, the focus at this stage will be upon the *SS-Regiment Deutschland,* fighting with the *3rd Panzer Division* further east. More specifically, *Combat Group Witt*, under the command of *SS-Sturmbannführer* Fritz Witt, who was the *Commander* of the *Deutschland Regiment's, I Battalion*. This overall *Regiment* moved on the right flank of the *3rd Panzer Division* as it started its' attack upon Merville, southeast of the Forest of Nieppe. The final objective was to the northeast at Bailleul. Crossings were made across the Lys Canal between Merville and Estaires in the evening of the 27th of May. Fritz Witt's combat group was only able to cross their bridge on foot, without support from heavier weapons. It was just after they had made this crossing that an *Allied* tank attack landed on top of them. It was during this enemy tank attack that *SS-Sturmbannführer* Witt organized and led his infantry against this dangerous armoured threat. After intensive, close range fighting, they succeeded in driving off this attack and the *Allied* tanks retreated back northwards. This position was later reinforced with anti-tank guns (This action formed part of Witt's Knight's Cross recommendation and will be covered in full at the end of this chapter).

Further enemy tank attacks occurred the following day as the advance continued. The *SS-Regiment Deutschland* stayed with the *3rd Panzer Division* until the 29th of May, when they then moved back to the *SS V Division*. Merville had been cleared by then and the *3rd Panzer Division* continued their moves north.

Over the next couple of days, the *SS V Division's* three *Regiments* had a quieter time as they moved into new positions further north, around Cassel and the Steenvoorde area, close to the Belgian border.

In the first week of June 1940 the *SS V Division* moved further southeast as they joined the pursuit of the remaining *Allied* soldiers in France. They moved down to the Somme River, near Peronne. During the second week, they continued their advance in a southeasterly direction through St. Quentin, Soissons and around the right hand side of Paris, through Romilly. They reached Romilly on the 14th of June 1940, the same day that the French capital surrendered. Their advance up to this point was not without incident and many firefights marked their route. With the surrender of Paris, it was becoming evident that the end of the campaign was on the horizon.

The advance southeast had to continue and the *SS V Division* continued through Troyes and beyond. Not only were they clearing the enemy from this area, but in addition, they were preventing the enemy from escaping as the enemy tried to move from the northeast to the south. A particularly heavy engagement took place around the 16th and 17th of June 1940, southeast of Troyes, in an area near Arthonnay and Channes. Fritz Witt's *I Battalion*, within the *SS-Regiment Deutschland,* were involved in blocking the escape route of large enemy formations (This action and its' subsequent success formed the second half of Fritz Witt's Knight's Cross recommendation and will be covered at the end of the chapter). In the afternoon of the 17th of June, Witt and the rest of the *Regiment* reached their objective of Chattilion.

After this pause, the southwardly advance carried on towards Autun and Le Creusot, reached on the 20th of June. From there, their orders took them northwest towards the French Atlantic coast. Three days later, they were in Orleans, they then carried on further southwest to Ambroise. From there, south to Poitiers and by the time of the French surrender on the 25th of June 1940, they were in Augouleme. Once the ceasefire was concluded, the *SS V Division* moved further southwest to Bordeaux, with lead elements crossing the French/Spanish border and also reaching Bayonne and Biarritz on the coast. The end of June brought a well earned rest for the *SS V Division*. This concludes the intensive and varied actions of this *Division* in the western campaign during 1940.

Army Group A and the *SS Totenkopf Division*

In March 1940, *Totenkopf* were ordered to Korbach, west of Kassel, and this was followed by a move to Cologne in early May. During the first seven days of the campaign, from the 10th to the 17th, this *Division* was held in reserve. This was changed on the 17th of May 1940, when they were ordered to take an active part and thus help Army Group A's further advances westwards. They moved west from Cologne on the 17th and by the early hours of the following day, they had crossed into enemy territory. Their first location was Sittard in Holland, west of Cologne. Over the next two days they advanced over the Belgian border and also the French border, moving in a southwesterly direction from Maastricht. They were placed under the operational control of the *7th Panzer Division*, commanded by Erwin Rommel. They assisted in the attacks against the enemy who were mounting an attack from the direction of Arras, *Totenkopf* were south of Arras. During the western offensive, this enemy action was considered the biggest threat to the entire campaign. The attack itself was launched by the enemy on the 21st of May 1940 and involved British and French tanks. Over the next two days, elements of *Totenkopf* did participate in the successful efforts to stop, and then defeat this enemy armoured thrust.

SS-Mann Paul Tanzer, serving then in the *II Battalion, Regiment 1,* was present when this enemy tank attack hit the men of *Totenkopf*. He recalled that they were moving so fast as part of the *Blitzkreig* fighting, that their *Aufklarungs* unit did not have the chance to do their defined role, nor did the men of *Totenkopf* have any anti-tank weapons. They were very surprised and concerned when the British tanks arrived in their area and started firing at them. Paul and his *Kameraden* had to withdraw and wait for the *Heer Stugs* to come up to their positions and engage these enemy tanks and remove this critical threat.

Once this action was over, the advance continued and *Totenkopf* moved from an area southwest of Arras towards the la Bassee Canal and Bethune, which was to the northwest. This was followed by a move to an area between Lille and Armentieres, towards the northeast. These moves were made between the 24th and the 27th of May. By the 29th they were northwest of Armentieres, this was in a direct line towards Dunkirk. It was also on this day that *Totenkopf* linked with elements of the German forces pushing from the east, thereby closing the ring around Dunkirk. *Totenkopf* temporarily halted offensive actions.

Returning briefly to the recollections of *SS-Mann* Paul Tanzer, he recalled the difficult fighting at La Bassee Canal. The men of the *II Battalion* suffered the most casualties from *Totenkopf* at that time, mainly due to their inexperience and also their young age – most of them aged around eighteen.

At the start of June 1940, they were given orders that moved them to the Boulogne area and gave them responsibility for the area stretching from Gravelines to the north down to Etaples in the south. No rest was allowed and the emphasis was placed upon repair of the vehicles, receiving replacements and teaching them as much as possible. On the 10th of June the *Totenkopf Division* was ordered to the southeast towards Peronne; This was to assist in the second phase of the conquest of France. Their advance was rapid and by the 16th of June they had crossed the Seine River at Nogent, southeast of Paris. Two days later they were in Nevers, over 110 miles southwest of Nogent. It was around this time that the end of this campaign became apparent, with *Marshall* Petain asking for surrender talks with the Germans. On the 19th of June they fought a hard battle in l'Arbresle, northwest of Lyon. The French surrender was signed the following day – the 20th of June 1940, the official end came on the 25th of June.

What was the cost to the *Totenkopf Division* in their first campaign? They lost a total of 1,234 dead and wounded men.

When the campaign concluded, they moved south of Bordeaux and conducted extensive training exercises during the autumn, winter and spring of 1940 and 1941. This *Division* would not participate in the next campaign in Greece, so their training continued until mid-1941.

Army Group A and the *Polizei Division*

This *Division* was moved to an area close to Freiburg at the start of February 1940. Here they helped to provide security for the southwestern corner of Germany, close to the Rhine River. They continued extensive training and, although officially they were not engaged in combat, they managed to inflict losses to the enemy stationed on the opposite side of the Rhine! In mid-April they were moved to an area south of Stuttgart and placed in reserve. With the start of the campaign in the west, they were on the move once again. This time, the *Division* moved to the northwest close to the border with Luxembourg during the latter part of May 1940. These moves continued through Luxembourg and brought them to the Ardennes Canal by the 4th of June 1940. The first taste of battle was not far away, and on the 9th of June they attacked across the canal, near Sedan. After engaging the enemy in battle, they continued westwards for the next few days. The advance then moved southwards. Further fighting ensued in Les Islettes, west of Verdun in mid-June. At the time of the official armistice on the 24th of June 1940 the *Polizei Division* were in Langres. Their brief, but bloody, introduction to battle had cost this unit over 130 dead and at least a further 520 wounded. To think that some history books state that this unit had only limited involvement in the western campaign!

When the fighting stopped, the *Division* was placed as part of the occupation forces in France. They moved to an area close to Paris in August 1940 and remained there until June 1941. Therefore, they did not take part in the campaign in the Balkans in early 1941. During this time, control of the *Division* was taken over by *Generalleutnant* Artur Mulverstedt.

The First Knight's Cross Recipients of the *SS*

Joseph 'Sepp' Dietrich

Date of birth: 28.05.1892
SS Number: 1 177
Sepp Dietrich was born in Hawangen, Bavaria. His military experiences began before the outbreak of the First World War, when he served briefly with the *Bavarian Army*. His experiences continued with the outbreak of the First World War in 1914. He joined the *6th Bavarian Reserve Artillery Regiment* and stayed with the artillery until late 1916. He followed this by a posting to the *Storm Troops* that lasted until early 1918. It was whilst with the *Storm Troops* that Dietrich was awarded the Second Class Iron Cross on the 14th of November 1917. His final posting was a move to one of Germany's tank units, the *Bavarian Storm Tank Detachment 13*. He saw action with this tank unit in various engagements up to the end of the war in November 1918. He ended the First World War with the rank of *Unteroffizier* and holder of the First and Second Class Iron Crosses (when the First Class Iron Cross was awarded is not listed).

He went to Bavaria after the war and joined the *Landspolizei*. He was also a member of the *Freikorps Oberland* and took part in the battles in Upper Silesia, against the Poles in 1921, winning both the Second and First Class of the Silesian Eagle award. Various sources state that Dietrich took part in the Putsch of 1923 and he was awarded the Blood Order by Hitler later on, actual date of the award was the 9th of November 1933 and Dietrich became the 10th person to receive this award. In addition, various sources also state that he was a member of the *Stosstruppe Adolf Hitler* in 1923. He stayed with the *Landspolizei* until 1927 and then on the 5th of May 1928 joined the *Schutzstaffel*, or *SS*. He was quickly promoted to *SS-Sturmführer (SS-Untersturmführer)* on the 1st of June 1928 and then on the 1st of August he was given command of the *Sturmbann I, Munich* and promoted to *SS-Sturmbannführer*. This was followed by a promotion to *SS-Standartenführer* in November 1929 and also command of the *SS* in the whole of Bavaria. The promotions did not stop there and on the 11th of July 1930 he would find himself as *Commander* of the *SS Group South* and holding the rank of *SS-Oberführer*.

SS-Obergruppenführer Sepp Dietrich (left) photographed in the autumn of 1940 in France, after his award of the Knight's Cross to the Iron Cross.

Dietrich was promoted further still, prior to Hitler becoming Chancellor. On the 18th of December 1931 he was raised to the rank of *SS-Gruppenführer.* As can be seen from these regular promotions, Dietrich was obviously doing something right and in addition to being close to Hitler, he must also have impressed the new head of the *SS*, Heinrich Himmler.

The 17th of March 1933 would see an important change for Sepp Dietrich. Hitler decided that he once again wanted a specific and smaller bodyguard unit and he ordered the formation of that unit on this day. He also selected Dietrich as its' *Commander* and from that date it is hard to mention Dietrich without mentioning the *LAH*. The details of the early years of that unit are contained in the preceding pages and there is no need to repeat them here. The next notable date for Dietrich was the 'Night of the Long Knives' when the leadership of the ever-growing *S.A.* was killed. Dietrich himself was present in Munich during this period. His loyalty was tested on this occasion and he stood by his oath to the Führer. As a measure of thanks to Dietrich, Hitler promoted him to *SS-Obergruppenführer* on the 1st of July 1934.

The *Leibstandarte Adolf Hitler* was transformed from a bodyguard unit to a military unit during the next five years. Under the direction of Sepp Dietrich, they acquired the skills necessary to ensure that they were present in all of the formative events leading up to the outbreak of World War II. This was balanced with maintaining their physical presence as a guard unit during all of the important public occasions and at all of the key locations. To give an idea, Dietrich and his men were responsible for the re-occupation of the Saarland in 1935; an event that could have went very wrong. They followed this by providing personnel for the Olympic Games in 1936. They continually provided guards at the Chancellery, Berlin's airports, the Obersalzburg and houses of high-ranking people such as Himmler. Dietrich, being an old front line fighter from World War I, was keen to ensure that his unit was also seen as militarily capable. Where possible he ensured that training with *Army* units was conducted and links with *Army* officers were maintained. The *LAH* were used as part of the forces sent to Austria during 1938 and also the Sudentenland. In 1939 the *LAH* were present when Hitler's troops marched into Bohemia and Moravia. Dietrich would not only see his importance within the Third Reich increase during these years, but the number of men under his control increased significantly up until the outbreak of the war. By August 1939, the *LAH* contained three *Battalions*; Dietrich had come a long way since his NCO days in 1918.

He had been keen to demonstrate that his men were up to the job when it came to military endeavors. He got his next chance to test this on the 1st of September 1939 with the invasion of Poland. As described in previous pages, the *LAH* took part in this campaign and they performed well. They suffered high casualties but earned some valuable lessons, as no doubt Dietrich did himself. The fighting he and his men took part in was a world away from the fighting he had endured over twenty years previous. His successes were rewarded with the bestowal of the Clasp to the Second Class Iron Cross on the 25th of September. This was followed just over a month later by the award of the Clasp to the First Class Iron Cross on the 27th of October 1939. In the months between the end of the campaign in Poland and the start of the next campaign in the west, Dietrich focused on ensuring his men were trained well and they also had to contend with a growth in numbers. During Christmas of 1939, Dietrich got to present the *LAH* to Hitler when the Führer made a visit to them at Bad Ems.

The next military test came in 1940 when the Dietrich took his *LAH* west through Holland, Belgium and France. They fought very well and successfully secured all of their tasks in Holland and Belgium, France was to provide a few challenges however. The first big challenge came on the 25th of May 1940 when the *LAH* were starting their attack upon the Dunkirk area. On this day they were around the town of Watten and its' nearby high ground known as the Wattenberg Heights. Adolf Hitler had issued the order to halt the attacks in the west to allow time to re-group. This was considered as madness by some, as the enemy was definitely on the run and close to collapse. It can be assumed that Dietrich was one of these men as he decided to ignore the order. He issued his own order for an attack to be made upon the Wattenberg Heights. This order was executed, and in a short space of time the Heights were firmly under the control of the *LAH*. This did not end the affair as despite Dietrich's closeness to Hitler, his decision to ignore a Führer Order was a dangerous decision for anyone. In the event, Dietrich had to explain his decision to Heinz Guderian and part of his explanation was as follows, "the Wattenberg sat on the opposite bank, looking us right in the belly". Upon receiving the explanation, Guderian confirmed the decision and provided support. Indeed, it is worth pointing out that Dietrich had realised that due to its location, the capture of this area would help in the defense of the nearby canal and also allow an unhindered launch of any subsequent attack from the canal area. A successful attack was launched from this precise area two days later and the pursuit towards Dunkirk continued.

So, was this action worthy of recognition? *General* von Brauchistch certainly thought so when he put forward the recommendation for the award of the Knight's Cross to the Iron Cross for Sepp Dietrich. Part of the recommendation read:

> '*SS-Obergruppenführer* Sepp Dietrich, through his resolve in capturing a bridgehead across the Aa canal near Watten, had a decisive influence on

> the rapid continuation of the operations in northern France and, in addition, distinguished himself, as he had earlier in Poland, by personal courage and by close comrade-like cooperation with the *Herr's Panzer* and motorised units'.

This recommendation was approved and on the 5th of July 1940. Joseph 'Sepp' Dietrich became the first soldier within the ranks of the *SS* to be presented with this new award. He had accurately guessed the importance of this objective to both sides and had ensured that the control of it lay with his men and not that of the enemy. In fact, the enemy tried to re-take this area, but were beaten back. It is also worth noting that the recommendation had highlighted the close cooperation between the *Army* and the *SS*. It is also fair to say that it took courage to decide to ignore a direct order from the Führer. What would the outcome have been if the attack had not been successful?

The next challenge for Dietrich came on the 28th of May, his 48th birthday, when he was close to the Dunkirk area at Esquelbecq. He was being accompanied by Max Wunsche, then holding the rank of *SS-Obersturmführer*. They came under close range fire and spend most of the day in a ditch close to the burning remains of the car that they had been travelling in. They were eventually rescued by men of the *LAH,* but this entanglement almost brought Dietrich's life to an end. It is doubtful that the enemy soldiers knew whom they were attacking. If they did, would their efforts have been increased?

The successful conclusion of the battle for northern France and the subsequent battle for the southern area of France would gain Dietrich, and his *LAH,* further valuable battle experience. The award of the Knight's Cross was a confirmation of his valuable contribution during this campaign. This would be not be the last award Dietrich would receive, but for now he focused on the job at hand, further training and getting ready for the next task.

Georg Keppler

Date of birth: 07.05.1894

SS Number: 273 799

Born in Mainz, he served during World War I as an infantry officer, was wounded three times and was awarded both the Second and First Class Iron Crosses. This was followed in the post war years with service in the police. He joined the *SS* in 1935, was given the rank of *SS-Obersturmbannführer* and served in *Deutschland's, I Battalion*. He moved to the command of the *Der Führer Regiment* in 1938 when this *Regiment* was being formed. At the start of the campaign in the west, he was holding the rank of *SS-Oberführer.*

SS-Oberführer Georg Keppler photographed after being awarded the Knight's Cross.

Georg Keppler received his Knight's Cross to the Iron Cross on the 15th of August 1940, for actions that took place between the 12th and 14th of May 1940. These actions are described very well in the recommendation document written by Paul Hausser, then holding the rank of *SS-Gruppenführer*:

> "*SS-Oberführer* Keppler and his *SS-Regiment 'Der Führer'* the only *Infantry Regiment* in the *X Army Corps*, forced a penetration of the Grebbe Line. The success of this *Regiment* had far reaching operational results. *SS-Oberführer* Keppler distinguished himself extraordinarily during reconnaissance, combat and while leading his *Regiment*. He personally dictated the *III/SS Der Führer's* forced crossing of the Ijssel and storming of the Grebbe Mountain against heavy enemy machine gun and artillery fire. Breaking through this key position of 'Fortress Holland' had significant operational value. *SS-Oberführer* Keppler withstood this difficult battle during the closest personal action with his *Regiment*".

Within the context of this book, Georg Keppler did not receive any further grades of the Knight's Cross. The question could be asked, why not? His continued career within the ranks of the *Waffen-SS* took him through the full duration of World War II and into the post-war uncertainty. After he received his Knight's Cross, he stayed with *Der Führer* until July 1941. This was followed by temporary command of the *Totenkopf Division* that lasted until late September 1941. Keppler then suffered his first illness in the form of a brain tumor that removed him from active duty until the start of April 1942. Whilst recuperating, he was promoted to *SS-Gruppenführer und Generalleutnant der Waffen-SS*.

His first posting upon returning to active service was command of *SS Division Reich*, or the *2nd SS-Panzergrenadier-Division 'Das Reich'*, as it soon became known. This command lasted until February 1943, when he fell ill once again in Russia. This illness kept him from duty until the end of August the same year. He then moved to the command of the *Waffen-SS* in Bohemia and Moravia until March 1944. This was followed by him moving to the command of the *Waffen-SS* in Hungary, which he retained until September that year. He also gained further promotion to the rank of *SS-Obergruppenführer und General der Waffen-SS*. Further temporary posting came along, the first of which saw him as *Commander* of the *I SS Panzer Korps* from August to October 1944. He then briefly returned to his Hungarian command position before being posted to the command of the *III Germanic Panzer Korps*, that took him to February 1945. His last command was that of the *XVIII SS Army Korps* and this lasted until the end of the war.

Like most other surviving *Waffen-SS* soldiers, Georg Keppler was placed in an Allied prisoner of war camp until 1948. He returned to civilian life in Germany until his death in June 1966. He epitomized the spirit of the *Waffen-SS* soldier and *Commanding Officer*, always at the front. As described in his Knight's Cross recommendation, he was in the thick of the fighting with his men and was able to assess the situations at hand and devise a battle winning strategy. His skills continued to be called upon throughout the war in the many varied commands he held. The soldiers under his command would have no doubt benefited greatly from the skills and capabilities of this very gifted person.

Felix Steiner
Date of birth: 23.05.1896
SS Number: 253 351
Born in Ebenrode, East Prussia, Steiner served in World War I as an officer and *Kompanie Commander*. He was wounded once and was also awarded the Second Class Iron Cross in November 1914. The award of the First Class Iron Cross came in 1917. He ended the First World War with the rank of *Oberleutnant*. He followed this by service in the inter-war *German Army*, reaching the rank of *Major*. He joined the *SS-VT* in 1935, with the rank of *SS-Obersturmbannführer* and was placed in charge of forming *Deutschland's III Battalion*. He assumed overall command of the entire *SS-Regiment Deutschland* in 1936. By the start of World War II he held the rank of *SS-Oberführer*. The campaign in Poland gave him the chance to win the Clasp to both classes of the Iron Cross. His Second Class Clasp was awarded on the 17th of September 1939, the First Class Clasp on the 26th of September. On the 17th June 1940, whilst the campaign in the west was still raging, Paul Hausser wrote the following recommendation for the Knight's Cross to the Iron Cross:

> "*SS-Oberführer* Steiner's *Regiment 'Deutschland'* was the only *Infantry Regiment* of *Battle Group Hausser* that took part in capturing the island group Seeland from French troops. *SS-Oberführer* Steiner's superior leadership was instrumental in the *Regiment's* swift, three day thrust to Vlissingen and the storming of two powerful defensive positions. He distinguished himself personally throughout this endeavor and employed his *Battalions* and *Stuka* support against heavy enemy fire at the Beveland Canal and the causeway to Walcheren Island. This swift success had far reaching influence upon the fighting in Belgium, especially at Antwerp, which was now accessible from the Schelde. *SS-Oberführer* Steiner also distinguished himself during the

Felix Steiner (right) photographed wearing his Knight's Cross. Unfortunately, the date and location of this photograph are unknown.

> fighting in northern France, at La Bassee Canal, at the Lys and the southern front"

Felix Steiner's award of the Knight's Cross to the Iron Cross was approved and he received this medal on the 15th of August 1940, the same day as Georg Keppler. This would not be Steiner's only association with the Knight's Cross, but more details of this will follow in later chapters and volumes.

Ludwig Kepplinger
Date of birth: 31.12.1911
SS Number: 116 879
Born in Linz, Austria, Kepplinger joined the *S.A.* in May 1930, followed by entry into the *SS* in September 1933. He moved to the *Deutschland Regiment* in 1935, at that stage holding the rank of *SS-Unterscharführer.* By the time of moving to the *Der Führer Regiment* in April 1938 he held the rank of *SS-Oberscharführer.*

Ludwig Kepplinger photographed sometime after January 1942, following his promotion to SS-Hauptsturmführer. He won his Knight's Cross two years earlier as an SS-NCO.

He was promoted further to *SS-Hauptscharführer* on the 1st of May 1940, whilst serving with the *11. Kompanie*. He was awarded the Second Class Iron Cross on the 16th of May 1940, followed by the First Class Iron Cross on the 2nd of August 1940. The recognition for his bravery was elevated further on the 4th of September 1940, when he was awarded the Knight's Cross to the Iron Cross. *SS-Oberführer* Georg Keppler recommended Kepplinger for the Knight's Cross on the 18th of July 1940 and his document contained the following summary:

> "Kepplinger distinguished himself through exceptional bravery during the *III/SS 'Der Führer's'* attack across the Dutch border at Elten and crossing the Ijssel at Arnhem. With only two other men, Kepplinger climbed across the destroyed (300 metre long) Ijssel Bridge with the intention of occupying the town of Westervoort, which bristled with machine guns. Kepplinger and both his men came under heavy fire while crossing the river. Although the chances for his success were exceptionally small, Kepplinger used all available cover to successfully sprint into Westervoort. Short, violent, close combat erupted between the ninety-man occupation force and the three approaching Germans. Kepplinger succeeded in forcing one portion of Westervoort after another to surrender".

It is also interesting to note that during the storming of the Grebbe Line, Kepplinger received multiple wounds, causing extensive blood loss. He was wounded twice in the stomach, twice in the thigh and once in the hand. It was whilst in hospital recovering from these wounds that he received both classes to the Iron Cross.

Ludwig Kepplinger's recommendation for the Knight's Cross to the Iron Cross was approved on the 4th of September 1940. This award was the first to be made to an *NCO* from the *SS,* although by the time he received the award, he had been promoted to the rank of *SS-Untersturmführer.* He had also been awarded the Silver Wound Badge for the wounds suffered in the Grebbe Line attack.

Soon after receiving the Knight's Cross from the hand of Paul Hausser, Ludwig Kepplinger moved to the newly formed *SS-Regiment 'Westland'*. At the end of January 1941 he was promoted to *SS-Obersturmführer* and given command of the *10. Kompanie*. He spent a brief spell at Bad Tolz and then returned to *SS-Regiment Westland*. On the 28th of February 1942, Kepplinger was awarded the German Cross in Gold. There are no details on his file to indicate why the award was made, although it is known that *Westland* were enduring very tough battles against the massed ranks of Russian soldiers at that time. He was no doubt awarded this medal as a further recognition for his continued bravery. One point to note, he is listed as holding his *SS-Obersturmführer* rank at the award of his German Cross in Gold, but his file shows that he was promoted to *SS-Hauptsturmführer* on the 30th of January 1942.

In late 1942 he moved to the tank training ground in Wunsdorf. What then followed was extensive training and various posts all connected with tanks. This included time learning the technical aspects of tanks, training with Panthers and Tigers and also a spell at Fallingbostel training grounds. In January 1944 he was promoted to *SS-Sturmbannführer.* In April 1944 he moved to the *SS-Panzer-Abteilung 17*, within the *17th SS-Panzergrenadier-Division 'Gotz von Berlichingen'*. He assumed command of this *Abteilung* at the start of August, during the intensive Normandy battles. It was with this unit that he was killed on the 7th of August 1944 during a battle with American soldiers near Laval in France.

Fritz Vogt
Date of birth: 17.03.1918
SS Number: 270 386
Born in Munich, he joined the *SS-VT* in April 1935. He attended the *SS* officer training school in Braunschweig pre-war and achieved the rank of *SS-Untersturmführer* on the 20th of April 1939. He was awarded the Second Class Iron Cross on the 23rd of September 1939 during the Polish campaign. He was performing the role of *Kompanie Commander* in the *Aufklarungs Abteilung*, within the *SS V Division,* when the campaign in the west started.

His recommendation for the Knight's Cross to the Iron Cross was written on the 18th of July 1940 and read as follows:

> "*SS-Obersturmführer* Vogt was an officer in the *SS V Division's Aufklarungs Abteilung*. He distinguished himself during the Polish campaign as *Platoon Leader* of a *Motorcycle Infantry Platoon*. He was the first in his *Battalion* to receive the Iron Cross Second Class and recommendation for the Iron Cross First Class for various reconnaissance actions.
>
> At the start of the great battle for France, his assault force received the mission of capturing and holding a bridge across the Maas-Waal Canal. Although the bridge was destroyed, he carried out his mission with daring and great success. He succeeded in reaching the enemy occupied bank with four men. Despite being wounded, he rolled up many bunker positions and caused soldiers in neighboring positions to surrender. This successful endeavor enabled the following units of a machine gun *Battalion* to cross the canal. An additional result was that the Dutch had to give up their heavily

Fritz Vogt pictured holding the rank of SS-Hauptsturmführer in 1943. His actions that resulted in the award of the Knight's Cross were conducted whilst an SS-Untersturmführer

fortified bunker positions along the canal. In the days that followed, Vogt led over twenty additional patrols that made contact with the enemy. These were also very successful. Award of the Iron Cross First Class and subsequent promotion to *SS-Obersturmführer* for bravery in the face of the enemy were the exterior symbols of this recognition."

As highlighted above, Vogt had been promoted to *SS-Obersturmführer,* on the 23rd of May 1940, after his successful actions. Fritz Vogt received the Knight's Cross to the Iron Cross on the 4th of September 1940 from *SS-Gruppenführer* Paul Hausser. In addition to the above awards, he received the Black Wound Badge on the 10th of May 1940. His association with the Knight's Cross and its' higher grades would continue beyond 1940, but details of that will follow later.

Fritz Witt

Date of birth: 27.05.1908

SS Number: 21 518

Born in Hohenlimburg, Westphalia, he joined the *SS* in 1931 and served with the *1. Sturm, II Sturmbann, SS-Standarte 30.* He was one of the first 117 men hand-picked to form Hitler's new personal protection squad. He moved to the *LAH* on the 17th of March 1933. Holding the rank of *SS-Scharführer (SS-Unterscharführer)* at that stage, rapid promotions followed. The 1st of April 1933, promoted to *SS-Truppführer (SS-Oberscharführer).* The 15th of September 1933, *SS-Haupttruppführer (SS-Hauptscharführer).* On the 1st of October 1933 he was promoted again to the rank of *SS-Sturmführer (SS-Untersturmführer)* and the following day he became a *Platoon Leader* in the *2. Kompanie* of the *LAH.* On the 9th of May 1934 he was promoted again, this time to the rank of *SS-Obersturmführer.* On the 12th of January 1935 he moved to the *Deutschland Standarte,* and by the 17th of May the same year, he was in command of the *3. Kompanie* within this *Standarte.* On the 1st of June 1935 he was promoted to *SS-Hauptsturmführer* and during the following month he attended a course at the infantry training school at Doberitz.

He advanced into Poland as a *Kompanie Commander* in September 1939 and quick recognition of his bravery soon followed. He was awarded the Second Class Iron Cross on the 19th of September 1939. This was followed on the 26th of September with the award of the First Class Iron Cross, this was in fact the very first one to be awarded to a soldier of the *SS.* At the end of 1939 he attended a *Battalion Leaders* course at Erfurt. He was promoted to *SS-Sturmbannführer* on the 25th of May 1940, during the campaign in the west, whilst commanding

Fritz Witt (right) photographed with his brother Franz (left) in the autumn of 1940, not long after his presentation of the Knight's Cross. This is prior to his move to the LAH. His brother was killed in Greece in April 1941 whilst serving as a Platoon Commander within Fritz Witt's I Battalion, LAH.

the *I Battalion* within the *Deutschland Standarte*. It was with this *Battalion* that Witt was awarded the Knight's Cross to the Iron Cross. His recommendation was written by his *Regimental Commander*, Felix Steiner, on the 18th of July 1940 and contained the following passages:

> "*SS-Sturmbannführer* Witt was one of the first to receive the Iron Cross First Class during the Polish Campaign. The *Commander* of the *I/SS 'Deutschland'* and his *Battalion* were attacked on the evening of the 27th of May, from the direction of Estaires, by twenty British tanks supported by infantry. At least ten enemy tanks succeeded in breaking into the *Battalion's* positions, because it was without anti-tank weapons at that time due to the lack of bridges.
>
> The *Battalion* conducted such a fanatical defense with all available light and heavy infantry weapons, that the British were unable to break through the position. The unit immobilized nine enemy tanks. *SS-Sturmbannführer* Witt provided his troops with a fine example of fearlessness and the will to endure. They attacked the enemy tanks from ditches, hedges, holes in the ground and cellars. He was the soul of resistance.

On the 17th of June the *Battalion* defended against a greatly superior enemy force, which sought to break through onto the Langres Plateau, near Arthonnay. It repulsed hour after hour of French attacks throughout the night of 16-17th June, in some cases, in bitter close combat. This provided a foundation for the *Regiment's* success over the days that followed, during which it captured almost 20,000 prisoners.

Witt led the defense from the front-most line and took a decisive part in the breaking up of the passionately conducted enemy breakthrough. In the Western Front he conducted his *Battalion* always with excellent leadership. In the battles for Zeeland he was the first to force a crossing over the Beveland Canal, tenaciously defended by a superior number of Frenchmen, and penetrated deeply into their positions with disregard of the Frenchmen staying at both flanks of the breakthrough. He captured about 1,000 prisoners".

Fritz Witt was presented his Knight's Cross to the Iron Cross on the 4th of September 1940. His connection with this medal would continue and further details will follow in future volumes.

Summary of the Campaign in the West 1940

An overview of this campaign shows that the Germans executed a brilliant plan that shattered the hopes for the enemy in another *Allied* victory. The inter-war years had seen the Dutch rely on their natural defenses in the shape of their numerous rivers and bridges, backed up with concrete emplacements. The Belgians and French placed their faith in the massive forts of Eben Emael and the Maginot Line. The Dutch defenses provided a brief thorn in the side of the Germans, but they were not enough to halt the advance. Eben Emael was captured in a stunning aerial raid and the Maginot Line was by-passed in the first instance and then mopped up later on. The relentless march of the combined German forces outclassed anything that the combined nations of Holland, Belgium, France and Britain could throw at them. Driving the British and *Allied* troops into the sea at Dunkirk and pursuing the remaining *Allied* troops through southern France sealed this spectacular victory. The Germans had shown that expensive fortifications were of limited use and the new fast, mobile type of warfare was the way forward. There would be no return to the miles of trenches and long drawn out battles for the sake of a mile of ground, like it had been twenty years earlier. What was the contribution of the *SS* in this complete and crushing victory of the German army over its' western enemies at that point?

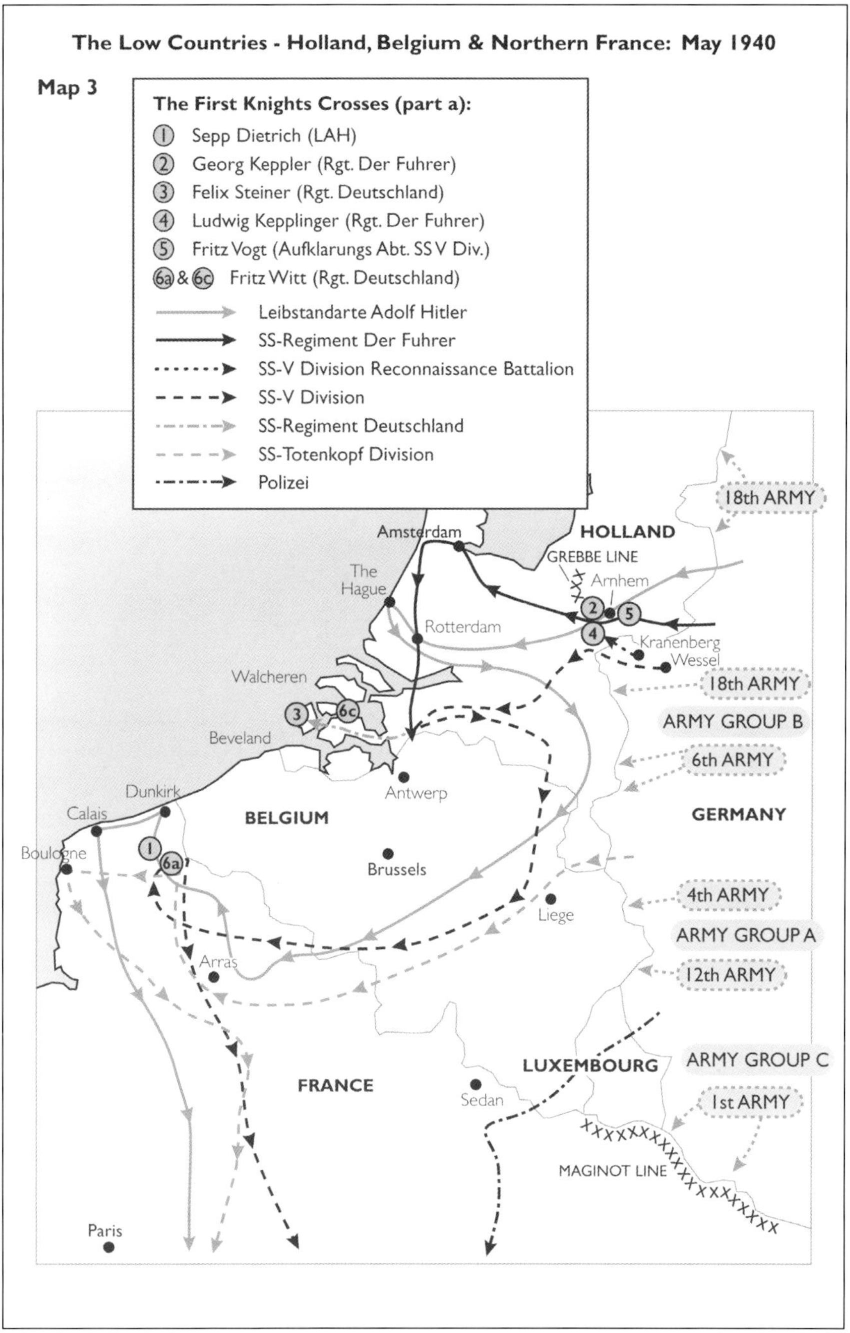
The Low Countries - Holland, Belgium & Northern France: May 1940
Map 3
The First Knights Crosses (part a):
1 Sepp Dietrich (LAH)
2 Georg Keppler (Rgt. Der Fuhrer)
3 Felix Steiner (Rgt. Deutschland)
4 Ludwig Kepplinger (Rgt. Der Fuhrer)
5 Fritz Vogt (Aufklarungs Abt. SS V Div.)
6a & 6c Fritz Witt (Rgt. Deutschland)
Leibstandarte Adolf Hitler
SS-Regiment Der Fuhrer
SS-V Division Reconnaissance Battalion
SS-V Division
SS-Regiment Deutschland
SS-Totenkopf Division
Polizei
18th ARMY
Amsterdam
HOLLAND
GREBBE LINE
The Hague
Arnhem
Rotterdam
Kranenberg
Wessel
Walcheren
18th ARMY
ARMY GROUP B
Beveland
6th ARMY
Antwerp
Dunkirk
Calais
BELGIUM
GERMANY
Boulogne
Brussels
4th ARMY
Liege
ARMY GROUP A
Arras
12th ARMY
LUXEMBOURG
ARMY GROUP C
FRANCE
Sedan
1st ARMY
MAGINOT LINE
Paris

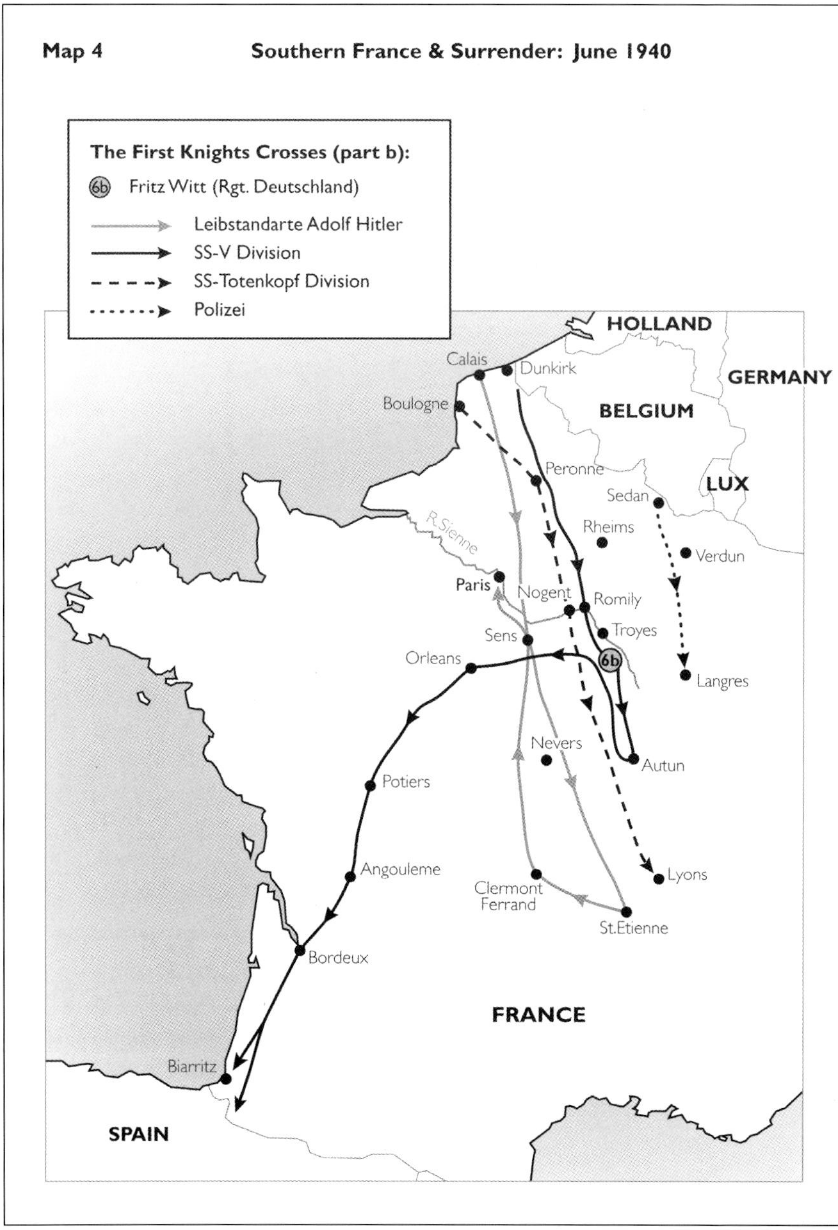

Map 4
Southern France & Surrender: June 1940
The First Knights Crosses (part b):
6b Fritz Witt (Rgt. Deutschland)
Leibstandarte Adolf Hitler
SS-V Division
SS-Totenkopf Division
Polizei
HOLLAND
GERMANY
BELGIUM
LUX
Calais
Dunkirk
Boulogne
Peronne
Sedan
Rheims
Verdun
R.Sienne
Paris
Nogent
Romily
Troyes
Sens
Orleans
6b
Langres
Nevers
Autun
Potiers
Angouleme
Lyons
Clermont Ferrand
St.Etienne
Bordeux
FRANCE
Biarritz
SPAIN

The various units of the *SS* had assisted in the defeat from day one and had made a significant contribution to the overall victory. From the *SS V Division's* capture of the Dutch bridges at the opening stages, through to the pursuit through Holland and Belgium and into the Walcheren Islands. Followed by the capture of the Wattenburg Heights and then, withstanding the determined efforts of the enemy, who launched tank attacks against the *SS* infantry at Arras and the Lys Canal, finishing with the final pursuit of the remaining enemy soldiers in the south of France. Each one of these focal points is a testament to the bravery and fighting skills of the still very young 'front-line' *SS*. This bravery and those skills would be displayed many times during the next five years, but for now it was time to enjoy the victory and remember fallen *Kameraden*.

With the end of the second major campaign the *SS* could now count themselves as having *Ritterkreuzträger* within their ranks. The awards covered three *Regimental Commanders*, one *Battalion Commander*, one *Kompanie Commander* and an *NCO*. The *LAH, Deutschland* and the *SS V Division's, Aufklarungs Abteilung* now contained Knight's Cross holders in their ranks, as did *Der Führer,* who in their first taste of combat earned two Knight's Cross holders.

In just over seven years the *SS* had risen from a small group of personal bodyguards to front line soldiers, whose deeds of bravery had been recognized at the highest level. Senior *Army Commanders* were beginning to change their opinions too, as they realized the contribution that the fighting *SS* had made and could make in future battles. Adolf Hitler agreed with this viewpoint and authorized a further expansion and creation of new *SS* units. The term *Waffen-SS*, or *Armed-SS* came into being just after this second campaign and would be used from that time to describe the front-line fighting *SS* soldiers. In the coming months and years, the *Waffen-SS* would be called upon in many situations, but for now the focus would be on forming new units and preparing them for the forthcoming campaigns.

CHAPTER FOUR

NEW FORMATIONS AND NEW ENEMIES

SS-Totenkopf-Reiterstandarte

Unlike the rest of the front line *SS* units, who were sent west in 1940, the above unit remained in Poland during October 1939. They grew slightly in size and by December of 1939 they received a name change to the *1. SS-Totenkopf-Reiterstandarte* and could now count almost 600 men within their twelve different squadrons. The overall unit contained replacement and heavy squadrons. All of the squadrons were situated at various locations within Poland.

As their *SS Kameraden* were fighting their way across Holland in the second week of May 1940, the *1. SS-Totenkopf-Reiterstandarte* had grown to almost 2,000 men. A dividing of these men into two main *Standarte* took place, the new units being named the *1. SS-Totenkopf-Reiterstandarte* and the *2. SS-Totenkopf-Reiterstandarte*. They contained 6 squadrons each and had motorcycle, engineer and signals troops in their ranks. Fegelein retained command of the *1st Reiterstandarte* and *SS-Sturmbannführer* Franz Magill took command of the *2nd Reiterstandarte*. Police and security duties continued, as well as combat training exercises.

In November 1940 they expanded further and the two *Reiterstandarte* were placed back into one unit, which by January 1941 was known as the *SS-Totenkopf-Kavallerie Regiment 1,* quickly changed to *SS-Kavallerie Regiment 1* before January ended. Hermann Fegelein remained in overall command and had two half *Regiments* under his control. He retained command of the first half *Regiment* and Magill commanded the second. They both had 9 squadrons each. Like *Totenkopf* and *Polizei,* they would not take part in the forthcoming campaign in Greece. Around the start of the Greek campaign, the basis of the *2nd Regiment* was being set up, with Franz Magill's half *Regiment* being used as the foundation.

SS-Division Wiking

Also during November 1940, a new formation was ordered. The basis of this new *Division* was established around the *SS-Regiment Germania*. This *Regiment* was detached from the *SS V Division* at the start of December. This new *Division* was initially known as the *Germania Division*, but this was quickly changed to the *SS-Division Wiking*. Command of this new *Division* was given to the recently promoted *SS-Brigadeführer und Generalmajor der Waffen SS* Felix Steiner. Alongside the *SS-Regiment Germania,* under the command of *SS-Standartenführer* Reichritter von Oberkamp, the following two new *Regiments* were established; *SS-Regiment Westland,* under the command of *SS-Standartenführer* Hilmar Wackerle and *SS-Regiment Nordland,* commanded by *SS-Standartenführer* Fritz von Scholz. *SS-Regiment Westland* contained volunteers from the recently conquered country of Holland, and their formation took place in Vienna and Klagenfurt in Austria, whilst *SS-Regiment Nordland* contained Danish and Norwegian volunteers and were formed in Munich.

The initial four months in the life of this new formation were spent incorporating the new recruits and managing the difficulties of the various language barriers. It must be pointed out that Norway and Holland had been defeated only months earlier. To think that former soldiers of those defeated countries had decided to volunteer to fight for their victor is a testament to their belief in the cause of Hitler's Germany. This cause was the defeat of communist Russia. These foreign volunteers would not have to wait long for their chance to fight this ultimate enemy and take part in the cause they had volunteered for.

In April 1941, whilst the *LAH* and *Division Reich* were heading south, the various elements of the *SS-Division Wiking* were assembled together at the Heuberg training grounds, near Ebingen. The sole purpose was to ready the *Division* for combat.

SS-Kampfgruppe Nord

Just prior to this, on the 28th of February 1941, a new *SS Mountain Brigade* was formed. This new unit was formed in the Norway area and used the *SS-Totenkopf's 6th, 7th and 9th Regiments* as a basis. *SS-Brigadeführer und Generalmajor der Waffen SS* Richard Hermann was placed in command at the outset. Their immediate focus was upon training and we will return to this unit after the Greek campaign.

Leibstandarte Adolf Hitler

The *LAH* spent the majority of July 1940 in the Paris area then, on the 24th of July, they were ordered to the Metz region. At the start of August, the *Regiment* was reorganised and increased to a *Motorised Brigade*. They were also to be known as *Verstarkte (re-inforced) Leibstandarte S.S. Adolf Hitler*, or *verst. LSSAH*. Notable highlights during this period were preparing for the planned invasion of England and receiving their new field insignia, a copy of Hitler's personal pennant. From August to December the *LAH* stayed in Metz. On the 10th of January 1941 the *LAH* were ordered to move to the Balkans. An advance party was sent out a few days later, with the bulk of the *LAH* staying in Metz until the start of March. The emphasis during those months had been on the expansion and incorporation of the new recruits.

SS V Division

After their initial stint of occupation duties in southern France, they were then moved to the Netherlands in July and stayed in that area until December 1940. In those months this *Division* lost various elements to help bulk out or form new units. Some elements were sent to the *LAH* to aid their expansion, whilst the entire *Germania Regiment* was detached to form a new *Division*, as detailed above. To replace the loss of this entire *Regiment*, the *11th SS-Totenkopf Regiment* were attached to the *SS V Division*. Also around this time, the *Division* was renamed the *SS-Division Reich*. In addition to losing an entire *Regiment*, they also lost Felix Steiner; with *SS-Obersturmbannführer* Wilhelm Bittrich assuming command of the *Deutschland Regiment*. In December 1940 they once again went to southern France and remained there until March 1941. Like the *LAH,* the emphasis had been on incorporating the new units and building new ones, which included the *Motorcycle Infantry Battalion* and the *Assault Gun* unit.

The Third Campaign – Greece and Yugoslavia, April 1941

The start of this campaign can be traced back to October 1940, when Mussolini invaded Greece from the west. He anticipated a quick victory, but this proved to be wishful thinking. Not only did the victory not arrive, but his Italian troops had to give ground and were on the verge of being defeated. The British offered assistance to the Greeks from March 1941, and at that stage Hitler decided that he had no option but to remove this potential threat from the south, before his intended move east into Russia. This new campaign would delay the start of the invasion of Russia. Although no-one knew it at the time, this decision would have far reaching implications on the direction of the war and its' final outcome.

He revived a plan that was first drafted in November 1940. The plan was code named Operation Marita and involved the use of the *German 12th Army*, under *Field Marshall* Wilhelm List, positioned in Bulgaria. Just prior to the start of this campaign, the Yugoslavians overthrew their rulers and changed sides, thereby taking a stance against Germany. With this development, Hitler then added a further element to his plans and ordered Operation Strafe, the plan to defeat Yugoslavia. The *German 2nd Army,* under *Colonel-General* Maximillian von Weichs, were positioned in the north around southern Germany, Rumania and Hungary. The focus of this book will only look at the actions of List's *12th Army,* as the only two participating *Waffen-SS* units – the *LAH* and *SS-Division Reich* – were contained within that *Army*

Their respective parts in the forthcoming campaign were as follows; the *LAH* would move through southern Yugoslavia, aiming for Sofia and from there they would swing south into Greece. *SS-Division Reich* would strike towards the Yugoslavian capital of Belgrade. So, how did they perform?

Leibstandarte Adolf Hitler

The *LAH* left Metz in the first week of March 1941 and moved to an area north of Bucharest. Here, they were attached to the *12th Army*. During the rest of March, they moved through the southern edge of the Transylvanian Alps and then into Bulgaria, being placed in the north of Sofia. Here, they were placed within the *XXXX Army Korps*.

On the 30th of March, the *LAH* were moved to the Radomir area. On the 5th of April, new orders were issued that detailed a simultaneous attack on Greece and Yugoslavia. The attacks were to begin the following day. The *LAH* did not cross the Yugoslavian border until the 8th. By the 10th of April, the town of Niki was reached; This was the first town to be reached on Greek soil. The advance route was in a southeasterly direction, from Niki towards Vevi and on to the Kliddi Pass. Vevi was captured on the 11th of April and the attack upon the Kliddi Pass was ready to begin.

The attack (towards this pass) was launched on the morning of the 12th of April. This attack was made against very stiff resistance, with defense being provided by Australian troops. The *1. Kompanie*, under the command of *SS-Obersturmführer* Gert Pleiss, took Hill .997 with the rest of Fritz Witt's *I Battalion* providing close support and capturing Hill .1009. The *1. Kompanie* went on later that day to capture the village of Klidi itself in the late afternoon (the capturing of this pass by Gert Pleiss resulted in him being awarded the Knight's Cross, covered in more detail at the end of this chapter). Fritz Witt and some of his officers stood at the opening to the Macedonian Plain and observed the enemy retreating southwards.

The *LAH*'s part in this battle came to an end on the following day, the 13th of April 1941. The cost had been 35 dead and almost 100 wounded.

Their fighting in Greece was by no means over and the next objective was already earmarked. This was the Klisura Pass, and for this attack *SS-Sturmbannführer* Kurt Meyer would lead the way. The recently mauled *I Battalion* were allowed some well earned rest. The attack was started on the 13th, and by the afternoon his men had reached a key bridge near Lehovon. The bridge had been destroyed by the defenders, and as Kurt Meyer's men tried to advance towards the remains, they came under intense heavy enemy machine-gun and grenade fire from the surrounding hills. This resulted in them having to wait until the early hours of the following day to resume their planned advance. The next attempt began in the early hours of the 14th, and by using small groups of men and mounting a three-pronged attack, Meyer (and his small group of men) captured the summit that evening (This action earned Kurt Meyer the Knight's Cross and will be covered in more detail at the end of the chapter).

Over the next six days the *LAH* fought further south, and their advance took them through Lake Kastoria, Argos-Orestiakon, Kivotos, Grevena and Joanina. The summit of the Katara Pass was reached on the 20th of April 1941. It was here that the advance guard was offered the surrender of the *Greek & Macedonian Army*. When Dietrich arrived on the scene, he was taken to meet *General* Tzolakoglou and negotiate peace terms. The final negotiations were held with *General* Jodl on the 21st. Kurt Meyer carried on with his actions and on the 25th he executed a crossing of the Gulf of Patras. On the 30th the *II Battalion* reached Pyrgos thereby bringing the campaign in Greece to an end.

SS-Division Reich

SS-Division Reich began their moves south at the start of April, advancing through southern Germany, Austria, Hungary and Rumania. They stopped in the town of Temesvar on the 7th of April 1941; this town is located around 90 miles north of Belgrade. They were also attached to the *12th Army*, being placed within the *XLI Army Korps*.

Reconnaissance troops crossed the Yugoslavian border on the 9th, with the main advance beginning on the 11th of April. The advance was made along the main road to Alibunar with the *Motorcycle Battalion* leading the way, other divisional elements supported on the left, with the *Heer's GrossDeutschland Division* advancing on the right. The *Korps Commander* had stated that the first to reach Alibunar would be permitted to lead the advance into Belgrade. Therefore, what developed was a race between *Division Reich* and *GrossDeutschland*.

The first part of the attack towards Alibunar was very difficult and slowed the rate of advance for *Division Reich*. The first major objective was reached in the late afternoon, and the first troops to get there were elements of *SS-Regiment Deutschland*. This automatically placed *Division Reich* in the lead for the second phase of the attack, the assault on Belgrade. The *Motorcycle Battalion* led the way again on the 12th of April, and they were the first to reach the River Danube at Belgrade. The main bridge was destroyed, so the request was made to cross by other means. This request was denied by the *Korps Commander*, but prior to the reply being received back, the *Motorcycle Battalion's, 2. Kompanie Commander*, *SS-Hauptsturmführer* Fritz Klingenberg, decided to press ahead. He made use of a nearby small boat and together with ten men, he made the trip across the river and set foot on the opposite bank. From here, he walked ahead and started to enter the city. After some well placed luck, he had the chance to gain the surrender of this capital city. He convinced the mayor to agree to this (This action will be covered in more detail at the end of this chapter as part of the overview of why Klingenberg received the Knight's Cross).

News of Klingenberg's success was passed back to the rest of the German soldiers on the other bank; *Heer* units entered the city later that day. The *Reich Division* remained in the Belgrade area for the next five days and conducted security duties and clearing up operations, along with *Grossdeutschland* and other *Heer* units. The Yugoslavian surrender was announced on the 18th of April 1941, thereby closing the brief, but spectacular campaign in this country.

The Balkan Knight's Cross Recipients

Gert Pleiss

Date of birth: 20.04.1915

SS Number: 323 807

Born in Remscheid, he joined the *LAH* in April 1936, being placed with the *1. Kompanie*. Very little is known about Pleiss over the next couple of years, but he must have impressed his superiors, as he was sent to the officers training school at Brunswick during the second half of 1938. In the spring of 1939, he left that school with the rank of *SS-Untersturmführer*, returning to the *1. Kompanie* in March 1939. He became one of the *Platoon Commanders* in January 1940, under Martin Gross. During the campaign in the west, he temporarily took command of the entire *Kompanie* when Gross was wounded, on the 27th of May 1940. He was promoted to *SS-Obersturmführer* at the start of June 1940. Gross reassumed command once his wounds had healed and Pleiss went back to *Platoon Commander*. He received

Gert Pleiss (right) photographed in Greece in May 1940, not long after his award of the Knight's Cross. This photograph was taken during an official visit to the LAH, by Reichsführer-SS Heinrich Himmler.

the Second Class Iron Cross on the 8th of June 1940, followed by the First Class Iron Cross. The award date was the 17th of July 1940 and was for actions during the second phase of the French Campaign when he forced a crossing over the river near the Pont du Chateau.

By the start of April 1941 he was in command of the *1. Kompanie,* and it was with this *Kompanie* that he entered the Balkan campaign. He led his men during the attack on the vital Klidi Pass, fighting up a 1000-foot high hill more suited to mountain troops than infantry. The capturing of this first important gateway into Greece was accomplished within two hours. The fight itself was made against enemy troops, who watched every move that Pleiss's men made. The battle for this high ground was intense and numerous enemy machine gun nests had to be cleared, fixed bayonets being the order of the day. Gert Pleiss himself was wounded during this attack, but stayed with his *Kompanie* throughout. The enemy defenders were completely overwhelmed by the speed and ferocity of the *1. Kompanie's* attack. This stunning, quick and very important victory led onto the subsequent capturing of other major objectives, such as the Klisura Pass two days later. Recognition of his actions was not long in coming. On the 20th of April 1941, *SS-Obersturmführer* Gert Pleiss was awarded the Knight's Cross to the Iron

Cross. The original recommendation does not survive, so it is not known when the recommendation was made or who made it, although it can be assumed that Sepp Dietrich was the person who put this forward.

So what happened to Gert Pleiss after the Balkan Campaign? He remained with the *LAH*'s, *1. Kompanie* and led them into the first stage of the invasion of Russia in late 1941. By August 1941 he was holding the rank of *SS-Hauptsturmführer,* although the exact date of this promotion is not known either. On the 17th of November 1941, the *LAH* began their assault on the city of Rostov. In the early stages of this attack, a Stalin Organ rocket exploded near where Gert Pleiss was standing. The explosion blew both of his legs off. He was tended to immediately and taken to a nearby hospital. The wounds however, were too severe and he died soon after. He was the seventh member of the *Waffen-SS* to be awarded the Knight's Cross to the Iron Cross.

Fritz Klingenberg

Date of birth: 17.12.1912

SS Number: 51 487

Born in Rowershagen, Klingenberg was an early entrant into the *SS,* joining in 1932. In October 1933 he was serving with the *LAH.* He was sent to the officer's training school at Bad Tolz in April 1934, reaching the rank of *SS-Standartenoberjunker* by February 1935. This was quickly followed by promotion to *SS-Untersturmführer* on the 20th of April the same year; at this stage he was serving with *SS-Regiment Germania.* He was holding the position of *Adjutant* to the *II Battalion* in January 1936. Promotion to *SS-Obersturmführer* came on the 9th of September 1937. He was promoted further on the 30th of June 1939 to the rank of *SS-Hauptsturmführer,* by that stage he was serving as Paul Hausser's *Adjutant.* He was awarded the Second Class Iron Cross on the 23rd of June 1940 and the First Class Iron Cross award came the following day, both during the campaign in the west. He moved to command of the *SS-Regiment Der Führer's 15. Motorcycle Kompanie* at the start of August 1940, then onto the command of the *2. Kompanie,* within the newly created *Motorcycle Infantry Battalion.* It was with this *Kompanie* that he would enter the next campaign, that in the Balkans in April 1941.

As mentioned in the preceeding pages, Klingenberg led his men up to the banks of the River Danube facing Belgrade. He successfully crossed that river and negotiated its' surrender. So how did he actually accomplish this? It is probably best to read an overview of the recommendation document that secured his award of the Knight's Cross to the Iron Cross. This recommendation was written by Paul

Fritz Klingenberg photographed in early 1944 during his time as Commander of Bad Tolz

Hausser on the 18th of April 1941, the same day the Yugoslavian Government surrendered, an overview reads as follows:

> '*SS-Hauptsturmführer* Klingenberg, then leader of a small vanguard of the *Motorcycle Battalion*, had the assignment to capture the bridge across the Danube River near Belgrade in a surprise attack. At 08:00 hours Klingenberg reached Pancevo and found that the bridge spanning the Tamis River had been blown. He crossed that river in fishing boats, taking some motorcycles and sidecars with him. On these motorcycles he reached the bridge across the Danube River at 11:30. This bridge had been blown earlier that morning. Klingenberg succeeded in getting a motorboat running and used that to cross the river along with ten men, with two machine guns and five sub-machine guns. The boat did get stuck on sand during the crossing, but it was freed up and they successfully reached the southern bank. He formed a bridgehead and then advanced into the city on foot. Klingenberg reached the Ministry of War, which was empty. From here he summoned the Mayor of Belgrade and gained his agreement to surrender the city. The Mayor was under the impression that there were heavier German troops in the city and Klingenberg threatened to call in the *Luftwaffe* to bomb the city. The surrender was agreed in the evening, besides gaining this surrender, Klingenberg and his men captured around 1000 enemy prisoners.'

The actual award recommendation and the recorded history of the *Das Reich Division*, differ in some detail. The recommendation states that he came across a Serbian soldier and used this soldier to summon the Mayor, whereas the *Das Reich* history states that he met a German Consulate official who took him to the consulate. It was from here that the German Military Attache summoned the Mayor. Although the actual details may vary, the facts remain unchanged. Fritz Klingenberg successfully gained the surrender of a major European Capital city without the need for a long drawn out battle that would have undoubtedly led to the deaths of German and Yugoslavian soldiers, along with the civilians of Belgrade. This was done by bluff and courage, but led to one of the most notable victories of the entire war. Adolf Hitler could recognize the significance of this victory and he approved the award of the Knight's Cross to the Iron Cross for *SS-Hauptsturmführer* Fritz Klingenberg on the 15th of May 1941.

Klingenberg would not receive any further grades of the Knight's Cross, but would certainly have a notable career in the *Waffen-SS* for most of the remainder of World War II. He assumed command of the *Motorcycle Infantry Battalion* towards the end of June 1941, a post he held until January 1942. He received a further award during that time; the Infantry Assault Badge in Bronze, awarded on the 3rd of July 1941. He was then promoted to *SS-Sturmbannführer* at the start of September 1941. In March 1942 Klingenberg took his skills and experiences to the officer training school at Bad Tolz in Bavaria. Here, he performed the role of instructor to the various *SS* officer candidates, readying them for what they may face at the front. Further promotion came on the 21st of December 1943, when he moved to the rank of *SS-Obersturmbannführer.* As mentioned above, he did not receive any further grades of the Knight's Cross, but on the 28th of April 1944 he was approved for the award of the German Cross in Gold. This recommendation was once again written by Paul Hausser and covered no less than seven different actions that spanned an almost two-year period. Just prior to this, Klingenberg had assumed overall command of Bad Tolz during mid-March 1944. His final promotion to the rank of *SS-Standartenführer* followed in December 1944. His final command came in January 1945, when he took over the *17th SS Division Gotz von Berlichingen*. It was with this *Division* that he was killed, on the March 22nd 1945.

Not only had he been one of the earliest holders of the Knight's Cross, but he had the opportunity to pass on the benefits of his experiences to the future officers of the *Waffen-SS*. Some of these future officers would become holders of the Knight's Cross themselves.

Kurt Meyer

Date of Birth: 23.12.1910

SS Number: 17 559

Born in Hexheim, he entered service in the *SS* on the 15th of October 1931, within the *22. Standarte*. Within his first year of service he gained promotion to *SS-Sturmführer (SS-Untersturmführer),* this taking place on the 7th of October 1932. He entered into the *LAH* in May 1934, following this with further promotion to *SS-Obersturmführer* on the 3rd of October 1935. He gained the command of the *Leibstandarte's 14. Kompanie* in September 1936, and remained at that command until late 1939. A further promotion had come along during that time, when on the 9th of December 1937, he moved to the rank of *SS-Hauptsturmführer.*

He fought in Poland and he was awarded the Second Class Iron Cross on the 25th of September 1939, having earlier been awarded the Black Wound Badge for a wound received in the first week of the campaign. By the time of the fighting in the west, he was commanding the *15. Motorcycle Kompanie*. During that campaign, he won the First Class Iron Cross on the 31st of May 1940. After this campaign he was presented with the Infantry Assault Badge in Bronze on the 3rd

SS-Sturmbannführer Kurt Meyer photographed after his award of the Knight's Cross

of October 1940. Just prior to this, at the start of September 1940, he was promoted to *SS-Sturmbannführer.* He had proved his bravery and skills up to the end of 1940 as it was, but the next campaign would allow him to demonstrate this further, it would also help forge the reputation that became known as 'Panzer' Meyer. Like Gert Pleiss, Meyer's Knight's Cross recommendation does not survive on his file, so the summary below is taken from Meyer himself.

He found himself as the advance guard in early April 1941 during the campaign in Greece. After elements of the *I Battalion* captured the Klidi Pass and suffered heavy casualties in the process, a different unit was needed to continue the advance. This job was given to Kurt Meyer and his *Aufklarungs Abteilung*.

Their assault upon the Klisura Pass started on the 13th of April 1941, and from the outset, they came up against difficulties. As outlined in the preceding pages, they came across a destroyed bridge, and attempts to get close to it were met with gun and grenade fire from the defenders in the mountains above. This prevented further advances on that day; Limited advances were made during the hours of darkness. For the second day of this assault, Meyer launched a diversionary attack along the road as well as two main attacks towards the high ground. As with the Klidi Pass, the fighting was close range and very hard.

Meyer was with the group advancing along the road. The three pronged attack got under way in the early morning and progress was made. Meyer's group advancing along the road, were surprised to have the road in front of them destroyed by a mine. The attack proceeded on foot, but in a matter of seconds, a further mine was exploded. The main attack was proceeding above them, and the intensity of the noise and the confusion must have made for a very difficult situation. It was at this stage that Meyer made a decision that became a myth. He found himself and his men pinned down behind some rocks and under intense enemy fire. The fear being felt by all of them was forcing them to stay put, a situation that Kurt Meyer knew could not continue. He therefore used the weapons at his disposal to force a continuation of the advance. He removed one of the grenades he was carrying and, in clear view of one of his *Platoon Commanders*, threw this at the feet of his men. They leaped into action and rushed forwards and advanced towards the summit, aided by their *Kameraden* above them. This relentless attack, made against very stiff and determined resistance, could only have one outcome. By the evening, this objective was under the control of the *LAH*.

The successful capture of this important objective resulted in the award of the Knight's Cross to the Iron Cross for Kurt Meyer, approved on the 18th of May 1941. It can be assumed that Dietrich would have made the recommendation, but this is not certain. This award would not be Meyer's last association with the various grades of this new medal, but details of that will follow in later

Map 5 The Balkans - Yugoslavia & Greece: April 1941

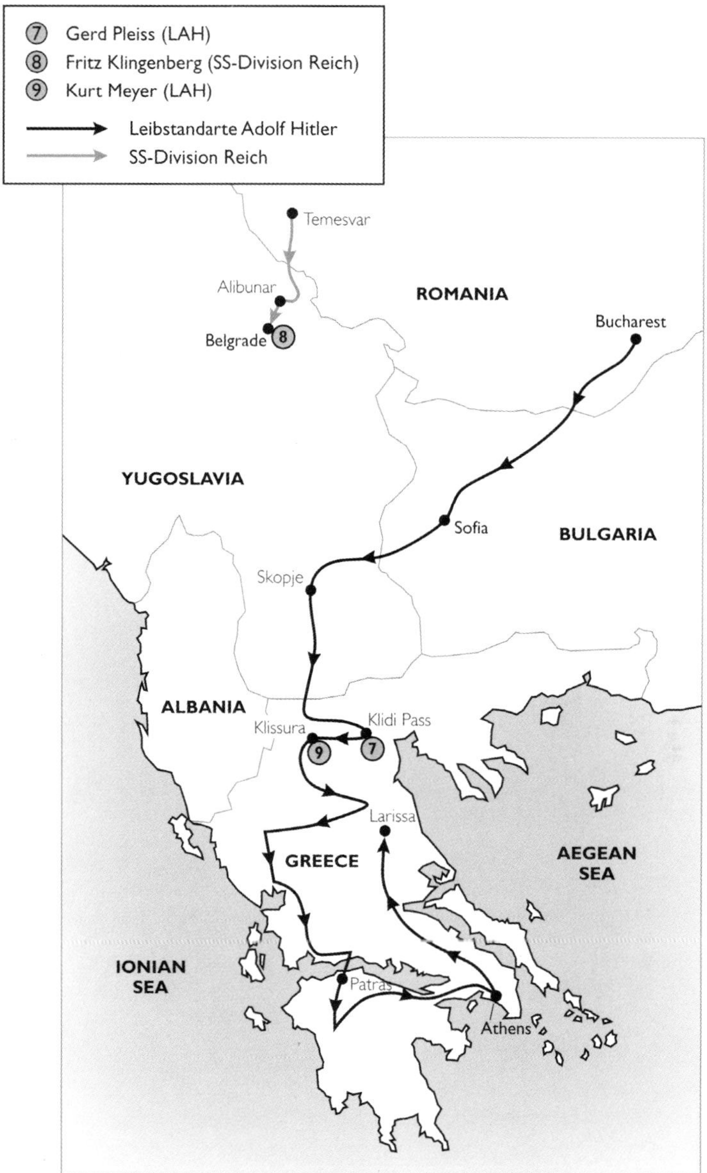

volumes. For now he could take pride in a job well done, even if achieved using controversial tactics.

Summary

The Balkan campaign overall, took less than one month to complete. Within the first week of crossing the Yugoslavian border, the capital city of Belgrade was in German hands, as were the formidable objectives of the Klidi and Klisura Passes in Greece. After being on Yugoslavian and Greek soil for less than two weeks, the surrender of both of these enemies was agreed. This was surely a stunning victory and another example of the workings of *Blitzkrieg*. So what about the part played by the *Waffen-SS?*

As highlighted above, Fritz Klingenberg had gained the surrender of the Yugoslavian capital city by using skill and a lot of luck, not to mention cool headed bravery and bluff! On the same day, the 12th of April 1941, Gert Pleiss secured the Klidi Pass in Greece. This was quickly followed by Kurt Meyer's capture of the Klisura Pass two days later. The capture of these three objectives led directly to the weakening of the enemy's resolve and ultimately, to the final surrender of both Yugoslavia and Greece. To add to this, it was Sepp Dietrich that was first offered the surrender of the *Greek Army*.

Therefore, not only had the *Waffen-SS* been involved heavily in this campaign, they had led the way and secured significant objectives. The individuals responsible were justly rewarded by the presentation of the Knight's Cross to the Iron Cross, bringing the *Waffen-SS* tally since the start of the war to nine, three within the *LAH* and six for the *SS-Division Reich*. The next campaign would give them ample chances to add to this tally and for some of the other *Waffen-SS* units to gain awards too, all of them would not have long to wait.

The skills employed were a further demonstration of the fighting skill of the *Waffen-SS*. They fought over difficult roads and steep mountains, not letting stiff resistance from natural barriers such as rivers or steep mountains, or well-emplaced defenders get in their way. They forged ahead and delivered what was expected of them in a very short space of time. They not only fought Yugoslavian and Greek troops, but also British and Commonwealth troops. These victories were only possible whilst fighting alongside their *Kameraden* within the *Heer* and with the support of the *Luftwaffe*.

CHAPTER FIVE

OPERATION BARBAROSSA - JUNE TO SEPTEMBER 1941

Preparing to Finish the War

With the end of the campaign in the Balkans Region, Adolf Hitler and his *Army* could class themselves as masters of Western Europe, apart from Britain. In less than two years they had defeated Poland, Norway, Holland, Belgium, France, Yugoslavia, Greece and Crete. This left Britain alone on the other side of the English Channel. Although Hitler had not gained the surrender of Britain, he knew that the formidable barrier of the Channel would prevent the British from launching any major attack into Europe in the foreseeable future. Britain would have to rebuild her severely weakened forces, and this would take time, as well as gain help from others. Even at this early stage, and despite America's proclamation of neutrality, it was estimated by all that their entry into the war was inevitable over the next one or two years.

In the east however, there was no formidable sea barrier between Germany and its' neighboring major power, the Soviet Union. Josef Stalin's Soviet Union had plans of their own, and 'negotiations' had been taking place between Germany and Russia since 1938. The most notable of these were the non-aggression pact and the agreement to divide Poland between them. Now however, Russia was pressing for more dominance, and expressed interests northwards in Finland and also southwards in Romania. Hitler was opposed to these interests and he clearly stated so. He saw a war with the Soviets as inevitable and, as early as July 1940, he ordered plans to be drawn up for such an attack. The plans were drafted between the summer of 1940 and the spring of 1941. With the successful conclusion of the

Balkan Campaign, Hitler decided that the time was right to launch his invasion of the Soviet Union.

The Overall Plan

To defeat Russia would require a monumental effort on the part of Hitler's *Army*. Any plan could draw on the experiences of previous invaders into Russia's vast land mass. Hitler knew that the campaign would have to be won swiftly, and one of the major objectives would be to prevent the escape of the Russian troops eastwards. Huge encirclements were called for, and a massive accumulation of men, machines and supplies would be needed. The plans would have to target strategically important areas and command structures. To aid in all of these needs, Hitler's troops were divided into three main groups.

Army Group North, under *Field Marshall* Ritter von Leeb contained the *16th Army, 4th Panzer Army* and the *18th Army*. There were a total of eighteen *Divisions* within this army group. Their primary objective was to advance on and seize control of Leningrad. Army Group Centre was under the control of *Field Marshall* Fedor von Bock. It contained the *3rd Panzer Group*, the *9th Army*, the *4th Army* and the *2nd Panzer Group*, which totaled over forty-five *Divisions*. Their primary objective was to push into Belorussia and advance onto Smolensk. Army Group South was under *Field Marshall* Gerd von Rundstedt, who had a total of fifty-two *Divisions*. These were split between the *6th Army*, the *17th Army*, *Panzer Group 1* and the *11th Army*. Their primary objective was to advance to the Black Sea, towards Odessa and the Crimea. In Finland, was *General* von Falkenhorst's *Norwegian Army Command*. They were to assist in the push on Leningrad. Of note is the fact that not one of these massive Army Groups had Moscow as their primary objective. The total number of soldiers amassed for this new offensive stood at around three-million.

So, what Soviet formations faced this formidable line up on the other side of the fence? Facing Army Group North was the North West Front, with the Kalinin Front placed close behind this. Opposite Army Group Centre was the West Front with the Reserve Front to the rear. In the south the South-West Front with the South Front in reserve faced Army Group South. Some estimates place around two-million Soviet troops in the immediate front line area, with a further one-million in reserve. The main Russian strength was in the south. Although Stalin had virtually ignored all of the warnings that he was given regarding the German attack, he certainly ensured that he had adequate men and materials in the western part of Russia to face any potential offensive. He did not expect an attack by Hitler so soon after the Greek campaign. In some respects, he was probably hoping that there would be no attack, as his own *Army* was in such a poor state after his bloody purges of 1937 and 1938.

Moving the *Waffen-SS* from West to East

As mentioned earlier, Hitler would have to amass as many troops as he could for this huge undertaking. The men of the *Waffen-SS* would be part of that undertaking, but at the start of the last campaign, they were either widely dispersed or in new formations undergoing training. It is now worth looking at how these various formations were moved towards the east and readied for their next challenge. It is important to mention that none of the front line troops were informed of where their next mission would take them. Intense speculation took place as the thousands of troops tried to guess what lay ahead.

The *LSSAH* spent May 1941 in the Greek area and then, during early June they moved to the Bohemia and Moravia Protectorate, in the Wischau area. At the end of the first week in June 1941, the *LSSAH* were ordered to begin their restructure into a full *Division*. However, unlike their *Waffen-SS* counterparts who formed their Divisions in the rear lines, the *LSSAH* would have to begin their formation whilst at the front line and whilst starting another major offensive. They spent the rest of June 1941 preparing for this next offensive as best as they could. The *LSSAH* were placed within *Panzer Gruppe 1*, part of Army Group South. Their first specific objective was to advance on Kiev and the Dnjeper River.

SS-Division Reich spent the remainder of April 1941 in Yugoslavia performing security duties. At the end of that month they moved to Austria, positioned around the Linz area. They stayed there until early June before being moved again. These moves took them through the eastern part of Germany and into Poland, initially around the Warsaw area and then slightly southeast of there to Lublin. *SS-Division Reich* was placed with *Panzer Gruppe 2*, within Army Group Centre.

SS-Division Totenkopf, if you recall, stayed in France after playing their part in the successful campaign in the west during the summer of 1940. They performed security and occupation duties and also focused on training. In early June 1941, they were moved from France and sent eastwards. They ended up on the East Prussian border with Lithuania. They were placed with *Panzer Gruppe 4*, within Army Group North.

The *Polizei Division* also remained in France during 1940, being situated around Paris. During November 1940 *SS-Gruppenführer und Generalleutnant* Arthur Mulverstadt took over command of this *Division*. Towards the end of June 1941, they were also sent east. They followed their *Totenkopf Kameraden* into *Panzer Gruppe 4*, within Army Group North. They however, were not placed on the front line, but instead were placed further back and assigned security duties.

SS-Division Wiking had focused on intensive training since their formation in late 1940. They were moved from Ebingen to Wurtemburg in the spring of 1941. They were then classed as combat ready in early June 1941, despite their relatively short training time. They were also ordered eastwards, and their moves took them via Czechoslovakia, Silesia, and then onto the Lublin area. They were assigned to *Panzer Gruppe 1*, part of Army Group South.

SS-Kampfgruppe Nord initially remained in Norway in the lead up to Barbarossa. As the start date approached they were moved to Finland, being placed in the Salla area in the northeast. They were given a new *Commander* in the form of *SS-Brigadeführer und Generalmajor der Waffen SS* Karl Demelhuber. They too were about to be used to help the assault on Soviet Russia. They were placed with *General* von Falkenhorst's *Norwegian Army Command.*

SS-Kavallerie Regiment 1 and the newly created *SS-Kavallerie Regiment 2* remained in the Polish region in early June 1941. They became part of the newly created security formation, *Kommandostab Reichsführer-SS*. They were placed as part of Army Group Centre and assigned security duties, although they would not participate in the opening stages.

1. SS-Infantry-Brigade (mot.)

As the battle in Greece was entering its' final stages, a new *SS Brigade* was raised. This unit was formed in late April 1941, and used the *8th* and *10th SS-Totenkopf Regiment's* as a foundation. Originally called the *1st SS-Brigade*, this was rapidly changed to the title of, *1. SS-Infantry-Brigade (mot.)*. This new unit was placed around Crakow in Poland and they stayed there until July 1941. They were assigned to Army Group Centre, but like the *SS-Kavallerie Regiment's,* they would not participate in the opening stages of this new campaign. *SS-Brigadeführer und Generalmajor der Waffen SS* Richard Hermann was placed as their *Commander*, after moving from *SS-Kampfgruppe Nord.*

2. SS-Infantry-Brigade (mot.)

This second new *SS Brigade* was raised at the start of May 1941, and contained the *4th*, *5th* and *14th SS-Totenkopf Infantry Regiment's*. The first *Commander* was *SS-Brigadeführer* Karl von Treuenfeld. Like their *1. SS-Infantry-Brigade Kameraden*, they would not be employed in the early stages of Barbarossa, but instead they remained in Crakow, Poland.

SS-Legion-Flandern & SS-Legion-Niederlande

Formed in mid-July 1941, these two units contained volunteers from Western Europe. They were stationed in Poland – *Flandern* in Radom and *Niederlande* in Cracow, where they began their formation and training. They were known collectively as *Germanic SS Volunteer Regiment Nordwest*. At the start of September 1941, *Niederlande and Flandern* were moved to the Ayrs camp, the same location as the *2. SS-Infantry Brigade (mot.)*. They stayed there as the *2. SS-Infantry Brigade (mot.)* moved to Army Group North in September 1941; therefore, they did not take part in the opening stages of Barbarossa. We will cover them again at a later stage.

On the Start Line

We have listed the various *SS* formations that existed in June 1941. Although they have been listed in chronological order of existence, I feel it would be beneficial to once again list their positions, only this time I will do so in relation the main army groups. Therefore:

> Norwegian Army Command – on the Finnish/Russian border stood around ten thousand *Waffen-SS* troops within *SS Kampfgruppe Nord*.
>
> Army Group North – stood in the region of thirty-six thousand *Waffen-SS* troops within the *SS Totenkopf Division* and the *Polizei Division*.
>
> Army Group Centre – contained approximately twenty-five thousand *Waffen-SS* troops within the *SS Division Reich* and the *SS-Kavallerie Regiments 1* and *2*.
>
> Army Group South – had around thirty-six thousand *Waffen-SS* troops within the *Leibstandarte Adolf Hitler, SS Division Wiking* and the *1. SS Infantry Brigade (mot.)*.

This totaled almost one hundred and ten thousand *Waffen-SS* troops. They stood ready to engage the next enemy. By the latter stages of June 1941 any uncertainty they had was dispelled and further guessing was not needed. The orders had been issued and everyone knew that they would be engaging the soldiers of the Soviet Union any time now. They knew that this would be a difficult battle and they were aware that this was the largest enemy they had faced to date. However, confidence was extremely high as they had swept all previous enemies to one side. There were no indicators for the men on the front line that this new enemy would be any different. A swift and stunning victory was the expectation, and as Adolf Hitler himself stated, '*the world will hold its' breath!*'

The forthcoming campaign would allow the men of the *Waffen-SS* to earn the highest number of Knight's Crosses in any one region. They did not know this at the time, nor did they know how high a blood-price would have to be paid. The last unknown factor was the fact that this advance into Russia would not end for nearly four years and the stop line would not be Moscow, but instead Berlin. For now however, let us begin to look at what took place in those intervening years, which started in late June 1941.

Army Group Centre

The First *Waffen-SS* Knight's Crosses of Barbarossa

The first *Waffen-SS* Knight's Cross of this new campaign would be awarded to a soldier within Army Group Centre, so we will follow the progress of that group first. At 03:15 a.m. on the morning of 22nd June 1941, the opening shots of Operation Barbarossa were fired. *SS-Division Reich* where in Brest-Litovsk at that stage and they would remain in their forming up area for the first five days of the campaign. They slowly moved up to the demarcation line through dense traffic jams. They finally moved over the front line on the 27th June 1941. They initially advanced towards Minsk then Citva, Dukova, Milovidy and Beresina, taking them up to the end of June, where they stood at Lubiasze. By this stage the first large pocket was closing around the Soviet forces between Bialystock and Minsk. This pocket netted over 300,000 enemy soldiers and thousands of tanks, some estimates list around forty enemy divisions being captured or destroyed.

The start of July had *SS-Division Reich* advancing to Tscherva, Puchoviece and reaching the town of Beresino by the 3rd of July. The fighting against the Soviets was increasing in intensity and included battles against infantry, tanks and anti-tank guns. This first seven days of Barbarossa for this *Division* had cost them almost 350 dead or wounded. After crossing the Beresina River they moved on towards the Dnjepr River, with the first objectives being Mohilev and Schlov. They ran into difficulties between the 6th of July and the 17th of July 1941 in between these two rivers. The Dnjepr River was crossed on the 11th of July by *SS-Regiment Der Führer* and the *11th Regiment*. The accompanying *10th Panzer Division* and the *GrossDeutschland Division* established a bridgehead on the eastern bank. Around this time the *Division* suffered some losses. The first was when Georg Keppler was transferred from command of *SS-Regiment Der Führer* to command of the *SS-Division Totenkopf*, *SS-Sturmbannführer* Otto Kumm took over *Der Führer*. Also, on the 13th of July *SS-Regiment 11* suffered almost fifty officers killed or wounded in Goski.

These losses had to be dealt with and the advance continued. By the 16th of July they were in Mstislavl and they had been harassed all the way by enemy infantry and aerial attacks as these enemy soldiers attempted to move further eastwards. Potschino was reached by the 18th of July and everyone was noticing

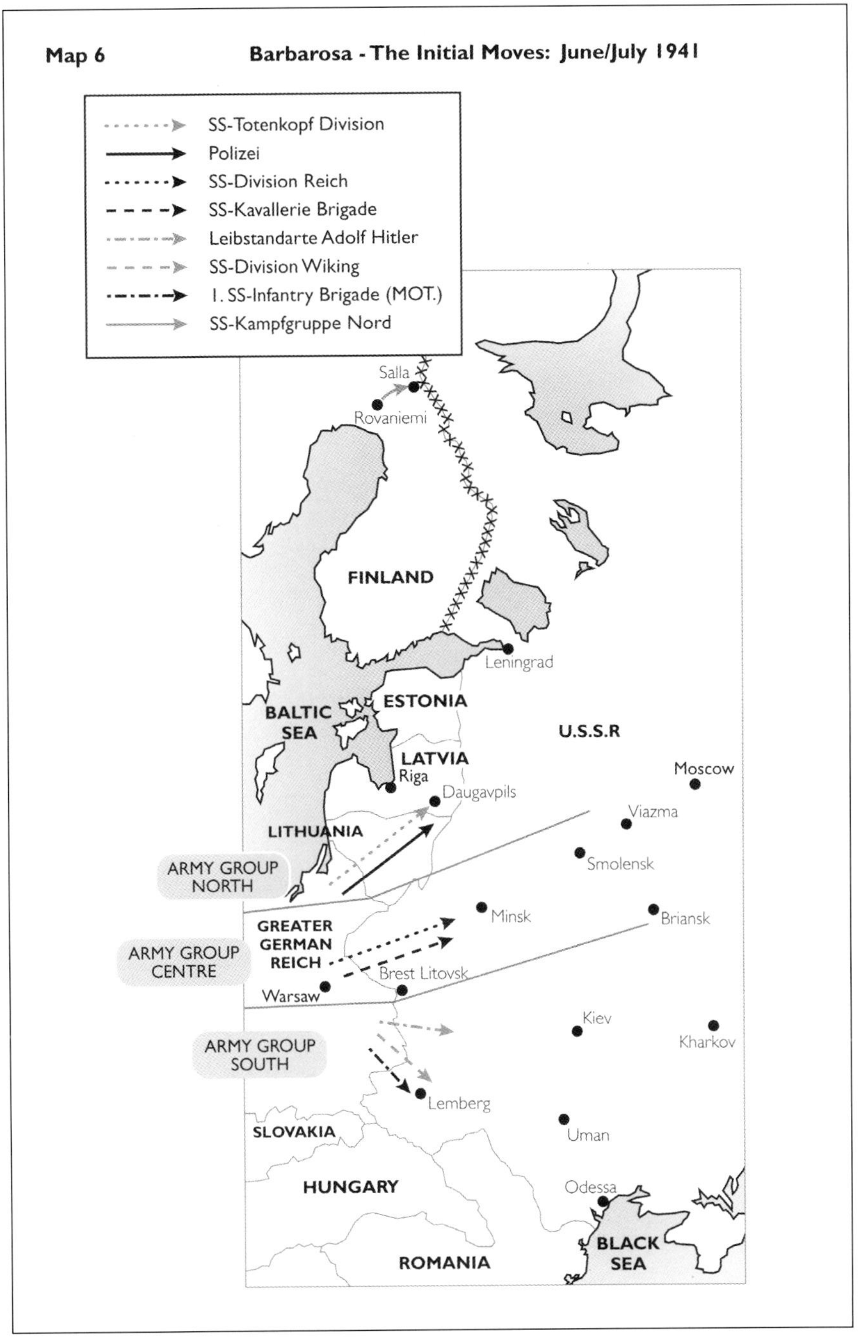
Map 6
Barbarosa - The Initial Moves: June/July 1941
SS-Totenkopf Division
Polizei
SS-Division Reich
SS-Kavallerie Brigade
Leibstandarte Adolf Hitler
SS-Division Wiking
I. SS-Infantry Brigade (MOT.)
SS-Kampfgruppe Nord
Salla
Rovaniemi
FINLAND
Leningrad
BALTIC SEA
ESTONIA
U.S.S.R
LATVIA
Riga
Moscow
Daugavpils
Viazma
LITHUANIA
Smolensk
ARMY GROUP NORTH
Minsk
Briansk
GREATER GERMAN REICH
ARMY GROUP CENTRE
Brest Litovsk
Warsaw
Kiev
Kharkov
ARMY GROUP SOUTH
Lemberg
SLOVAKIA
Uman
HUNGARY
Odessa
BLACK SEA
ROMANIA

the increasing intensity of the enemy resistance as they moved deeper and deeper into Russia. By the 20th of July elements of *SS-Division Reich* reached the Yelnya – Dorogobusch road. Their advance up to this point had taken them south-southeast of Smolensk and they were part of the southern wing of the encirclement attempts around this significant city. It was now almost one month since the start of this campaign and already they were only 200 miles from Moscow.

At Yelnya there is a stretch of high ground and this became the next target. The Russians had set up their main defensive lines at Yelnya and they controlled the dominant high ground. By the end of the 22nd of July the *Division* had succeeded in taking control of this high ground, despite heavy fighting, now they switched to the defensive. Heavy counter attacks were launched by the enemy all along the twenty-five mile front held by *SS-Division Reich*. The intensity of the fighting can be gauged by the fact that virtually all of the elements of the *Division* were committed to either strengthening defenses or defending against a variety of attacks, including enemy tank attacks.

One such enemy tank attack was launched with eight tanks on the 24th of July against Yelnya from the north along the main Yelnya to Dorogobusch road. At this place there was a natural ravine flanked by steep cliffs. *SS-Unterscharführer* Erich Rossner, from the *SS-Division Reich's, Tank Destroyer Battalion's, 2. Kompanie,* held this defensive point. He managed to defeat this enemy tank attack in a short space of time (Knight's Cross action that will be covered in more detail later).

The enemy tank attacks did not stop around Yelnya that day and further probing attacks were put in by the enemy. Slightly north of Yelnya is the village of Uschakova and it received the focus of the Russians later on the 24th of July 1941. The pressure they exerted succeeded in pushing back an *Army Pioneer Battalion*, which exposed the left flank of the *SS-Motorcycle Infantry Battalion*. The *First Staff Officer* of *SS-Division Reich, SS-Obersturmbannführer* Werner Ostendorff, gathered together a few *Sturmgeschutze,* anti-tank guns and some men and together they moved to this village. They arrived that evening and began to take up positions. On the following day, the 25th of July 1941, they successfully dealt with the enemy incursion and restored the situation back to a favorable one for the Germans, all under the careful command of Ostendorf who led and coordinated the counter attack (Knight's Cross action covered in more detail later).

The intensity of the enemy attacks in this area continued, with both sides fully aware of the importance of this sector and therefore the importance in controlling it. The Russians pushed everything they had in this area towards Yelnya. *SS-Division Reich* held the most forward point within Army Group Centre at this stage and the enemy focused on trying to blunt this point. Over the following days the *Division* had to deal with intensive tank, artillery and infantry attacks.

They also had to cope with ammunition shortages, no relief, no reserves and no rest or respite. One positive occurrence around this time was the closing of the Smolensk Pocket on the 27th of July 1941. This encirclement netted over 300,000 enemy soldiers, 3,000 tanks and a similar number of anti-tank guns. The cost to *SS-Division Reich* in this first month of fighting in Russia was around 2,500 dead and wounded.

The closing of the Smolensk Pocket did not end the fighting. The remaining Soviet soldiers still applied relentless pressure upon the sector around Yelnya. The fact that *SS-Division Reich* held this area against this extreme pressure is a testament to their fighting abilities, skills, bravery and determination. Many individual acts of bravery were performed during this period. One new aspect came to the fore around this time, the knocking out of enemy tanks by individual soldiers. As an indication, between the 23rd and 25th of July over fifty enemy tanks were knocked out, in and around Yelnya.

With the closing of the pocket and the fact that Yelnya was held against the enemy helped to improve the situation for the Germans. Around this time, new units arrived and fresh supplies were sent to the front. The holding of the Yelnya sector lasted until the end of the first week in August 1941, only then did the relief begin. During the time in between, the enemy continuously tried to seize Yelnya. The intensity of these attacks slowly decreased. By the 9th of August the relief was complete and *SS-Division Reich* moved slightly backwards to the west for an intended rest period. This rest did not materialize until after the middle of the month. This was due to the fact that between the 9th and the 17th of August, they had to deal with more enemy attacks in their new positions. These new attacks were not as intensive as those at Yelnya, but they were costly none the less. Total casualties suffered by *SS-Division Reich* up to the middle of August amounted to almost 4,000 dead and wounded.

They had fought odds of 7-to-1 in very intensive battles and gained valuable battle experience, a large degree of this division's reputation began from the Yelnya battles. Their accomplishments were recognized at the highest level and three Knight's Crosses were awarded for the fighting actions of partial actions around Yelnya. Two of these have been indicated above and will be covered in more detail. The third Knight's Cross came on the 8th of August 1941 for Paul Hausser and the recommendation covered actions as far back as the campaign in the west during 1940 (more details to follow). To sum up the overall views of *SS-Division Reich's* achievements within Army Group Centre in the first six weeks of Operation Barbarossa, what better person to quote, but none other than the most recent Knight's Cross winner, *SS-Gruppenführer* Paul Hausser. He issued an 'order of the day' on the 10th of August 1941, which gave a very good overview of what had been achieved and lost! The final short paragraph read as follows:

> 'The *Division* can be especially proud of the achievements and successes for which it was recognized by its' superiors! We are awaiting orders for continued action. The men of *SS-Division* "Reich" could drive the devil from burning hell itself.'

It is a good point to leave the actions of *SS-Division Reich* for the time being and to have a look at the other *SS* unit fighting within this army group. However, before doing this, I will give details of the Knight's Cross winners up to this date.

Paul Hausser

Date of Birth: 07.10.1880

SS Number: 217 862

Born in Brandenburg, Haval, his extensive military career began aged just twelve when he joined the *Prussian Cadet Corps*. One of his early schools was the future home of the *LAH,* that of Berlin Lichterfelde. Seven years later, in early 1899, he achieved the rank of *Leutnant*. He served as an *Adjutant* in west Prussian over the next eight years. Further training courses and a stint with the *Navy* covered the time up to his next promotion. This was in 1912 when he was promoted to *Oberleutnant,* also in 1912 he joined the *Army General Staff.* Fifteen years after receiving his first officer rank he achieved the rank of *Hauptmann,* in March 1914. Prior to the start of the First World War he moved to the *Bavarian Army* under the command of Crown Prince Rupprecht, again as a *Staff Officer*. By the end of the war he was holding the rank of *Major* and had been awarded both classes of the Iron Cross, as well as at least seven other awards!

The inter-war years saw Paul Hausser serve with a host of different units including border protection in the east and a spell as *First Staff Officer* for *Brigade Number 5*. Promotion to *Oberstleutnant* came in mid-November 1922. This was followed by command of an *Infantry Battalion*, *First Staff Officer* with a *Division* and then command of an *Infantry Regiment*. The same year as serving as a *Regimental Commander*, 1927, he was promoted to *Oberst*. He also spent time as the *Commander* of the troop training area in Munsingen during 1930. Further promotion to *Generalmajor* came in early 1931 and then again to *Generalleutnant* before retiring from the *Reichswehr* at the end of January 1932. Then the work really began!

In 1934 he had a spell with the *S.A*. and then on the 1st of November the same year he moved to the fledgling *SS* as part of the *SS-VT.* Heinrich Himmler had been keen to make use of Hausser's extensive skills and employing them in helping to train the men of the *SS*. His first posting was as *Commander* of the *SS* officer school in Braunschweig, at that time holding the rank of *SS-Standartenführer.*

A signed photograph of Paul Hausser showing him after his award of the Knight's Cross. He can also be seen wearing his eye patch, necessary after his severe eye injury in 1941.

Within a year he was given the title of *Inspector of SS Officer Schools* and promoted to *SS-Oberführer.* 1936 would see further career advances with a move to *Inspector of the SS-Verfugungstruppen* and promotion to *SS-Brigadeführer und Generalmajor der Waffen-SS*. Just prior to the outbreak of the Second World War, Hausser was promoted to *SS-Gruppenführer.* Paul Hausser is often referred to as the 'Father of the *Waffen-SS*' and was often called 'Papa' Hausser. It was during his five-year inter-war service with the *SS* that he earned this reputation. He can be regarded as the person who ensured that the *SS* were readied for the next possible conflict. He overseen the officer training schools at Braunschweig and Bad Tolz through which, many of the men that formed the excellent fighting reputation of the *Waffen-SS* passed through. These individual men included many of the *Kompanie, Battalion, Regimental* and *Divisional Commanders* of the *Waffen-SS* during World War II, not to mention countless Knight's Cross holders! It is fair to say that his formal military training that began forty-seven years earlier made a huge difference to the pre-war *SS* and ensured that it had the skills and knowledge to engage the armies of the rest of the world. Even after achieving all of this, his work was far from over. In 1939 he entered Poland with his *SS-VT,* at the grand age of fifty-eight, in what became known as the Second World War.

Service in Poland earned him the Clasp to the Second Class Iron Cross. In between Poland and the end of 1939 he assumed command of the newly formed *SS V Division*. His new *Division* performed excellently during the campaign in the west during 1940. No fewer than five of his soldiers were awarded the Knight's Cross to the Iron Cross, some of the recommendations were written by Hausser himself. He personally received the Clasp to the First Class Iron Cross for this campaign. Yugoslavia would see his men perform equally as well in this short, but significant campaign. A further Knight's Cross went to one of his men after this campaign. It was in Russia however, that his men of the re-named *SS-Division Reich* came to the fore. Even in the early stages, his men proved their abilities as covered in the preceding pages.

It was on the 8th of August 1941 however, that *SS-Gruppenführer* Paul Hausser received a Knight's Cross to the Iron Cross for himself. The recommendation was endorsed by Heinz Guderian, the *2. Panzer Gruppe Commander*, whose words contained the following: 'He always remained at the focal point of the battle and led his troops without regard for himself, despite the threat on the flank and from the rear.' *General* von Vietinghoff, the *XXXXVI Panzer Korps Commander*, who focused on Hausser's successes during the campaign in the west the previous year. *Field Marshall* von Kluge, the *4. Panzer Army Commander,* and Feder von Bock, the *Commander* of Army Group Centre. The *Commander* of the *OKH* himself, von Brauschitsch penned the overall recommendation, approved on the 5th of

August 1941. The recommendation mentioned the campaign in the west during 1940, but focused heavily on the successes in the early stages of Barbarossa. It contained the following points:

> 'Proved himself an excellent leader during the Western campaign, taking command of the situation always at the most dangerous position. Great confidence and calm and mastering the most difficult situation set him apart from others.
>
> His battle leadership won decisive influence during the battles between the Beresina and Dnjepr Rivers. After crossing the Beresina, the *Division* received the task of relieving the threatened *10. Panzer Division*. In order to find the enemy's position and to annihilate the opponent which had skillfully retreated to the east, the *Divisional Commander* decided to push forward the *Motorcycle Infantry Battalion* on the 7th of July. This *Battalion* pushed into Esmon and on towards Oslik, they also had to secure the area. The bulk of the *Division* was to attack the enemy head on. Near Somry, the enemy offered *SS-Regiment 'Der Führer'* strong resistance. The *Divisional Commander* rushed to the forward most *Battalion* in order to personally get a look at the strength of the enemy. Despite being wounded by shrapnel from a grenade, he remained at his post. He used all available artillery to push the enemy back into a forested area.
>
> The skillful and energetic leadership of the *Divisional Commander* brought successes in this extremely difficult terrain. He was able to throw back and almost annihilate the enemy who attacked on all sides. The quick advance to the Dnjepr River during this engagement; ensured that the Russians were not able to organize effective defenses. These actions enabled the *Korps* to cross the Dnjepr River and the *10. Panzer Division* to follow up quickly, which later proved to be a decisive event for the entire operation.'

This award was not the only link to the various grades of the Knight's Cross for Paul Hausser, but more of that later. With the above award, Hausser became the tenth recipient of this prestigious medal and the second overall unit *Commander* within the *Waffen-SS,* the other being Sepp Dietrich. It is worth drawing a comparison between these two personalities at this point.

Josef Dietrich had reached *NCO* rank by the end of the First World War and was always considered a rough and ready type of person. His unquestionable loyalty was one of his main strengths and one that Adolf Hitler made extensive use of. His other abilities as a leader of men and a father figure were also put to good use. His physical abilities were used during the early days of Hitler's power struggles. In later years, there were question marks raised over his ability to command larger military formations, but his achievements with the *LAH* were there for all to see up to start of Operation Barbarossa and would continue beyond that point.

Paul Hausser on the other hand had received formal military training from an early age and had moved up the officer ranks in the years prior to World War II. This training included staff officer courses and it could be argued that Hausser was better equipped to handle the commands he was given. His age was not a hindrance and he proved to men many years his junior that he still had something to offer. The men under his command held the highest number of Knight's Crosses, even as early as mid-1941. Like Dietrich, the achievements of his unit were there for all to see and recognize.

Although these two men had taken different paths up to this point and they would continue to do so, the both played a huge part in the forming of the *Waffen-SS* and its' fighting ability and they would continue to have a decisive influence for the remainder of the war.

To finish this overview of Paul Hausser up to early August 1941, what better quote to finish with, than that of the man himself from his 'order of the day' dated the 17th of August, "The Führer bestowed upon me the Knight's Cross of the Iron Cross. I consider this award recognition for the *Division's* achievements in all theatres of battle, especially against Soviet Russia."

Erich Rossner

Date of Birth: 26.05.1918

SS Number: unknown

Born in Helmbrechts, Pfalz on the above date. He joined the *Hitler Youth* and moved up the ranks in that organization during the early 1930s. On the 3rd of July 1937 he joined the *SS-Verfugungstruppe* and took part in the march into Austria and also the Sudetenland prior to the outbreak of the war. He also seen service in the west during 1940 and his tank killing skills were put to good use in France, where he is listed as knocking out three tanks in one day alone. At that time he crewed a *Pak .37*. One source lists him as having successfully knocked out at least thirteen enemy tanks in Russia alone. As highlighted earlier in this chapter, he found himself in a natural defensive position on the main Yelnya to Dorogobusch road, facing northwards. From this direction came eight Russian tanks. They were looking for weak spots and hoped that their weight in numbers would help them punch through at this position. What they had not counted on was the determination and skill of *SS-Unterscharführer* Erich Rossner and his crew, who were manning a *Pak .38* anti-tank gun.

Probably the only known photo of Erich Rossner, pictured prior to his death in July 1941.

As the tanks approached, Rossner issued the following orders, "let them get to fifty metres, hit the first tank and then the rear one, then the rest". His crew started to do exactly that and successfully destroyed the first enemy tank. The second enemy tank was a flamethrower version and it ejected a jet of flame towards Rossner's gun. The gun crew all managed to get out of the way and avoided being incinerated by this flame. The enemy tank crew assumed that they had scored a hit and killed the crew, so they stopped, got out of their tank and walked towards the gun. At this point Rossner and his men descended upon their gun and attacked this enemy tank crew. Using grenades, hand-held weapons and shovels, they defeated this enemy and then re-manned their anti-tank gun. They carried on with the orders issued by Rossner and successfully knocked out all eight of the enemy tanks. This entire engagement lasted around five minutes from start to finish! The enemy was sent a clear message from these actions and no further attempts were made to break into Yelnya along this point in the road.

The intensive battle for Yelnya was far from over and Rossner and his men continued to fight after this engagement. The following day, the 25th of July 1941, Erich Rossner was severely wounded by an enemy shell fragment and moved to a field hospital. It was there that he died on the 30th of July 1941. He was awarded the Second Class Iron Cross on the 25th of July 1941 and the First Class Iron Cross on the 3rd of August 1941. His actual award of the Knight's Cross to the Iron Cross was approved on the 25th of August 1941 and was the first posthumous award of this medal, awarded to a soldier of the *Waffen-SS*, but would not be the last. It is not known who wrote the recommendation, but it can be assumed that it would have been Paul Hausser. It is also not known what other awards Erich Rossner held up to his death. He became the 11th *SS* soldier to receive the award of the Knight's Cross to the Iron Cross and the first *Waffen-SS* Knight's Cross holder to die during the war, but certainly not the last.

Werner Ostendorff

Date of Birth: 15.08.1903

SS Number: 257 146

Born in Konigsberg, he was not quite old enough to see service in the First World War. He did however, help to repel the rise of communism in the after war years in Germany during 1919-20. He joined the *Reichsheer* on the 5th of November 1925, seeing service with the *1st Prussian Infantry Regiment*. He became an officer candidate less than six months later in April 1926. He became a *Leutnant* in June 1930, having been promoted through the ranks during the intervening four years. His first role as *Leutnant* was that of *Platoon Commander* in the *II Battalion*. His next promotion came in July 1933 to *Oberleutnant,* by then Adolf Hitler had

SS-Obersturmbannführer Werner Ostendorff pictured shortly after his award of the Knight's Cross for actions in July 1941.

come to power. At the start of March 1934 he began a stint with the *Luftwaffe*, qualifying as a pilot. His time with the *Luftwaffe* ended in October 1935 when he transferred again, this time to the *SS-VT*.

He retained his rank and on the 1st of October 1935 he held the rank of *SS-Obersturmführer*. He then moved to the *SS* Officers School at Bad Tolz in the role of teacher and stayed there until the end of March 1938. He had been promoted further to *SS-Hauptsturmführer* whilst at Bad Tolz, at the end of January 1936. Upon leaving there he then took command of the *4. Kompanie* within the newly formed *SS-Regiment Der Führer*. Just prior to the start of World War II, he was promoted to *SS-Sturmbannführer*. He saw service in Poland during 1939, then, when the *SS V Division* was formed towards the end of that year, he was chosen as the *First Staff Officer*. His service during the campaign in the west during 1940 earned him the Second Class Iron Cross, on the 19th of May 1940 and also the First Class Iron Cross on the 23rd of June 1940. In mid-December 1940 he was promoted further to *SS-Obersturmbannführer*. He saw service in Yugoslavia and then with the rest of the *Division*, he entered the abyss of Russia in June 1941.

An indication of his actions at Yelnya on the 25th of July 1941 is listed on the previous pages. As a result of these actions Paul Hausser wrote a recommendation for the award of the Knight's Cross on the 29th of July 1941. This was approved and awarded on the 13th of September 1941. Although he became the 13th *SS* soldier to win this award, with a soldier from Army Group North coming before him, it is worth covering his actions here as they followed the day after Erich Rossner's actions and were performed during the same battle. The recommendation contained the following:

> "The battles focused on the main road to Dorogobusch, which the enemy used to move troops. A Russian success at this open flank would have endangered the positions of the entire *XXXXVI Army Korps*, *10. Panzer Division* and *SS-Division Reich*. On the 24th of July 1941 the *Korps Engineer Battalion* lost possession of Ushakowo, twice. A counter attack restored the situation, but once again the enemy attacked and cut-off the engineers. The attached heavy weapons battery also ran short of ammunition. The *Division*, with a twenty-five-mile front, did not have any reserves and as the situation was critical, requested a tank *Kompanie* from the *Korps* as a last reserve.
>
> *SS-Obersturmbannführer* Ostendorff drove to this area and took all necessary measures. The situation was only saved due to bold actions by him. He reconnoitered the enemy himself, sent out reconnaissance parties, extricated one unit to a more favorable attack position and personally directed the tanks, assault guns, infantry and heavy machine guns. He advanced

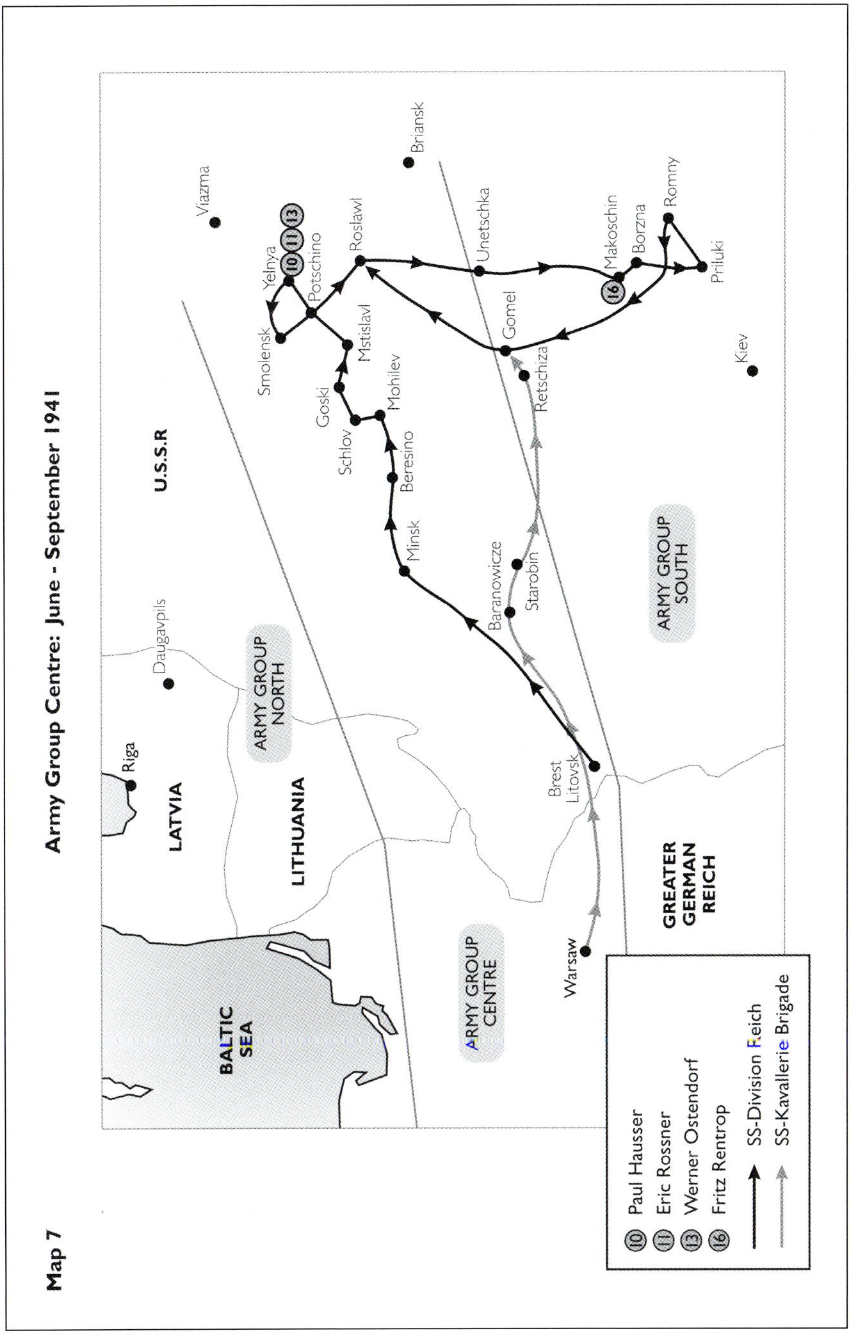

Map 7

Army Group Centre: June - September 1941

forward with the unit up to the enemy defensive fire zone. He succeeded the next morning in taking the positions and eliminated the danger of the enemy breakthrough along the entire northern boundary."

Like many of his Knight's Cross winning *Kameraden*, this would not be his only link with this award. More details of his subsequent actions will follow.

SS-Kavallerie Regiments 1* and *2

On the 21st of July 1941, just as *SS-Division Reich's* intensive battle at Yelnya was beginning, *SS-Kavallerie Regiments 1* and *2* were moved further eastwards to the north-western reaches of the extensive Pripet Marsh. Their first stop was Baranowicze (Baranavicy), over 250 miles southwest of Yelnya. Around 100 miles further east at Sluck, a large group of Partisan/Russian troops were advancing westwards. This was around the start of the last week of July 1941. *SS-Kavallerie Regiments 1* and *2* would be tasked with linking with a cut-off element of another *Regiment* and then engaging this enemy force. The overall *Commander* in this area was *SS-Brigadeführer* Erich von dem Bach. This operation began on the 29th of July and continued until August the 13th, and was considered successful. Back at the start of August, *SS-Kavallerie Regiments 1* and *2* received the official orders to reorganize and rename themselves into the *SS-Kavallerie Brigade*. They were in the western sector of the Marsh at this stage.

We will leave the actions of this unit at this stage and now move onto the Army Group North's sector for details of the next Knight's Cross winner and his actions.

Army Group North

The Push Towards Leningrad and the Next Knight's Cross

Although the first Knight's Cross for a *Waffen-SS* soldier within the above army group was awarded to a member of the *Polizei Division,* this unit moved behind the main lead advance troops. Therefore, to fully understand the circumstances that resulted in the next award of the Knight's Cross, we will cover the initial stages of Operation Barbarossa in the north. Within the context of this book, that means covering the *SS-Totenkopf Division's* actions.

SS-Totenkopf Division

Totenkopf began their moves on the 24th of July 1941. They crossed the Lithuanian border at Jurbarkas and moved in a northeasterly direction. By the 28th of

June elements were south of Utena. Movement continued through Dunaburg (Daugavpils) and onto Kraslava, towards the end of June 1941. Enemy resistance intensified along the way. Even at this early stage of Barbarossa it was evident that this would be a difficult battle. The *Totenkopf Division* had also suffered its' first losses in the Russian campaign. By the end of the first week in July the *Division* was fighting in Sebesh, further east of Kraslava. After securing this difficult objective, they moved northwards to Opotschka (Opocka). This objective was finally secured on the 10th of July 1941. Up to this point, the *Division* had suffered the loss of around 1,850 dead and wounded; one of these wounded was the *Divisional Commander* Theodore Eicke. These casualty figures give a very good indication of the intensity of the fighting in these first two weeks, and to think that tougher objectives lay ahead!

SS-Standartenführer Kleinhesterkamp temporarily replaced Eicke as *Divisional Commander*. The main advance continued northeast with the *3rd Infantry Division* and *8th Panzer Division's* in the lead; *Totenkopf* also continued in this line of advance. By mid-July elements of *Totenkopf* were supporting the *8th Panzer Division* near Borowitschi, other elements attacked towards Dno. Around this time, on the 19th of July, *SS-Brigadeführer* Georg Keppler returned as *Divisional Commander*, in place of the wounded Theodore Eicke. The attack continued northeast towards the Mschaga River. With the move northeast, other *Divisions* were moved through the towns previously won by *Totenkopf* and their *Army Kameraden*. One of these 'second line' units was the *Polizei Division*. We will now shift to give an overview of their actions as this is where the next Knight's Cross was awarded.

Polizei Division

As highlighted previously, the *Polizei Division* where on the Lithuanian border towards the end of June 1941, as part of the *4. Panzer Gruppe*. The phenomenal advances by Army Group North had taken them as far as Opotschka (Opocka) by the end of the first week in July. The left wing of the army group had moved through Lithuania, Latvia and then slightly northeast to Pleskau (Pskow), reached on the 10th of July. This gave Army Group North control of the three Baltic provinces of Lithuania, Latvia and Estonia.

Behind this advance moved the *Polizei Division*. They moved initially eastwards over the Lithuanian border and then north of Kauen (Kaunas), then south of Dunaburg then on across the Duna River at Dryssa on the 13th of July 1941. After crossing this river, the *Division* moved northwards towards Opotschka (Opocka), Ostrow (Ostrov) and Pleskau (Pskow), which was reached on the 26th of July. At this stage they were now part of the *18th Army*, within the *LVI Army*

Korps. They had covered over 550 miles since crossing the Lithuanian border. At the end of July 1941 the *Polizei Division* began their part in the first attacks around the greater Luga area. This city is on the main advance road to Leningrad (St. Petersburg) and control of it would open the road to the north coast.

The first stages of the attack started on the 10th of August 1941, to the south of Luga, around Kut. This was the same day that Paul Hausser was issuing his 'order of the day' at the end of their Yelnya battle – around 300 miles southeast of Luga. The first stage of the attack was to advance on Luga from both sides. This first day witnessed very intensive fighting around this area, which resulted in the death of the *Polizei Division's Commander, General* Mulverstadt along with many of his soldiers. There was no time to pause or find a replacement and the official history makes mention of the remaining units fighting as *Kampfgruppes*. By mid-August they had fought up to Stojanowtschina. They then moved eastwards over the next few days.

This started the second phase of the attack and it began on the 23rd of August 1941. They would attack the city of Luga from the east and southeast. *Regiment 1* where on the left, *Regiment 2* in the centre, with *Regiment 3* on the right. *Oberst* Hans Christian Schulze led *Regiment 2* into the heart of the city over the 23rd and 24th of August and by the evening of the 24th they raised the German flag in the city centre (Knight's Cross action). The capture of this city netted 5,000 enemy soldiers killed or captured and it also opened the direct route to Leningrad.

No sooner was this success achieved, than the *Division* had to continue their northwards movement. In the final days of August and into the first week of September, the *Polizei Division* moved through the Lugi swamps area, Wyriza, Krassnizy, Ssussanino and on towards Krassnogwardeisk. Along the way they had to deal with difficult terrain and a determined and desperate enemy trying to also reach the relative safety of Leningrad. The enemy was also trying to buy valuable time in order to further improve the defenses around this strategic objective. On the 9th of September 1941 Georgi Zhukov was appointed overall *Commander* of Leningrad and ordered by Stalin himself not to surrender the city.

On this same day the *Polizei Division* began the next phase of their moves closer to Leningrad. The objective was Krassnogwardeisk, which formed part of the outer defenses of Leningrad. As with the previous fighting in this sector, the Russians were resisting with all they had. The forward attack by the *Polizei Division* was harassed by the enemy, from woods along the advance route. Multiple concrete bunkers had to be taken along the way and despite all of the resistance put up by the Russians; Krassnogwardeisk was captured on September the 13th 1941 by *Regiment 3*, under the command of *Oberst* Wunnenberg.

It was also on this day that *SS-Brigadeführer und Generalmajor der Polizei* Hans Christian Schulze died. It is a good point to leave the advance of the *Polizei Division* within Army Group North.

2. SS-Infantry-Brigade (mot.)
This unit was last coverd in May 1941 as they were being raised in Crakow, Poland. Towards the end of July 1941, they were sent to Ayrs in East Prussia. They remained there until the start of September 1941. During mid-August *SS-Infantry Regiment 5* was removed from this *Brigade* and elements were sent to join *SS-Kampfgruppe Nord* in Finland. At the start of September, the remaining elements were sent as replacements to *SS-Division Reich*. In the first week of September, the *2. SS-Infantry-Brigade (mot.)* was sent to Army Group North, moving initially through Latvian territory. By the 8th of September they had reached Pleskau (Pskov) within the boundaries of Soviet Russia. Their first enemy contact came two days later and for a period of five days, they fought enemy forces in what was known as the Vyriza Pocket, south of Leningrad, it cost the *Brigade* almost 180 casualties. They were then moved further east to Tschudovo (Cudovo). In the last week of September, they were positioned northeast of Tschudovo at Tossno (Tosno) engaging in further smaller battles with enemy troops.

Hans Christian Schulze
Date of Birth: 15.07.1893
SS Number: 401 321
Born in Schwarzenbeck, Holstein, Schulze's military career began in 1912. By 1914 he was holding the rank of *Leutnant*. His service during the First World War took him from *Platoon Leader*, to *Kompanie Commander* through to an *Adjutant* at *Battalion, Regiment* and finally *Brigade* level. He was awarded both classes of the Iron Cross during the war.

In between the wars he transferred to the police in the Hamburg area. During the early Hitler years he transferred to *Infantry Regiment 47* with the rank of *Oberstleutnant*. He transferred once again, back to the police and began his service with the *Polizei Division*. He was given command of the *Polizei-Schutzen-Regiment 2.;* during the campaign in the west during 1940 he was awarded the Clasp to the Second Class Iron Cross on the 13th of June 1940. This was followed the next day with the award of the Clasp to the First Class Iron Cross. It was however, during the advances into Russia that his skills and abilities would come to the fore.

As previously covered the *Polizei Division's* advances, as part of Army Group North, took them on a route towards Leningrad. One of the major objectives on

One of the few known photos of Hans-Christian Schulze (centre). He is shown prior to his award of the Knight's Cross, made two days before his death in mid-September 1941.

this route was Luga. The file for Schulze does not contain a copy of his Knight's Cross recommendation, or many other details for that matter. It can be assumed that Hans Christian Schulze's recommendation was for his actions in capturing Luga on the 24th of August 1941. It is not known who wrote the recommendation or when it was written, an overview of his actions on the 24th of August are as follows: He led his *Polizei-Schutzen-Regiment 2* from the front as they advanced on their second attempt to seize Luga. This second attempt started on the 23rd of August with Schulze's *Regiment* in the centre of the overall advance line. They advanced over minefields, bunkers and destroyed bridges. The advance into the city centre involved crossing the main bridge, which ran over the Luga River. When crossing the bridge Schulze personally removed the fuses from demolition charges and carried on with his advance. His *Regiment* reached the city centre and by 5pm on the 24th they raised the German flag. With the fall of Luga the route straight to Leningrad was open. The city of Luga was a tough nut to crack and it had taken them two weeks from start to finish, gaining control of it. Many of their *Kameraden* had died along the way, including the *Divisional Commander*.

Hans Christian Schulze's rank at the time of the attack on Luga was that of *Oberst (SS-Standartenführer)*. The approval for the award of the Knight's Cross to the Iron Cross for Schulze came on the 11th of September 1941. At that

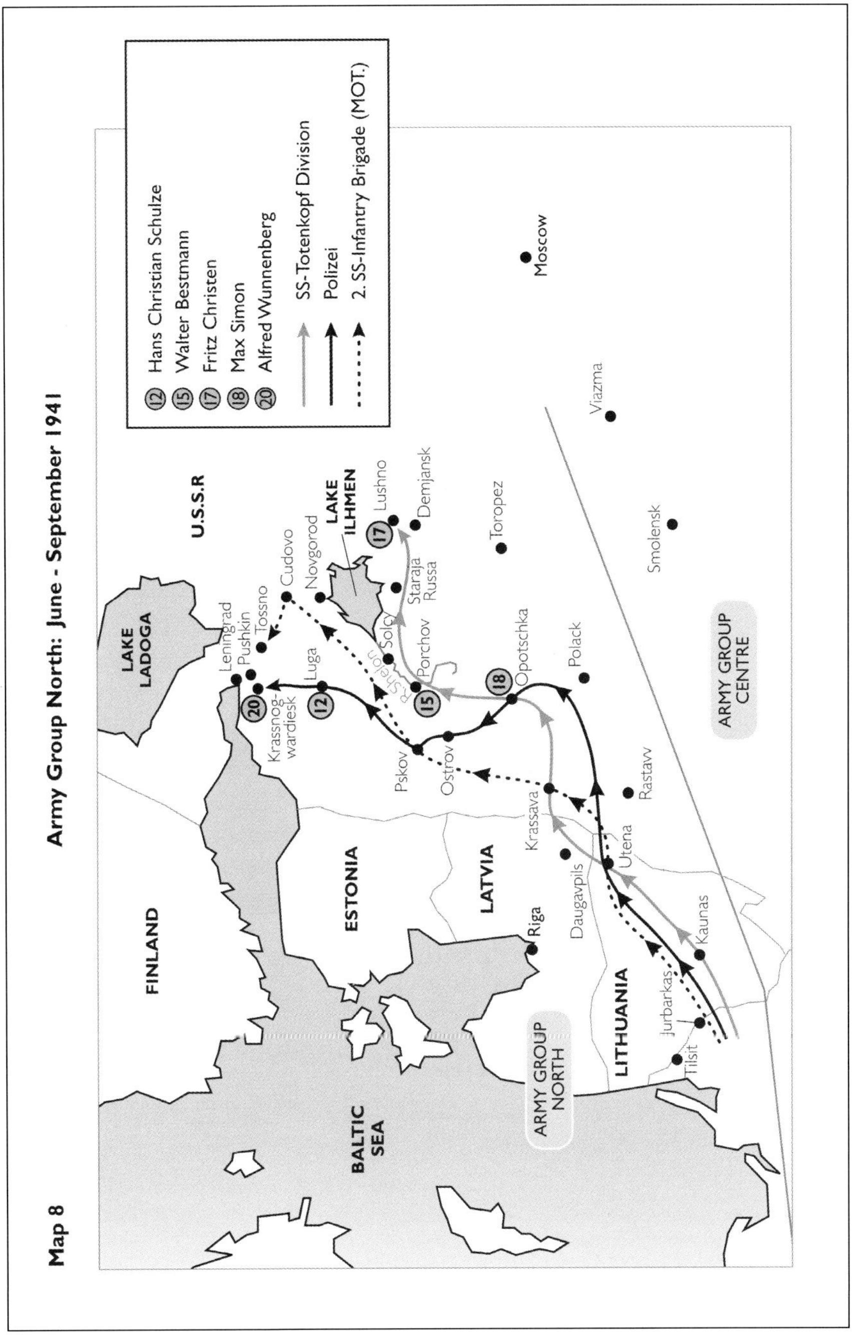
Map 8
Army Group North: June - September 1941
12 Hans Christian Schulze
15 Walter Bestmann
17 Fritz Christen
18 Max Simon
20 Alfred Wunnenberg
SS-Totenkopf Division
Polizei
2. SS-Infantry Brigade (MOT.)
FINLAND
BALTIC SEA
ESTONIA
LATVIA
LITHUANIA
U.S.S.R
LAKE LADOGA
LAKE ILHMEN
ARMY GROUP NORTH
ARMY GROUP CENTRE
Leningrad
Pushkin
Tossno
Krassnog-wardiesk
Cudovo
Novgorod
Luga
Pskov
Ostrov
Porchov
Solcy
R.Shelon
Staraja Russa
Lushno
Demjansk
Opotschka
Polack
Toropez
Smolensk
Viazma
Moscow
Riga
Daugavpils
Krassava
Rastavv
Utena
Kaunas
Jurbarkas
Tilsit

time he was fighting at Krassnogwardeisk. It was here that Schulze was heavily wounded by shrapnel on the 12th of September. He was moved to a field hospital at Nikolajewka, twenty kilometers southwest of Krassnogwardeisk. It would appear that along with the award of the Knight's Cross, he received a promotion to *Generalmajor (SS-Brigadeführer)*. He was informed of the award of the Knight's Cross whilst in the field hospital, but he did not have time to enjoy that fact. On the 13th of September 1941 Hans Christian Schulze died of his wounds. As he was aware of the award before dying, he became the first Knight's Cross holder of the *Waffen-SS* to die during the war, but he would certainly not be the last. Schulze was also the first member of the *Polizei Division* to be awarded the Knight's Cross to the Iron Cross.

Before moving to cover the actions within Army Group South, a brief overview of *SS-Kampfgruppe Nord* will follow.

SS-Kampfgruppe Nord

This *Kampfgruppe* took part in their first battle, which started on the 2nd of July 1941, their objective was that of Markajarvi-Salla. The Russians had been fighting the Finns in this area since 1939. They were experienced and used to the area and climate conditions. The untested men of the *Waffen-SS* within *SS Kampfgruppe Nord* were not. What developed was a short intensive battle in which the Russians gained the upper hand. Losses to *SS Kampfgruppe Nord* are listed in the region of 700! These brought to and end the involvement of *SS* troops in Finland for the time being. It was clear that an intensive and long training period would be needed before they were committed to battle once again.

Army Group South

The *LAH* and the Push Towards the Black Sea

Like the rest of their *Waffen-SS Kameraden* fighting elsewhere in Russia, the *LAH*, attached to *Panzer Gruppe 1*, did not move out at the very start of this new campaign. The days of the *Waffen-SS* leading the way were not yet in existence. The *LAH* moved from Poland at Ostrowiec, southeast of Radom and advanced eastwards to Samosz (Zamosc). These moves started on the 30th of June 1941. The other *Divisions* within this army group were fighting further eastwards at Dubno and towards Rowno, just south of the Pripjet Marshes. The *III Panzer Korps* were cut off at the start of July and the *LAH* were ordered in that direction to help relieve them. The enemy was striking down from the northeast. The *LAH* advanced from Luck towards Rowno, directly east and also southeast. They successfully punched forward and cleared the enemy from this area, they also linked with the *III Panzer Korps* headquarters over the 2nd and 3rd of July.

From there they moved further east and then southeast towards Shitomir (Zytomyr) over the second and third week of July. They covered the main road into this city from the west and the area south of the road. Some elements then moved northwards, with the *II Battalion*, under *SS-Sturmbannführer* Theodore Wisch, holding the most northerly point near Sokolow. This northerly position received heavy enemy attacks between the 11th and 15th of July. This town became the focus of defense for the *LAH* in the north and also the focus of the attack for the Russians. The *LAH* repulsed repeated strong attacks from three enemy *Divisions* (Knight's Cross action covered later). The other German units had pushed further eastwards towards Kiev in the third week of July 1941.

Towards the end of July the *LAH* were moved initially back towards Shitomir, then southeast and finally southwards towards Uman. By the end of July they found themselves north of this city, lead elements were ten kilometers north of there. Their objectives were to close a gap that had opened between the *11th* and *16th Panzer Divisions* from Sokolowka to Cybulow and then to help encircle Uman itself. These objectives were completed by the 7th of August. The fighting had been very intensive but the efforts were worth it. Over 3,200 prisoners were taken along with tanks, artillery and planes. From here they continued towards the Black Sea, with the towns of Wossnesensk, Nikolajew and Cherson. The town of Sasselje was reached by the lead elements of the *LAH* under Kurt Meyer. They found themselves cut-off for two days until the *II Battalion* reached them on the 16th of August. It was also on this day that Nikolajew was taken by the *16th Panzer Division* with a further 4,000 prisoners and enemy materials being taken. The Black Sea itself was reached on the 20th of August 1941.

During the first week of September, the *LAH* found itself split into two different groups. One group fought towards and through the Crimea area from mid-September until the 23rd of September. The other group found itself moving southwest into the peninsula below Cherson. They fought in that area from the 12th of September until the 23rd. As part of their attacks they were positioned at Tschulakowka. It was here on the 17th of September just before noon that Theodore Wisch was given official notification of his award of the Knight's Cross to the Iron Cross. We will leave the advances of the *LAH* at this point and briefly cover the advances of *Wiking* and the *1. SS-Infantry Brigade (mot.);* before turning northwards again.

Theodore 'Teddi' Wisch
Date of Birth: 13.12.1907
SS Number: 4 759

Born in Wesselburener Koog, he joined the *SS* on the 2nd of November 1930 and served with the *1. Sturm* within the *53. SS-Standarte*, in the Wesselburen area. He was one of the first 117 men selected to form the *Sonderkommando Berlin* – later the *LSSAH*. This was on the 17th of March 1933 and by that stage he had reached the rank of *SS-Truppführer (SS-Oberscharführer)*. He spent a few months as part of the squad who guarded the Berghof in southern Germany. Further promotion came on the 28th of July 1933 with a move to *SS-Sturmführer (SS-Untersturmführer)* and then again to *SS-Sturmhauptführer (SS-Hauptsturmführer)* on the 1st of October 1933. Shortly after that date he assumed command of the renamed *Leibstandarte Adolf Hitler's, 1. Kompanie*. He remained in this role until the early stages of the Second World War. He is probably as well known for that role as any recognition he received during the war. He was photographed extensively as head of this show-piece *Kompanie*, who were present at all of the major functions in the years leading up to the outbreak of the Second World War. The tallest members of the *LAH* were selected to be part of that unit and Theodore Wisch certainly looked the part at the head of that formation.

Like the rest of the men of the *LAH*, Wisch took part in the campaign in Poland during late 1939. He was awarded the Second Class Iron Cross on the 24th of September 1939 and then the First Class Iron Cross on the 8th of November 1939 for his actions during that campaign. In January 1940 he relinquished his command of the *1. Kompanie* and also received a promotion to *SS-Sturmbannführer*. He initially commanded the *IV Battalion* who had the role of honour guard, but then in May of 1941 he moved to the command of the *II Battalion*. Although he did not see service in the campaign in the west, he did enter Russia with the *LAH*, leading his *II Battalion*. He would not have to wait long until his *Battalion* would be put to the test against this new enemy.

As covered in preceding pages, the *II Battalion* were moved towards Sokolow, and found themselves north of there at Januszowka. Placed alongside the *Heer's, 25. Kradschutzen Battalion*, the *LAH* had some *Stugs* with them. Around midday on the 11th of July twenty-five enemy tanks attacked, but were driven off. The *II Battalion* then moved back to Sokolow itself. The following day heavy enemy artillery strikes landed upon the *II Battalion* positions during the morning, followed by tank attacks in the afternoon, ending with heavy fighting in and around Sokolow itself that evening.

Information gained from enemy prisoners revealed that there was three enemy divisions facing their positions, one of these was a tank *Division*. Further enemy

Theodore Wisch shown here with the rank of SS-Sturmbannführer and after his award of the Knight's Cross in Russia in September 1941.

attacks during the night and into the early hours of the 13th of July followed. Enemy thrusts and heavy attacks continued throughout the 13th. Individual *Kompanies* were being attacked by the enemy, in *Battalion* strength. Some successes came during the morning of the 14th of July, when hundreds of enemy prisoners were captured. This was off-set however, by heavy prolonged enemy artillery attacks in the afternoon and into the late evening. This marked the crescendo of the enemy attacks, but the *II Battalion* held their ground against everything the enemy threw at them. Sokolow remained in the hands of the *LAH's, II Battalion* under the expert leadership of *SS-Sturmbannführer* Theodore 'Teddi' Wisch. They were relieved during the 15th of July and moved to different positions. The fact that Wisch and his *Battalion* had forced the enemy to commit three *Divisions*, and suffer heavy losses, during this four-day struggle is a testament to his abilities as a *Battalion Commander.*

You may recall that he received official notification just over two months later, on the 17th of September, whilst fighting at the front with his men. The official award was approved on the 15th of September. This made Wisch the 14th *Waffen-SS* soldier to receive this award and the 4th within the *LAH*. It can be assumed that Sepp Dietrich wrote the recommendation, as this recommendation is not in his file it is impossible to verify this or the date of writing it. This would not be Theodore Wisch's only connection to this award or its' higher grades, but more about that later.

We will leave the advances of the *LAH* towards the end of September and follow the advances of the other *Waffen-SS* units fighting within Army Group South.

SS-Division Wiking

This newly formed and untested *Division* started their advance into Russia earlier than their *Waffen-SS Kameraden*. The *Germania Regiment* began actions in the first few days of Barbarossa, moving towards Luck. The entire *Division* then moved out of their forming up area, east of Cholm, on the 25th of June 1941 and headed south to Samosz (Zamosc), then southeast through Lemberg (L'viv) and Tarnapol (Ternopil) with the *SS-Regiment Nordland* in the lead. By the end of the first week of advance they were at Tarnapol. They then moved northeast towards Shitomir and by mid-July lead elements (*Nordland)* were in Radomysl, northeast of Shitomir. This was the same time that Theodore Wisch and his *II Battalion* of the *LAH* were fighting west of Shitomir. The rest of *Wiking* were southeast of Shitomir itself and by the 14th of July they were in Skwira (Skvyra). On the 18th of July, *Germania's, 2. Kompanie* fought a successful action at Saalischy, for which *SS-Obersturmführer* Helmut Pfortner would be awarded the Knight's Cross

Map 9 **Army Group South: June - September 1941**

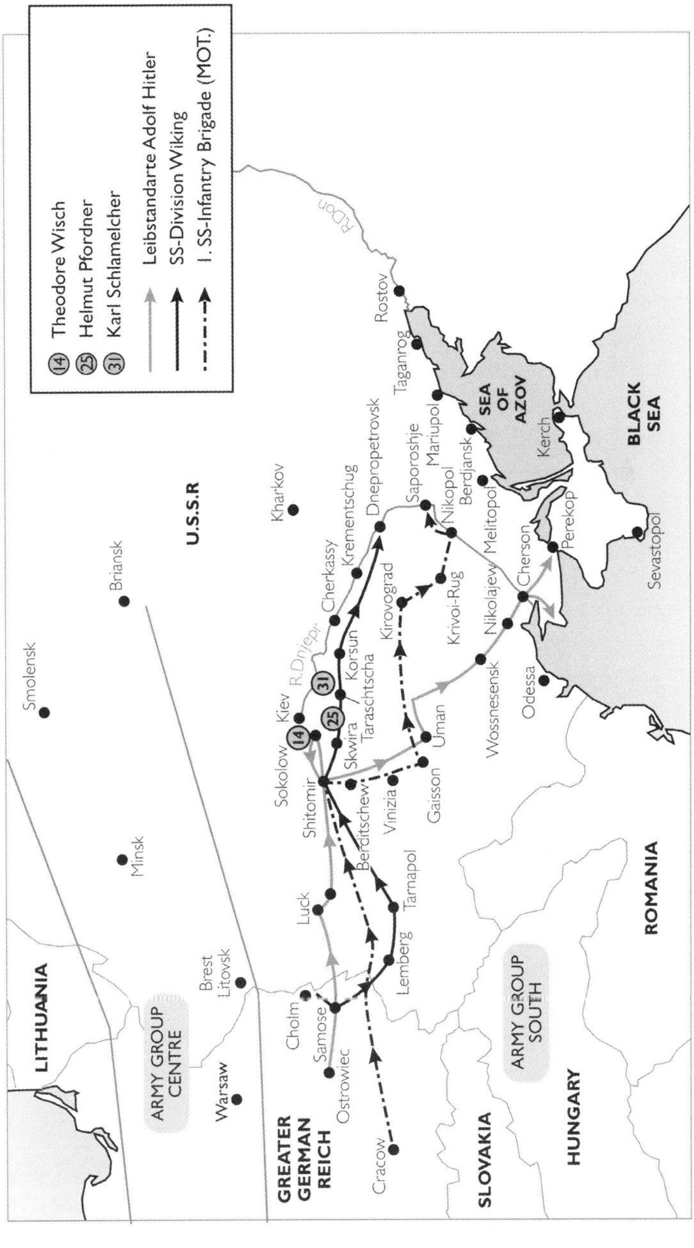

(the first one of these awards for this *Division* – these actions will be detailed later in this volume). By the 21st of July *Wiking* were at Taraschtscha (Tarasca), tough fighting took place around this area up to the Ross River. This fighting ended on the 25th of July and around 2,000 prisoners were taken. Losses to *Wiking* stood at 450 dead and wounded. This was the same time that Werner Ostendorff was battling at Yelnya, further north.

After this they moved eastwards to Korsun by the start of August. They got as far as Ssmela (Smila) and fought a difficult battle there for the next week. From there they moved further east and by the end of August they had advanced to the western outskirts of Dnepropetrovsk (Dnipropetrovs'k). *SS-Regiment Westland* had moved through Kirovograd (Kirovohrad), *SS-Regiment Nordland* had moved along the Dnjepr River directly to Dnepropetrovsk. They were there at the end of the first week in September when they prepared to advance on Kamenka.

We will leave the advances of *SS-Division Wiking* at this stage; briefly cover the actions of the *1. SS-Infantry Brigade (mot.),* then moved northwards to cover the award of the next Knight's Cross for the *Waffen-SS*.

1. SS-Infantry-Brigade (mot.)

In late July and into August 1941, this *Brigade* followed behind elements of Army Group South. By the end of the first week in August they were twenty-five miles north of Shitomir (Zytomyr). They operated between there and the southern reaches of the Pripjet Marshes. They met with successes and could count almost 8,000 prisoners taken around this time. They also crossed the Dnjepr River towards the end of August. Their advances took them south of Shitomir, onto Berditschev and on further to Gaisson (Hajsyn) by mid-September 1941. From there they moved further east and southeast through Krivovograd (Kirovohrad) and Krivoi-Rog (Kryvyj-Rih). At the end of September, elements were fighting on the bend of the Dnjepr River at Kamenka and also south towards Nikopol, with their main positions being between Nikopol and Saporoshje (Zaporizzja)

Army Group North

SS-Totenkopf Division and the Push Eastwards

If you recall, we left the advances of the *Totenkopf Division,* within Army Group North, around the 19th of July 1941, when they were advancing northeast to the Mschaga River. The moves up to and along this river continued throughout the rest of July and into August. The enemy had strong forces in this area and the advance rate became slower. Around this time, on the 28th of July, temporary

Divisional Commander, *SS-Brigadeführer* Georg Keppler, wrote a Knight's Cross recommendation that would result in the next award of this medal to a soldier of the *Waffen-SS*, but more of that later. By mid-August they had advanced to Szolzy and beyond, up to the area south of Lake Ilmen. A major Russian advance from Staraja-Russa westwards towards Dno was launched. *Totenkopf* would be used to blunt this enemy advance.

The bulk of the *Division* was back towards Dno, but the *Aufklarungs Abteilung* remained in its' forward positions due to the fact that it was engaged in combat. The main attack began on the 19th of August and the objective was to destroy the enemy and then advance, first to the Polisst River and then the Lowat River, east of Staraja-Russa. The Polisst River was reached the following day and with this the net around the enemy was tightening. At this time around 35,000 prisoners, hundreds of tanks and thousands of smaller weapons fell into German hands. This action by *SS-Totenkopf Division* and other *Divisions* in the area had managed to blunt the enemy advance, but there was no time for rest as the Lowat River beckoned.

The advances continued throughout late August and into September. The losses were mounting and despite loosing nearly 5,000 men, the *Division* still had orders to advance further eastwards. The Lowat River was crossed on the 25th of August and the *Division* moved on towards Demjansk. *Totenkopf's* area of responsibility was north of this town. Heavy rain was causing as many problems as the strong enemy forces in their way around this time. The area north of Demjansk was in *Totenkopf's* control by mid-September 1941. On the 19th, Theodore Eicke returned to lead the *Division* and by then his men were advancing towards Lushno. The Russians launched a further thrust into this area on the 24th of September. These attacks were made with tanks, artillery and masses of infantry, supported by hundreds of aircraft. The control of Lushno fell into Russian hands on and off over the next few days. The enemy attacks reached a crescendo on the night of the 26th and into the 27th of September. *Totenkopf* repulsed all of the enemy attacks and a brief pause for this exhausted *Division* came on the 27th of September 1941.

A review of the fighting and information obtained from Russian prisoners showed that at least three enemy divisions supported by armoured formations with around 100 tanks, all fresh into the front line, had crashed into the area held by *Totenkopf*, who were running at around 40% under strength. The losses to the enemy were around half of their strength, including their tanks. One successful anti-tank action was discovered on the 27th of September in Lushno concerning *SS-Sturmmann* Fritz Christen. Before we cover that action however, it is necessary to cover the actions of the next *Waffen-SS* recipient of the Knight's Cross, *SS-Sturmbannführer* Walter Bestmann. The recommendation for this was the one written by Georg Keppler back on the 28th of July 1941.

Walter Bestmann

Date of Birth: 02.10.1907

SS Number: 20 135

Born in Lubeck, his service history began at the age of nineteen when he joined the *Mecklenburg State Police*. He moved to the *SS* at the end of May 1933, also attending an officer's course during this year. By the 14th of May 1934 he was holding the rank of *SS-Untersturmführer,* serving within the *LSSAH*. This was followed at the start of 1935 by promotion to *SS-Obersturmführer* and then again on the 10th of March 1935 by a move to *SS-Hauptsturmführer.* He was a *Kompanie Commander* around this time and remained in that role until late 1939, commanding the *4. Kompanie*. Whilst with the *LSSAH* he advanced into the Saarland, Sudetenland and Bohemia & Moravia, receiving the respective medals for these actions. He also stayed with the *LSSAH* as they advanced into Poland at the start of the war. In this campaign he earned the Second Class Iron Cross on the 25th of September 1939.

In late October he moved to the *III Battalion, 1st Infantry Regiment* within the newly formed *SS-Totenkopf Division*. Promotion to *SS-Sturmbannführer* came on the 9th of November 1939 as did command of this *Battalion*. He went west with them in 1940 and was awarded the Black Wound Badge on the 20th of May, followed by the First Class Iron Cross on the 3rd of June 1940. In late March 1941 he moved to the command of *Totenkopf's, Aufklarungs Abteilung*. It was with this unit that he moved eastwards in June 1941. The purpose of the *Aufklarungs* is to go ahead of the main unit and determine the strength and positions of any enemy forces. In the early stages of Operation Barabrossa this involved contact with large numbers of well equipped and desperate enemy soldiers. Intense combat and losses were often the result.

As mentioned previously, *Totenkopf's* temporary *Divisional Commander*, *SS-Brigadeführer* Georg Keppler, wrote a recommendation for the award of the Knight's Cross to the Iron Cross for *SS-Sturmbannführer* Walter Bestmann. This recommendation covered multiple actions throughout July 1941 and it is more in line with a typical recommendation for the German Cross in Gold, multiple actions over a period of time rather than one single outstanding action. This new award however, did not come into being until late September 1941. An overview of the details within the recommendation is as follows:

> "27.6.41 03:00 in the morning the *Aufklarungs Abteilung* pushed into the Borowitschi area and came across an enemy regiment of around 700 men, advancing forwards on the bridge over the river was a German supply column and it was clear that the Russians would seize this column and take the supplies, which included petrol for the tanks.

Walter Bestmann seen here on the day of his Knight's Cross presentation.

Walter Bestmann shown after his Knight's Cross award, seen here presenting awards to some of his men.

SS-Sturmbannführer Bestmann set his *Aufklarungs Abteilung* immediately upon the enemy regiment and destroyed it. At the outset of the battle, the enemy held better ground, through the outstanding personal actions of *SS-Sturmbannführer* Bestmann, decided the outcome and losses to the enemy in the river area. Losses to the enemy were 137 dead. (Losses to the *Aufklarungs Abteilung* were thirty-seven dead and wounded).

1.7.41 at the lake area near Rageli where the lake narrows at the start, they had to determine if this was occupied by the enemy. This was only weakly held. A surprise attack on the 2/7 through a strong, silent, frontal attack would take place. The *Aufklarungs* assessed that two streets would be best for the advance and split the enemy. Bridge explosions would delay the advance, so the *Pioneer Kompanie* would have to erect a makeshift bridge. At 03:30 on the 2/7 the *Aufklarungs Abteilung*, along with subordinate *Batteries* and *Panzerjaeger Kompanies* fought in exhausting conditions due to the rain and unfavorable ground.

SS-Sturmbannführer Bestmann was personally at the front line directing the men and all the heavy weapons, the success against strong enemy forces, with only slight losses to themselves, allowed the *Division* to advance forwards.

7.7.41. In the battle at Sebesh, and isolated and cut-off near Opotschka, they destroyed heavy enemy tanks under heavy attacks they held the line until the arrival of other parts of the *Division*. In this area, they not only coped with attacks to their front, but also heavy attacks to their rear.

23.7.41. By reconnaissance against the Mschaga sector on the 23rd of July 1941, under the direction of *SS-Sturmbannführer* Bestmann making use of surprise in this area, captured heavy tanks and tractors, Bestmann himself shot up a medium enemy tank."

The recommendation also makes brief mention of his previous actions in Poland and the west, then it summarises:

"1. 30.6.41. On the dangerous Rollbahn, used by *Panzer Gruppe 4*, removed the dangerous opposition for the *Division* and facilitated fast forward advance.

2. 2.7.41. Through shining success, took the lake by Rageli, advance by the *Division* free of heavy losses was achieved.

3.7.7.41. Through his reduced losses, the basis for drawing near and entering Opotschka happened.

4. 23.7.41 The *Division* drew up to the Mschaga sector, through his surprise decisive actions near the river.

5. *SS-Sturmbannführer Bestmann* and his *Aufklarungs Abteilung* subordinated to the *1 Armee Korps* achieved outstanding reconnaissance."

The recommendation finishes by mentioning his three wounds. The approval for the award of the Knight's Cross to the Iron Cross came on the 29th of September 1941, two months after it was submitted. This was the first award of this medal to a soldier of the *SS-Totenkopf Division* and the 15th for the *Waffen-SS*.

Walter Bestmann was also awarded the Silver Wound Badge and the Infantry Assault Badge. At the start of December 1941 he became the *Commander* of the *Motorcycle Replacement Battalion*. This was followed on the 1st of September 1942 by promotion to *SS-Obersturmbannführer*. A spell at Bad Tolz for course leader's teaching began the following month. Towards the end of January 1943 he was serving with the *Panzer Regiment* within the *10th SS Panzer Division 'Frundsberg'*. At the start of December 1943 he became the *Commandant* of Klagenfurt's *SS* School in Austria. He survived the war and died on the 17th of June 1958.

Although out of sequence, we will stay with the actions of *SS-Totenkopf* as another two Knight's Crosses were awarded for actions up to the end of September 1941. We will then move to Army Group Centre.

Fritz Christen

Date of Birth: 29.06.1921

SS Number: Unknown

Born in Mecklenburg, he volunteered for service in the *Waffen-SS* in May 1940. By the time he went east in the summer of 1941 he was holding the rank of *SS-Sturmmann*. He was awarded the Second Class Iron Cross on the 20th of July 1941. Just over two months later he found himself in Lushno during the intensive battles around that area, serving with the *2. Kompanie* within *Totenkopf's, Panzerjaeger Abteilung*.

During the 24th of September 1941 he was manning his *Pak-38* anti-tank gun. The Russians launched one of their many tank attacks towards Lushno. During this, the rest of Christen's gun crew was killed, as well as the crews of surrounding guns. Fritz Christen remained alone by his *Pak* gun and knocked out six enemy tanks. This brought a respite for the Germans in this area and the remaining enemy tanks temporarily withdrew. He was cut off by this point and

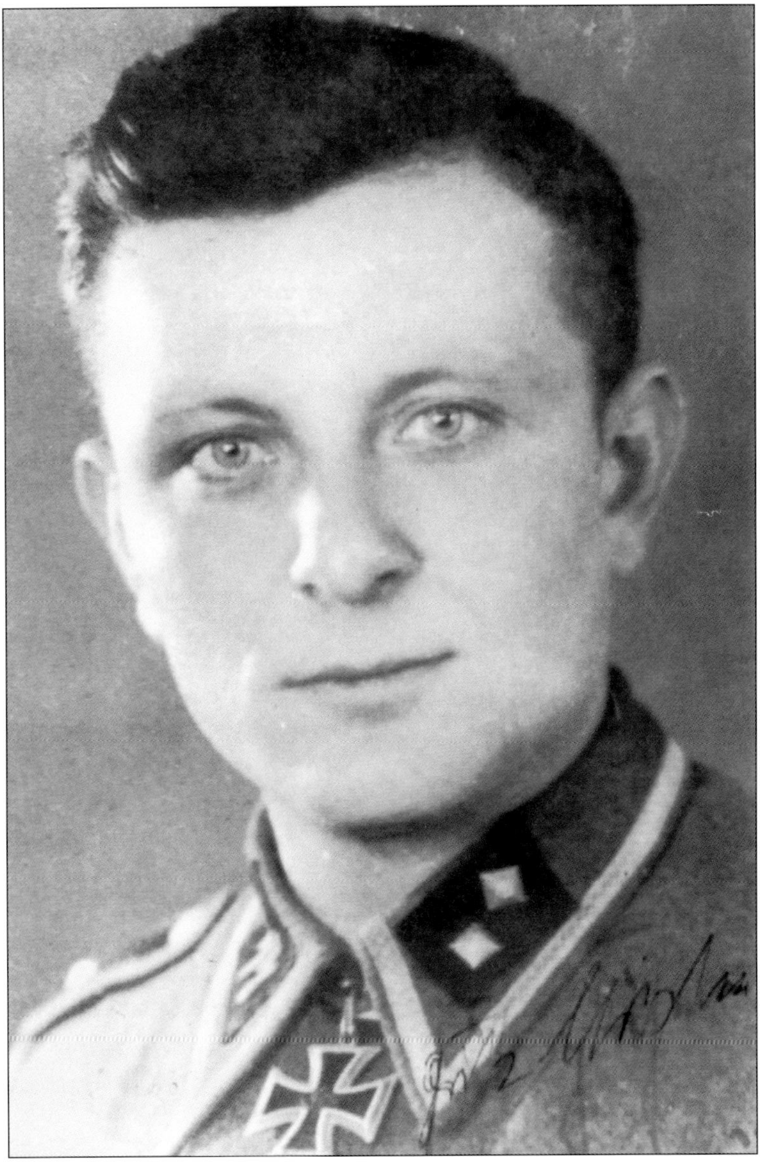

An autographed photo of Fritz Christen, taken late in the war and showing him with his final rank of SS-Oberscharführer.

was left with no option but to stay at his gun and fight it out to the end. As he was cut-off, he also ran out of food and water.

A further breakthrough of between twelve to fifteen tanks came out of the northern edge of Dubrowka, Christen smashed that attack also and destroyed a further six tanks. Not only had he to contend with enemy tanks, but also had to deal with enemy artillery and machine gun fire close by his position. On the 25th of September ten more enemy tanks broke through, Christen proceeded to destroy seven of them. He also defeated an accompanying infantry attack.

Two days later his *Kameraden* from *Totenkopf* launched a counter attack. They came across Fritz Christen and also the death and carnage that lay all around him. This scene bore testament to his skill, bravey, resoluteness and also his iron will. His ability to stop all enemy tank thrusts in this area had helped stem the flow of the enemy westwards and allowed a favorable counter attack to be launched.

The *Divisional Commander*, Theodor Eicke, awarded Fritz Christen the First Class Iron Cross. The official award date is listed as the 24th of September 1941. He did not stop there however and he followed this up by writing a recommendation for the award of the Knight's Cross for Christen. This recommendation was approved on the 20th of October 1941. This made Fritz Christen the lowest ranking *Waffen-SS* soldier to be awarded this medal; Adolf Hitler himself, presented the award to Christen. In addition, Fritz Christen was the youngest *Waffen-SS* soldier to be award the Knight's Cross, being aged only twenty at the time.

Little is known about Fritz Christen after this award date. He finished the war holding the rank of *SS-Oberscharführer.* He survived the war and lived up to the 23rd of September 1995, almost fifty-four years after his successful actions in Russia.

SS-Sturmmann Fritz Christen was not the only *Waffen-SS* soldier to be awarded the Knight's Cross on the 20th of October 1941.

Max Simon

Date of Birth: 06.01.1899

SS Number: 83 086

Born in Breslau, his military service began in 1917 and he seen action from then until the end of the First World War. He was awarded the Second Class Iron Cross during that time. He was one of the men who served in the much-reduced inter-war *German Army*, serving from 1920 to 1929.

He then joined the *SS* at the start of May 1933, serving with the *1. Sturm. I. 47. SS-Standarte*. He gained promotion quickly and within six months he had reached the rank of *SS-Oberscharführer (SS-Scharführer)*. His training for higher levels of command began towards the end of 1933. Further rapid promotions

Max Simon pictured after his award of the Knight's Cross and also after his promotion to SS-Oberführer.

followed in 1934 and by early November of that year he was holding the rank of *SS-Untersturmführer* and was commanding *SS-Sonderkommando Sachsen*. His promotions continued into 1935 and by mid-September he was moved up to *SS-Sturmbannführer*. His unit was incorporated into the various *Totenkopfverbande* before the outbreak of the Second World War. He was promoted further on the 12th of September 1937 to the rank of *SS-Obersturmbannführer* and then to *SS-Standartenführer* one year later. He took part in and was awarded the medals for the march into Austria and also the Sudetenland prior to the start of the Second World War.

When the *SS-Totenkopf Division* was formed in late 1939, Max Simon was assigned as the *Commander* of their *1st Infantry Regiment*. He went west with them during 1940 and was awarded the Clasp to the Second Class Iron Cross, plus the First Class Iron Cross. There is however, conflicting information, with some documents showing him as being awarded the Clasp to both Iron Crosses during late 1939, meaning that he was awarded both classes of the Iron Cross during World War I? Whatever the case may be, he was definitely holding the pre-requisites for the Knight's Cross by the time he moved east with *Totenkopf* in mid-1941. Theodor Eicke wrote the recommendation for Max Simon's Knight's Cross initially on the 6th of July 1941, but the submission must have been delayed for some reason as the recommendation covers actions dated two days later. The recommendation itself covered actions between May 1940 and contained the following information:

> May 19th 1940, ordered forwards at speed to assist the *7th Panzer Division* in the area between Landrecies and Cambrai (they were considered to be in a dangerous situation. This was the start of the enemy counter thrust from the north). Simon was informed, by Eicke, that his *Regiment* would be dispersed to a variety of villages. The enemy resistance was strong in these areas. The recommendation makes mention of the fact that the *1st Regiment* accomplished all of their orders and also defeated the enemy in this area. The town of Catillon is given special mention, as in this area, 1,300 prisoners, anti-tank guns and machine guns were also captured. These successes are credited to Max Simon's leadership skills. Mention is also made of his leadership at Arras and at La Bassee Canal.
>
> Moving onto the early stages of Operation Barbarossa, the recommendation then covers actions at Kreslau at the start of July 1941. At this location Max Simon and his *1st Infantry Regiment* defeated the enemy who were twice the number of Simon's men and they were supported by tanks. It highlights Simon's actions in deploying his *Regiment* in an enveloping attack at Kreslau,

which widened the bridgehead at Dunaberg and secured the flanks for the *SS-Totenkopf Division,* to quote, "The success of the attacks is to be credited only to the exceptional personal action of *SS-Standartenführer* Simon"

The recommendation then proceeds to the actions at Opotschka on July 8th 1941, mentioning the following, "*SS-Standartenführer* Simon distinguished himself again extraordinarily through his personal action in the critical situations". It also mentions the wounds he received at that time.

This recommendation for the Knight's Cross to the Iron Cross was approved on the 20th of October 1941, thereby making *SS-Standartenführer* Max Simon the 18th *Waffen-SS* soldier to receive this award. It also took *SS-Totenkopf Division's* total so far to three.

We now need to go back slightly in time and move to Army Group Centre to cover the actions of another *Waffen-SS* Knight's Cross winner.

Army Group Centre

SS-Division Reich and the move southwards

We last visited the advances of Paul Hausser and his *Division* in the middle of August 1941, after their difficult struggle at Yelnya in establishing the bridgehead there. As has been previously covered, this was a difficult task for the Germans, but a vital necessity for the further advance upon Moscow. The Soviets were well aware of this fact and they continued to push increasing numbers of soldiers into the Yelnya area to defeat the German advance. It was also around this time that Adolf Hitler issued orders highlighting the importance of capturing Leningrad and the securing of the entire southern sector of the Soviet Union, to the detriment of the continuing advance on the capital, Moscow. Hitler's *Generals* did not agree with his views, but had no options but to comply.

During the remainder of August *SS-Division Reich* were placed northeast of Smolensk as a reserve unit. They used this time to rest and refit as best they could. They also received a number of replacements. This rest period did not last long as orders arrived for them to begin marching once again, only not towards Moscow, this time they were going south towards Kiev. They were to assist in the destruction of the enemy in that area and would be moving in from the northeast.

At the start of September 1941, *SS-Division Reich* moved from Smolensk, south through Roslawl (Roslavl), Unetscha (Uneca) up to Awdejewka and then southeast of Gomel (Homel). This objective was reached on the 4th of September and with that, *SS-Division Reich* came under the control of the *XXIV Panzer Korps,* commanded by Heinz Guderian. The distance covered in these moves was around three hundred miles.

They fought in and around this area for the next two days, then on the 6th of September they moved further southwest to push over the Don River. This attack was launched by *SS-Regiment Der Führer* along with supporting elements. Led by the *Motorcycle Infantry Battalion,* they advanced towards Makoschin on the Desna River. The advance was fast and relentless. A railroad bridge at Makoschin was reached and the Russians began an intensive battle to hold this town. They were supported by tanks and armoured trains. It was during the opening phase of this attack that *SS-Obersturmführer* Fritz Rentrop stormed across the railway bridge and prevented its' demolition by the enemy (Knight's Cross action covered in detail later on). After an intense battle that raged until the 8th of September, the southwards advance continued.

SS-Division Reich began to play their part in what became the biggest encirclement in military history, that of the encirclement of Kiev. The objectives of Borsna (Borzna) and Bachmatsch (Bachmac) were reached; whilst *Heer* units were fighting further east. The relentless pursuit southwards against stiff enemy resistance continued and by the 14th of September 1941 the pocket around Kiev was closed tight. *Heer* units from Army Group Centre met with units from Army Group South. At this stage *SS-Division Reich* was at Itschnja (Icnja). Although this pocket had been closed the battle against the fifty or so enemy divisions within the pocket was far from over. *SS-Division Reich* moved further south (this was around the time that *SS-Totenkopf Division* had moved into the Demjansk area). By the 16th of September, *SS-Division Reich* was in Prilinki (Prylnky) and they battled for control of this objective for the next two days.

From here *SS-Division Reich* were ordered east to Romny to assist in its' defense against attacks coming in from the east. They fought around Romny during the third week in September 1941. It was during this time that the battle to control the Kiev pocket ended in favor of the Germans. Their accomplishments in this area could hardly be comprehended then and are difficult for people to envisage even now. Over 660,000 enemy troops entered German captivity, with half of that number again being killed or wounded. This totaled one million men, along with thousands of guns, hundreds of tanks and thousands of smaller weapons. These losses would have finished the offensive capabilities of many countries, but not that of Soviet Russia; but more of that later. It was a huge blow for the Russians and the Germans made the most of it. *SS-Division Reich* had played their part in this battle, they themselves taking 13,000 prisoners along with hundreds of guns.

After helping out at Romny, *SS-Division Reich* was ordered north once more, close to their old positions near Yelnya. Through the rest of September 1941 they moved northwest through Gomel (Homel), then northeast towards Roslawl (Roslavl), reached on the 28th of September 1941. There followed a few days of rest before the next assault began. This next assault would be towards the prize of Moscow. However, for now, we will leave the advances of *SS-Division Reich*. Before we do, we will cover in detail the actions that resulted in the award of the next Knight's Cross to the Iron Cross. Although the approval came in mid-October, the actions took place during the recent fighting in the south.

Fritz Rentrop

Date of birth: 19.11.1917

SS Number: 323 804

Born in Munster, he seen service with the *Hitler Youth* from 1931 to 1937, followed by a stint with the *R.A.D.* in late 1936 and into 1937. He then joined the *SS-VT* on the 1st of April 1937 serving with the *SS-Regiment Germania,* staying with them until the end of March 1938. He then took part in an officers training course at Braunschweig during the remainder of 1938 and into early 1939. By the 20th of April 1939 he had reached the rank of *SS-Untersturmführer.*

He spent May and June 1939 with the *SS-VT* at Ellwangen. From June 1939 until early September 1940 he was a *Platoon Commander* in the *Machine Gun Abteilung,* within the newly created *SS V Division*. Taking part in the campaign in the west during the summer of 1940, he was awarded the Second Class Iron Cross on the 18th of June 1940. At the start of September 1940 he was promoted to *SS-Obersturmführer* and then on the 27th of November 1940 he was awarded the First Class Iron Cross, presumably for actions during the campaign in the west. Before the end of 1940 he had moved to serve with the *Flak Abteilung* and by the start of 1941 he was the *Adjutant* for that *Battalion*. In early March 1941 he took command of the *2. Kompanie,* within the *Flak Abteilung*. It was with this *Kompanie* that he found himself at Makoschin on the 6th of September 1941. He was part of the group that was supporting the *Motorcycle Infantry Battalion's* advance.

As previously mentioned, as they pushed towards Makoschin, the enemy withdrew across the river. The German attack was supported by two *Stugs* and some armoured cars, fighting against enemy tanks and armoured trains. The focus for the Germans was the securing of the railroad bridge leading over the Desna River. Fritz Rentrop, along with some men from the *14. Kompanie,* advanced at speed across the bridge. Rentrop led the group who rapidly removed the fuses from the demolition charges. In addition they defeated the enemy demolition party

SS-Obersturmführer Fritz Rentrop pictured after his award of the Knight's Cross.

and then advanced to the opposite end of the bridge and set up a small bridgehead. The *Stugs* then moved up to the bridge. It was at this point that *Stukas*, which were expected earlier, arrived. They unleashed an aerial attack upon Makoschin focusing on both sides of the railway bridge, unaware that friendly troops were that far forward. This attack had two outcomes; firstly it caused around forty casualties within the *Motorcycle Infantry Battalion,* in addition it aided the defeat of the strong enemy forces within Makoschin.

The fighting did not end with this first *Stuka* attack, if anything it intensified. The battle raged into the late afternoon, once again the *Stukas* arrived, only this time they successfully targeted the enemy positions, which included the two armoured trains. Further German infantry elements made it across the bridge to support Rentrop's group. The difficult struggle around this area raged until the 8th of September. Rentrop's group kept their positions during friendly aircraft attacks and repeated enemy attacks over those two days. It was only on the 8th of September that the battle for the Desna bridgehead came to an end.

Fritz Rentrop's cool-headed actions on the 6th of September 1941 opened the way for the successful continuation of *SS-Division Reich's* southwards attack. Although he was a *Kompanie Commander* within the *Flak Abteilung,* this did not prevent him from playing his part during the *Motorcycle Infantry Battalion* led attack. It is not known who wrote the recommendation for this Knight's Cross. It was approved on the 13th of October 1941, making *SS-Obersturmführer* Fritz Rentrop the 16th *Waffen-SS* soldier to be awarded the Knight's Cross to the Iron Cross. This also gave *SS-Division Reich* their 10th Knight's Cross since the start of the Second World War.

In the years after this action he was promoted to *SS-Hauptsturmführer* and then further again to *SS-Sturmbannführer* in late December 1944. In the intervening years of these promotions, he spent time at Braunschweig from spring 1942 to the summer of 1943. He then moved to the Panzer Grenadier School at Prossetsignitz from late July 1943 to the start of 1944. He then spent time with the *LSSAH* in their battle around Cherkassy and Tarnapol up to April 1944. The remainder of 1944 saw him serve as an officer within the *XXXXVII Panzer Korps* and the *General Staff*. At the start of 1945 he was the *First Staff Officer* of the *IV SS Panzer Korps*. It was in this position that he was badly wounded and reported missing on the 2nd of February 1945, in Hungary. It is believed that he died as a prisoner of the Soviets soon after this date.

SS-Kavallerie Brigade

The actions of this second line unit were last covered whey they were in the northwest part of the Pripjet Marshes. They had been given orders to form into a *Brigade* and in August 1941 this process began. *SS-Standartenführer* Hermann Fegelein was appointed *Brigade Commander*. *SS-Sturmbannführer* Gustav Lombard was placed as *Commander* of *Regiment 1*, with *SS-Standartenführer* Hermann Schleifenbaum as *Commander* of *Regiment 2*.

Their next actions focused on Starabin, west of where they had been before. Partisan activity was taking place in that area and the surrounding areas. *Regiment 1* fought in and around here, with *Regiment 2* fighting southeast of here. Both actions lasted through the second half of August 1941.

In early September they moved further east towards Retschiza (Recyca) to conduct more security duties and mopping up of partisan groups. This lasted into the rest of September and ended with the *Brigade* being in Gomel (Homel). It was at the end of September that the *SS-Kavallerie Brigade* would be moved, this time northwards to Toropez (Toropec), over two hundred and fifty miles north of Gomel.

The first few months of this new campaign had been very eventful for the men of the *Waffen-SS*. They had not yet achieved success and the vastness of this region was becoming apparent to them all. It can be said that motivation and morale was still high and expectations of final victory were still in their minds; but how long would this take?

CHAPTER SIX

OPERATION BARBAROSSA - OCTOBER TO DECEMBER 1941

The Weather Changes

In the preceding chapter we have covered the advances of the *Waffen-SS* units within the various Army Groups up to the end of September 1941, three months into Operation Barbarossa. This chapter will cover their actions until the end of 1941, from October to December.

How had the advances gone up to the end of September? In the north, Krassnogwardiesk and Demjansk were reached. In the centre, Yelnya had been tamed, then a move south to Kiev and back up to Roslawl. In the south Kamenka and the Crimea lay as the next prizes. All of the objectives taken up to this point had been difficult to take, but the finer weather had helped. Almost two and a half million enemy soldiers had been taken prisoner in the pocket battles such as Smolensk, Kiev, Bryansk and Uman – the figure of dead and wounded is unkown, but can be estimated at around half of that again. These losses would have seen the defeat of many other nations, but the Russians were far from finished. The expectations were still high for the German troops as victory after victory was achieved. However, the prize of Moscow still awaited the Germans, as did Leningrad and the southern expanses. So let us take a look at what took place over the next three months as the Germans were introduced to the most difficult enemy of them all – the Russian weather.

Army Group South

The Leibstandarte Adolf Hitler

We last covered the advances of the *LAH* as they neared the Black Sea at Cherson and towards the Crimea area at Perekop, as the two groups separated throughout September. Towards the end of September the two groups were reunited.

The *LAH* did not move into the Crimea, although elements were engaged in difficult fighting around Perekop in the final week of September. From there the *LAH* were ordered northeast to Melitopol and Berdjansk. This advance took place into the first week of October, the initial advance was to the east, but due to a dangerous situation north of the coast, the *LAH* moved northeast. They then advanced south to Berdjansk, with this objective being approached from the northwest, the *Aufklarungs Abteilung* were in the lead. This objective fell to the *LAH* by the end of the first week of October. By reaching Berdjansk, the *LAH* were at the coast of the Sea of Azov. This was quickly followed by the capture of Mariupol on the following day, a success that slowed the advance for a few days. These were considerable achievements and one officer of the *LAH's, Aufklarungs Abteilung* was recognized for his part in these achievements (Gert Bremer's Knight's Cross actions covered later in more detail).

After spending from the 8th to the 10th of October mopping up Mariupol and counting their success, they handed control of this city to the *13th Panzer Division*. The *LAH* went further east towards Taganrog and by nightfall on the 12th of October, they had crossed the Mius River, near Nikolajewka. The battle to control this objective lasted two days. Once this was completed, the road was open to Taganrog. The advance to that target began on the 17th of October and by the end of that day, the *LAH* were firmly within the confines of the city limits. They had enveloped it from the west and north, with full control not coming until the 19th of October.

On the 20th they moved further east to capitalize on the successes to date. Rostov on Don was the next significant objective for the *LAH,* the capture of that city would open the way to the Caucausus for the Germans. The advance was initially to northeast, alongside the *13th Panzer Division*. The weather was worsening and the supply situation was not ideal at this stage either. This combination produced a slowing of the advance rate. Stiffening resistance in the towns and villages before Rostov also added to this slowing pace of the *LAH's* progress. This situation lasted through the rest of October and into the early part of November, by then the Russian cold winter had arrived. The snow and frost prevented any advances until the middle of November 1941. For now, we will leave the *LAH's* situation and cover the advances of *SS-Wiking Division,* also within Army Group South.

SS-Wiking Division

At the end of August 1941, *Wiking* were preparing to assault Kamenka. This objective is on the east bank of the Dnjepr River. The *Division* used the cover of darkness to cross the river at the end of the first week of September. On the 8th of September the attack began, first by a long drawn out artillery duel between the Germans and the Russians, with the infantry advancing in the afternoon. *Wiking* moved in to the north of Kamenka and by the end of this first day their positions were established and held. These positions were then expanded over the next few days.

In the last week of September the push further east began from the Kamenka bridgehead. One group under Fritz von Scholz advanced north of Podgorodnoje. By the 9th of October lead elements were as far east as Konstaninowka – this was around the same time that the *LAH* has reached the Sea of Azov further south. Once the battle for this area was complete, the *SS-Wiking Division* moved further south to Wolnowacha. It was at this time that the skies opened and the Russian rains began their downpour. This immediately presented problems for *Wiking* and for the next two weeks they made little or no movement.

The next successes came on the 24th of October 1941 when *SS-Regiment Nordland* took the city of Amrosiewka, further east; *Kampfgruppe von Scholz* was the successful group here. Further advance was made to Uspenskaja, this advance took them until the end of October.

On the 5th of November 1941 the next advance began. All *Divisional* elements had closed up around a bridgehead at Golodajewka, and they were to protect the northern flank, as the rest of the *Divisions* were to push further southwards towards Rostov. They managed to advance further eastwards and by mid-November lead elements were as far as Popowka and Astachowo. The rain had turned to snow and this did not help the morale of the men of *SS-Wiking Division*. We will leave the advances of this *Division* in mid-November 1941 as the final preparations for the assault on Rostov on Don were being made.

1. SS-Infantry Brigade (mot.)

We last covered this unit at the end of September when they were positioned between Nikopol and Saporoshje (Zaporizzja) on the bend of the Dnjepr River. They were performing security duties in this area, these varied in intensity, but one particularly heavy fight took place on the 9th of October 1941. This was the same day that Heinrich Himmler ordered the *1. SS-Infantry Brigade (mot.)* to move to the northwest and reach Konotop; around 200 miles from their current positions. Their march began the following day and lasted fifteen days, delayed due to the atrocious weather and subsequent impassable roads. (This was the same time that their *2. SS-Infantry Brigade (mot.) Kameraden* were fighting in the Vyriza Pocket further north). For the remainder of October and up to the middle of November 1941 they busied themselves with security, mopping up and anti-partisan duties.

We will detail Gert Bremer's Knight's Cross, then move back to Army Group North.

Gert Bremer
Date of birth: 25.07.1917
SS Number: 310 405
Born in Dusterntal, Bremer's service began in April 1933 when he joined the *Hitler Youth*, staying there until April 1936. He then served in the *R.A.D.* from April 1936 until the start of October 1936. He followed this by entering the *SS* on the 6th of October 1936, initially serving in the *III Battalion, SS-Regiment Germania*. At the start of October 1937 he went to Bad Tolz, staying there until the 1st of September 1938. His next move came on the 9th of November the same year when he moved to the *LAH,* the same day as he was promoted to *SS-Untersturmführer.* He went with the *LAH* into Poland during 1939 winning the Second Class Iron Cross on the 1st of October 1939. He then took part in the campaign in the west during the summer of 1940, winning the First Class Iron Cross on the 5th of June 1940. At the start of September 1940 he was promoted to *SS-Obersturmführer.* Just over one month later, he received the Infantry Assault Badge in Bronze. Just prior to the start of Barbarossa, on the 21st of June 1941, he was promoted further to *SS-Hauptsturmführer.* Bremer and the *LAH* then went east into Russia as part of Operation Barbarossa.

Their advances up to the end of September as part of that operation have been highlighted in the preceding pages. Bremer and the rest of the *Aufklarungs Abteilung* took Dnjeprowka at the very end of September. The following day they moved towards Mentschekur, Bremer's *1. Kompanie* were in Hf. Neuhof during this day. The next day he led his men in an attack against difficult opposition and took Jelissawetowka. By the end of the 3rd of October they had played their part in the defeat of two Russian Armies, fighting on the enemy's southern flank. Over ten thousand prisoners passed into captivity along with hundreds of guns. From there, the pursuit turned south and southeast.

The enemy had realized that they could not stop the advance of the Germans and those soldiers not already captured began a rapid flight eastwards. The importance of capturing objectives further to the east was essential for the *LAH* and their *Kameraden*. What developed was an intensive, fast paced race between the Russians and the *LAH,* led by Bremer's *1. Kompanie, Aufklarungs Abteilung*.

A smiling Gert Bremer photographed following his award of the Knight's Cross in Russia.

The first objective reached in the 5th of October was Fedrowka, where Bremer cleared the town of the enemy. Next on the list was an important bridge at Terpenje, over the Moltschnaja River (I recommend that you read through Kurt Meyer's, '*Grenadiers*' book to get a full idea of the intensity of this advance). Bremer and his men led the race towards the bridge and as they did so, they found themselves in amongst a mass of enemy soldiers and Russian civilians all vying for the same objective. Bremer's men began to shoot into the enemy ranks in order to cut a path through the throng. As they got close to the bridge, the Russians detonated their explosive charges on the bridge – it was full of their own soldiers at the time. This apparent disaster did not stop Gert Bremer. His men sought and found a suitable crossing further along the river. They raced across it and established a small bridgehead, all of this within one hour of reaching the bridge itself. This bridgehead was extended and the advance continued to the southeast.

On the 6th of October 1941 Astrachanka and Arechowka were taken and also an area near Nowospasskoje. The enemy was attempting to resist and the last two objectives were taken in close combat by Gert Bremer and his men. By the end of this day Romanowka was reached and senior Russian staff officers were captured. On the following day, early morning advances brought the *LAH* to within ten miles of Berdjansk. At Stanitsa Nowospasskoj, Bremer's *1. Kompanie* once again raced into dense enemy columns and successfully crossed the bridge. From here Berdjansk beckoned.

As the advance continued, the *Aufklarungs Abteilung* were made aware of retreating Russians coming from the west. They diverted, engaged and captured the enemy column containing two thousand enemy soldiers, with about five hundred being captured. Enemy survivors were surprised to be met by Germans this far eastwards. Once again, Bremer was in the lead here. As this took place *Army* units from *Battalion von Boddien* moved into Berdjansk. The *LAH* were to move upon Mariupol next. This objective was reached before midday on the 8th of October. Bremer's *1. Kompanie* had led the way and pushed through the outer defenses and straight through the sprawling city itself. This success surprised even the *German High Command*. Due to the size of the city, the advances slowed as the entire city had to be controlled. This lasted for the next few days with the help of accompanying infantry.

In summary, Gert Bremer had led most of the way from Dnjeprowka, through Fedrowka and on towards Berdjansk, finally reaching and seizing Mariupol. He did not do this alone and was helped by his *LAH Kameraden*, as well as *Kameraden* from the *Heer*. He did however show great courage and leadership abilities during this time, as well as extreme cool headedness and bravery. His advances had often overtaken the massed ranks of the retreating enemy, a situation that would have

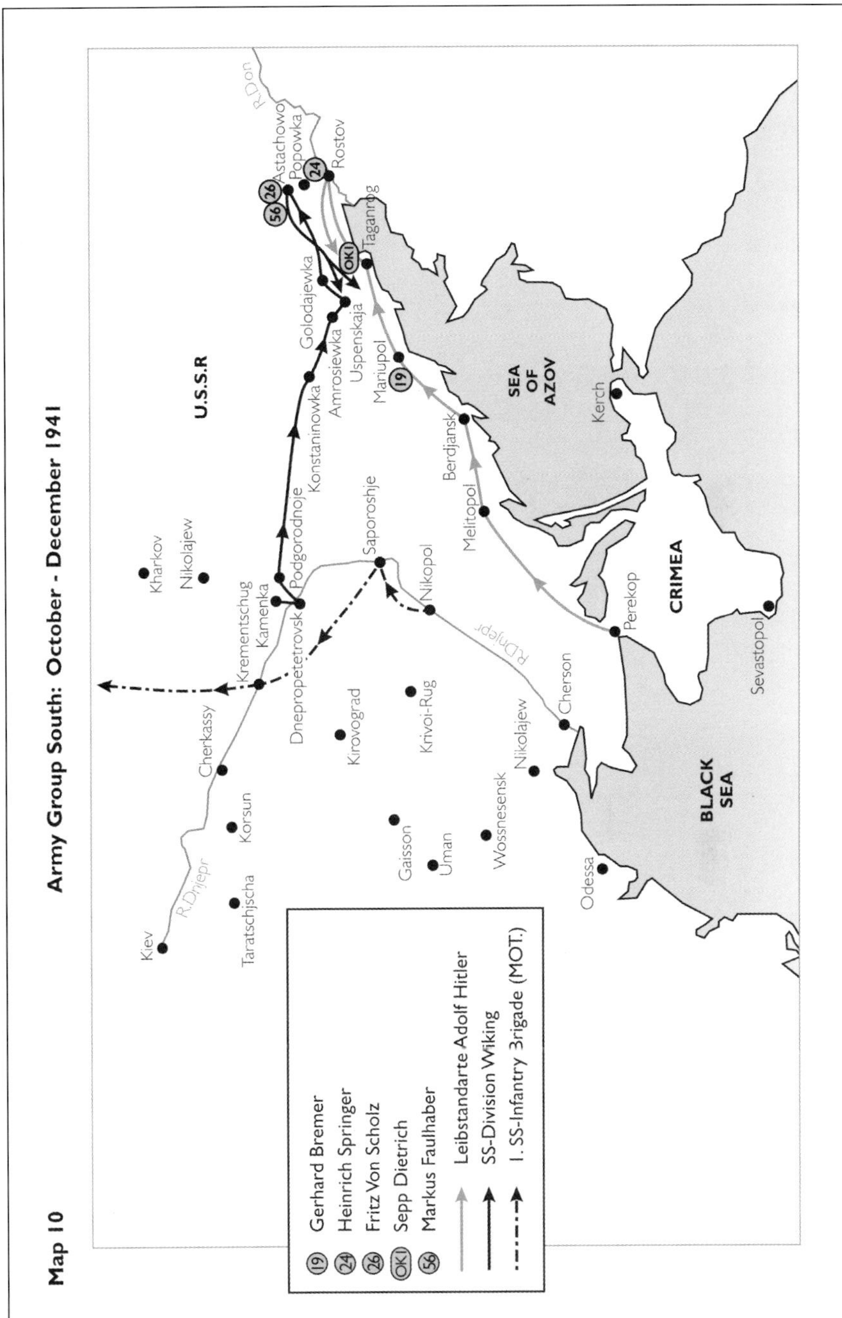
Map 10
Army Group South: October - December 1941
19 Gerhard Bremer
24 Heinrich Springer
26 Fritz Von Scholz
OKI Sepp Dietrich
56 Markus Faulhaber
Leibstandarte Adolf Hitler
SS-Division Wiking
1. SS-Infantry Brigade (MOT.)
U.S.S.R
SEA OF AZOV
CRIMEA
BLACK SEA
R.Don
R.Dnjepr
Kiev
Taratschjscha
Korsun
Cherkassy
Krementschug
Kamenka
Dnepropetetrovsk
Kharkov
Nikolajew
Podgorodnoje
Konstaninowka
Amrosiewka
Golodajewka
Uspenskaja
Astachowo
Popowka
Rostov
Taganrog
Mariupol
Berdjansk
Melitopol
Saporoshje
Nikopol
Kirovograd
Krivoi-Rug
Gaisson
Uman
Wossnesensk
Nikolajew
Cherson
Odessa
Perekop
Kerch
Sevastopol

had an incalculable psychological advantage. With Mariupol's capture, the 'Battle for the Sea of Azov' was considered to be over. Estimations placed one hundred thousand prisoners, along with hundreds of tanks and guns as the size of the booty. Gert Bremer certainly played a critical role in this success at the head of his *1. Kompanie, Aufklarungs Abteilung, LAH.*

His Knight's Cross recommendation is not on his file, therefore the author and the submission date are unknown, but it can be presumed that Sepp Dietrich would have written this? What is known is that it was approved on the 30th of October 1941. Considering that his actions finished on the 8th of October, this was a rapid approval, compared to his *Waffen-SS Kameraden*. This award made him the 19th *Waffen-SS* soldier and the 5th *LAH* soldier to receive this award. He was presented with his medal on the 5th of November by Sepp Dietrich, Kurt Meyer was also present.

Army Group North

Polizei Division

The advances and successes of the *Polizei Division* were covered up mid-September 1941, after they had taken Krassnogwardeisk. From here they opened the road ready for further moves northwards, but they were ordered slightly eastwards instead. From the 15th to the 17th of September *Regiment 2* seized control of Pushkin, directly south of Leningrad. An unsuccessful attack was put in against Pulkowo, closer to Leningrad. This took the *Division* up to the end of September 1941.

From October the overall emphasis shifted to attacking Moscow, the decision had been taken in mid-September to surround, cut-off, but not assault Leningrad itself. This resulted in a changing to a 'defensive posture' for the *Polizei Division*. They developed a style of harassing warfare against any identifiable enemy positions. The Russians also made harassing attacks against the positions of *Polizei*. None of these attacks were of significant size to change the positions of either side; the snow had also arrived in the north.

The next notable occurrence came around mid-November 1941. A further Knight's Cross was awarded to a *Waffen-SS* soldier within the *Polizei Division,* the name of the recipient was *Oberst* Alfred Wunnenberg. The actions that resulted in this award had taken place two months earlier, around Luga and Krassnogwardeisk, and will be covered in more detail later on.

This award was followed by another for the *Polizei Division,* but it came almost one month later in mid-December. Before we cover that award, we will cover the actions of this *Division* up to that point. The *Divisional* area of control remained in and around Pushkin. The enemy tried various attacks through the rest of November and into December 1941. The *Division* also assumed control of a wider area within the ring around Leningrad, as accompanying units were withdrawn and sent to other areas.

Around mid-December, the *Divisional Commander*, *SS-Brigadeführer* Walter Kruger was awarded the Knight's Cross to the Iron Cross. At the same time Walter Kruger moved back to the *Fuhrungshauptamt,* Alfred Wunnenberg took over command of the *Division*.

Over the preceding weeks more and more attacks were launched against the *Polizei Division*. This continued into the remainder of December. Towards the end of the third week of this month an enemy tank attack was stopped with the loss of nearly twenty tanks for the Russians. Further attacks continued until the end of 1941.

For now, we will move to cover the advances of *SS-Totenkopf Division,* also within Army Group North. Before doing so however, we will give an overview of Alfred Wunnenberg and Walter Kruger.

Alfred Wunnenberg

Date of birth: 20.07.1891

SS Number: 405 898

Born is Saarburg, he began his military service in early 1913 and by August 1914 he had obtained the rank of *Leutnant*. During the First World War he became a *Kompanie Commander*. Mid-way through the war he began training with the aerial component of the *German Armed Forces* and by August 1917 he was an aerial observer. Promotion to *Oberleutnant* came soon after in November 1917. By the end of the war he had been awarded the Second and First Class Iron Crosses, plus the Silver Wound Badge as well as the Observers Badge.

The end of World War I did not end his military service. By late 1919 he was a *Staff Aerial Liaison Officer*. The following year he was promoted to *Hauptmann,* the rank he left the *Army* with in September 1920. He then had a stint with the *Freikorps* before joining the police.

He stayed with the police until the start of October 1939. In those intervening years he held various posts that included teaching, administrative and command positions. By 1937 he was holding the rank of *Oberstleutnant*. On the 2nd of October 1939 he moved to the newly created *Polizei Division* as *Commander* of their *Regiment 3*. On the first day of 1940 he was promoted to *Oberst der Schutz Polizei*. This was the same day that he joined the *SS,* given the rank of *SS-Standertenführer.*

An autographed photograph of Alfred Wunnenberg showing him after his award of the Knight's Cross; seen here wearing his Polizei uniform, rather than his Waffen-SS uniform.

He seen action during the western campaign in 1940 and after that campaign he was awarded both clasps to the Iron Cross, 18th of June and 21st of August respectively. In early November 1941 he was promoted further to *SS-Oberführer.* Prior to this, on the 30th of October 1941, his *Divisional Commander*, Walter Kruger, wrote a recommendation for the award of the Knight's Cross to the Iron Cross for Wunnenberg. This recommendation contained the following details:

"*Oberst* Wunnenberg is a skilled and model *Regimental Commander*. Especially remarkable is his daring personal actions during the capture of the hills at Stojanowschtschina near Luga on the 11th of August 1941 seventeen enemy tanks and numerous heavy bunkers were also captured the same day.

On the 23rd of August 1941 Alfred Wunnenberg was ordered to capture Ssyrez, the hills west of there and also advance to the hills at Turowo, east of Luga. Throughout this day he led his *3rd Regiment* to Ssyrez and the hills west of Ssyrez and Wybor. Although his *Regiment* had been weakened due to heavy fighting in these areas, he pushed on to Nelaja and took the hills at Turowo. He advanced along the flanks and rear of the enemy, breaking their strong resistance. This made *Regiment 2's* capture of Luga possible.

On the 13th of September Wunnenberg's *Regiment* were tasked with taking Krassnowardeisk, advancing from the southwest. They had to secure the bridges and reach the fork in the road, north of this city. They captured four heavy bunkers, took four bridges intact and also reached the city centre ahead of some enemy tanks.

Oberst Wunnenberg, with his personal bravery, succeeded in breaking through the key positions of the outer defensive line of St. Petersburg (Leningrad). This ensured continued advance towards Pushkin, via the Ishora position."

This recommendation was approved on the 15th of November 1941, six days after his promotion to *SS-Oberführer,* it was not his only association with this award and its' grades.

Walter Kruger

Date of birth: 27.02.1890

SS Number: 266 184

Born in Strassbourg, within the Alsace region, his military career began on the 1st of April 1900 when he joined the *Cadet Corps*. By 1908 he had obtained the rank of *Leutnant*. Just prior to the start of the First World War he was performing the role of a *Battalion Adjutant* within the *2nd Baden Grenadier Regiment*. During the First World War he was a *Kompanie* and *Battalion Commander* within the above-mentioned unit. He was further promoted to *Oberleutnant* and then to *Hauptmann* by mid-August 1917. By the end of World War I he had been awarded the Second and First Class Iron Crosses and also the Wound Badge.

A formal portrait of Walter Kruger taken after his award of the Knight's Cross.

Like many of this World War I *Kameraden*, he served in the post-war *Freikorps* and other similar organizations until 1921. He then pursued a civilian career first in Germany and then in Austria. He joined the *S.A.* at the end of 1933 and the *SS* towards the end of April 1935, his rank at that time was *SS-Obersturmbannführer.* He was given command of the *II Batallion, SS-Regiment Germania*. This lasted until May 1937, when he moved to Bad Tolz as an instructor. Before the end of that year he was back with the *SS-VT,* commanding the *IV Battalion* within the *SS-Regiment Deutschland*. In January 1939 he achieved the rank of *SS-Standartenführer*, the rank he entered the Second World War with.

One year later he was promoted further to *SS-Oberführer* and became the *First Staff Officer* of the *Polizei Division*. During the campaign in the west during 1940, he was awarded the Clasp to both classes of the Iron Cross in quick succession, June the 13th and June 22nd 1940.

He was promoted to *Brigadeführer und Generalmajor der Waffen-SS* on Hitler's birthday 1941. By mid-August the same year he was in command of the *Polizei Division*. It was with this *Division* that he was awarded the Knight's Cross to the Iron Cross on December the 13th 1941 for his unit's successes during the fighting around Leningrad in 1941. A brief overview of these successes is as follows, but is contained in more detail in the preceding pages:

After the death at the front of Arthur Mulverstedt, an occurrence that had a deep effect upon the *Division*, Walter Kruger took over. Under his command he focused on keeping the unit sharp and combat capable. He led the *Polizei Division* as it took control of Luga, Krassnogwardeisk and Pushkin, thereby leading the way to Leningrad. He had seen two of his men being recognized for their bravery, through the award of the Knight's Cross – he had even penned one of these recommendations himself, now it was his turn. This made him the third for this *Division* and the twenty-first for the *Waffen-SS*.

Two days after being awarded the Knight's Cross he was taken back to the *SS Main Office*, in the department of *Arms Inspectorate*. His association with the Knight's Cross did not end there, but more details of that later on.

SS-Totenkopf Division

Also within Army Group North was the *SS-Totenkopf Division,* last visited at the end of September 1941, after their successful capture of Lushno, southeast of Leningrad.

At the start of October *Totenkopf* adapted a defensive posture. This was in some respects a fortuitous move as the Russian winter arrived in earnest just over one week later, delivering heavy snowfalls. Orders for continued attacks came in the second half of October. These attacks extended *Totenkopf's* area

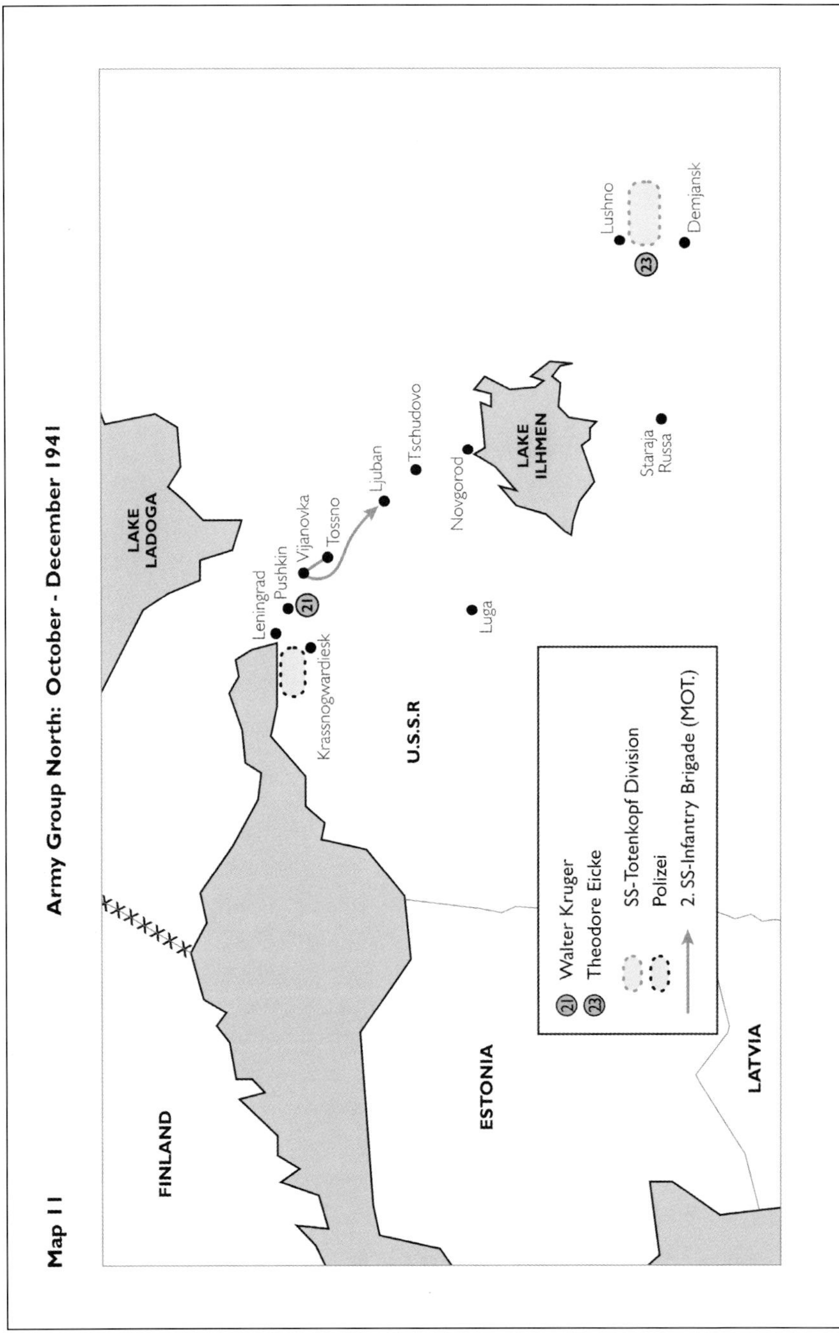
Map 11
Army Group North: October - December 1941
FINLAND
ESTONIA
LATVIA
U.S.S.R
LAKE LADOGA
LAKE ILHMEN
Leningrad
Pushkin
Vijanovka
Tossno
Ljuban
Tschudovo
Novgorod
Krassnogwardiesk
Luga
Staraja Russa
Lushno
Demjansk
21 Walter Kruger
23 Theodore Eicke
SS-Totenkopf Division
Polizei
2. SS-Infantry Brigade (MOT.)

slightly northwards. A combination of very poor weather, difficult defenses by the Russians and this extension of *Totenkopf's* area of responsibility made this task very difficult.

This *Division* remained in this general area for the rest of 1941. Intermittent enemy attacks were dealt with as well as *Totenkopf* sending localized missions. The worsening winter conditions forced a change in priority for the *Totenkopf Division*. They focused on building bunkers for themselves to protect them against the elements and the enemy artillery fire. The Russians maintained their harassing fire throughout, but neither side moved much for the rest of this first year of the war between Germany and Russia. *Totenkopf* had hoped for relief after their continuous and costly fighting since the 24th of July 1941, but this was not to be. They were instead given an even wider area to control and no additional units were sent to help them.

One highlight arrived for them before the end of 1941; this was an award of the Knight's Cross to another one of their ranks, but more of that in a little while.

2. SS-Infantry Brigade (mot.)

Last covered in September, whilst at Tossno (Tosno) and Vljanovka (Ul'janovka). At this stage they were placed in reserve; elements were also sent south of Ljuban. They were joined by the *SS-Flak Detachment 'Ost'*. There were skirmishes against the enemy in the area south of Ljuban during the first week of October 1941. Anti-partisan sweeping operations took place during the first half of October, one noticeable issue that they had to content with was the constant harassing aerial attacks by the *Soviet Airforce*. Anti-partisan search missions were conducted throughout the remainder of October and up to mid-November. On the 14th of November the *2. SS-Infantry-Brigade (mot.)* was joined by the *SS-Legion Flandern*.

With the help of this new *Legion*, they conducted many sweeps and engaged partisans of various strengths throughout the remainder of November and until the end of December 1941. The constant enemy aerial attacks did not relent during that time.

SS-Legion-Flandern & SS-Legion-Niederlande

Training continued for both of these units until early November 1941, when *Flandern* were ordered to join the *2. SS-Infantry Brigade (mot.)* at Tossno. They began to move from Ayrs on the 10th of November 1941, arriving at the designated destination seven days later. Their addition of around 1,100 men increased the overall strength of the *2. SS-Infantry Brigade (mot.)* to 5,300 men approx. These western European *SS* volunteers were a welcome addition to the existing German *SS* volunteers. They would be the first of hundreds of thousands of foreign volunteers to the ranks of the *Waffen-SS*.

We will leave this unit on the 17th of November 1941 (the same day as Army Group South started their advance on Rostov) and move to Army Group Centre.

SS-Legion-Niederlande remained in Ayrs until January 1942.

Army Group Centre

SS-Division Reich

After having been diverted southwards to help in the destruction of the Kiev pocket, they were back north in Roslawl (Roslavl) at the start of October 1941. They were to now take part in the push towards the Soviet capital of Moscow. This operation began on the 2nd of October, but *SS-Division Reich* was not among the lead elements during the opening phase. Their moves began on the 3rd of October, following the advance routes of the lead units. By the end of their fourth day of advance they had moved northeast of Roslawl, over the Desna River and all the way to Juchnow (Juchnov), on the Ugra River. From there they changed direction northeast towards Wjasma (V'az'ma) and Gshatsk (Gagarin), both objectives are positioned on the main road to Moscow.

After a brief pause, *SS-Division Reich* set out for Gshatsk on the 8th of October. This objective was reached and secured the following day. The advance was following on the heels of the retreating Russian soldiers. Although they offered no defined defense, the resistance they offered was increasing, causing further losses to the *SS-Division Reich*. As mid-October beckoned, the advance closer to Moscow came about. After Gshatsk the next objective on the main road to Moscow was Moshaisk (Mozajsk). In front of Moshaisk, the Soviets had erected the first of the defensive rings around their capital. By the end of the 12th of October 1941, elements of *SS-Division Reich* stood ready to move on this defensive line.

In the preceding days, *SS-Division Reich* had encountered more and more enemy attacks, backed up with tanks. They had overcome each of these, but it was anticipated that the Soviets would not allow the Germans to have an easy ride to the prize of Moscow. The lead element of the *Division* was one *Kompanie* of *SS-Regiment Deutschland* and on the morning of the 13th of October 1941 they moved to the village of Kolozkoje along with *Kameraden* from the *Heer*. After entering this village, they pushed on towards Rogatschewo. By reaching Rogatschewo, this *Kompanie* had broken through the defensive ring. The *Regimental Commander*,

SS-Brigadeführer Wilhelm Bittrich issued orders to exploit this situation. (Knight's Cross action covered in more detail later on). All available supporting forces were pushed into this area later that day, so the breech could be extended. As this was the first defensive line, the resistance was heavy. *SS-Regiments Deutschland* and *Der Führer* pushed on into this area over the 13th and 14th of October, dealing with hand to hand fighting. They had extended this breech by three kilometers by the end of the 14th. Fighting on these days was around another town by the name of Jelnya, it became evident that the name of Jelnya and Jelnya II would forever be connected to the *SS-Division Reich's* glory.

The fighting was very intense with many casualties, once of which was none other than *SS-Obergruppenführer* Paul Hausser, who was severely wounded by a tank shell fragment to his right eye. This wound forced him to be evacuated to Germany. *SS-Oberführer* Wilhelm Bittrich, who had achieved the successful breakthrough of Moscow's defenses the day before, took over command of *SS-Division Reich*.

Further *Heer* units were moved up and the push eastwards continued. The towns of Artemki and Siwkowka were reached over the next few days. By the end of the 18th of October the all important city of Moshaisk was reached, with *SS-Regiment Deutschland* in the lead. Losses had mounted along the way, with almost one and a half thousand dead and wounded in two weeks of fighting with heavy enemy defenses and appalling weather conditions to contend with. This took *SS-Division Reich's* casualties to almost eight thousand since the start of Barbarossa. Another indication of the heavy nature of these losses was the decision to disband the *SS-Regiment 11* in the third week of October, with the remaining troops being dispersed between the other two *Regiments*. The losses to the enemy had not been light either, with around one hundred and fifty enemy divisions being lost in the north alone since the end of June 1941!

In the closing stages of October Borisowo was reached, as was Schelkowka. By the end of this month *SS-Division Reich* was in Rusa, northeast of Moshaisk. Torrential rains had arrived, bringing to a halt all forward movement.

The first two weeks in November was one of no significant movement, but the orders came to continue the moves to Moscow. In the second half of November 1941 the advance towards the city of Istra was begun, via Gorodischtsche and Nikolskoje. After crossing the Istra River the city beyond was taken in the first few days of December. The furthest point of the advance by *SS-Division Reich* was Lenino. On the 3rd of December 1941 all forward movement stopped, but why?

The physical and mental strains, supplies and losses to enemy fire and cold weather had all taken their toll. Some of the *Battalions* were temporarily disbanded

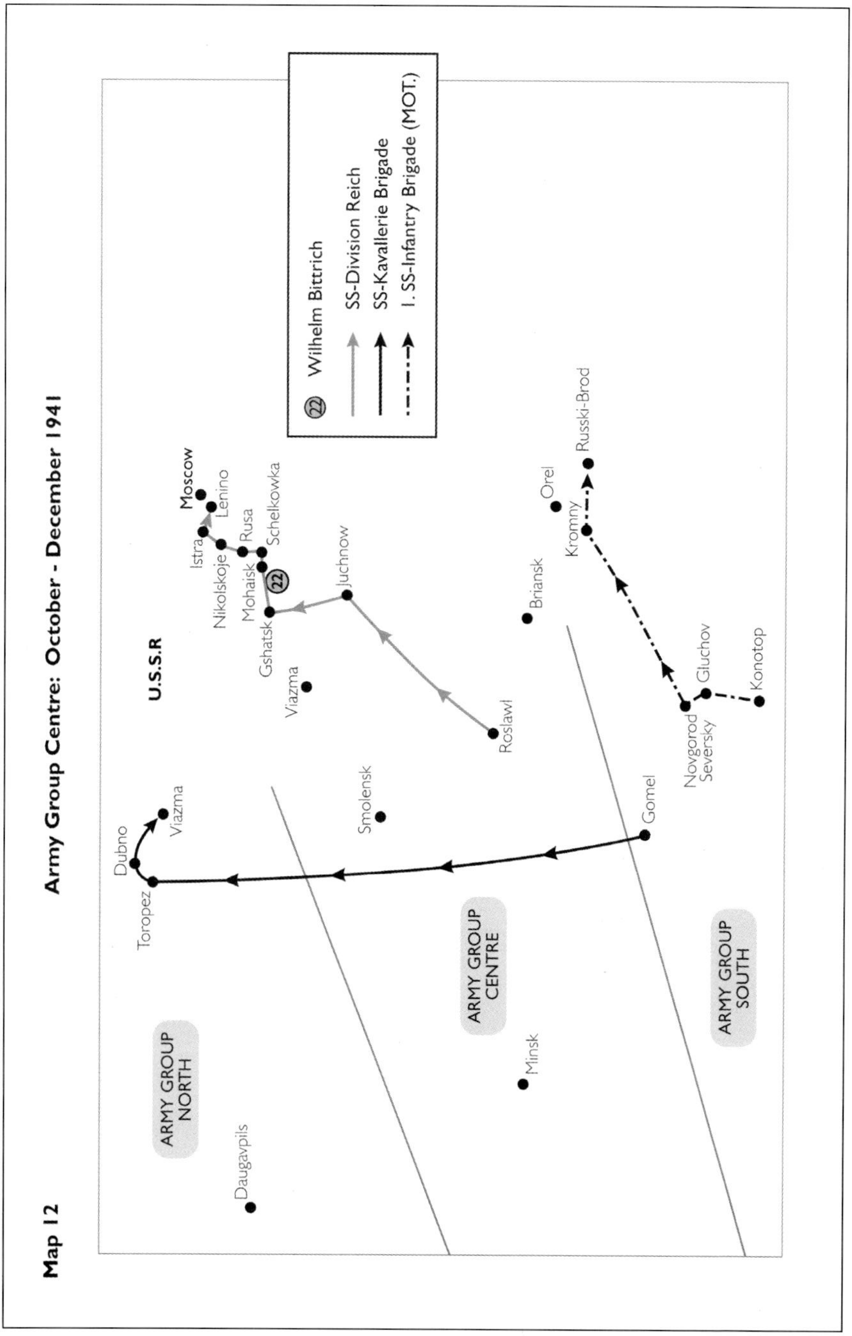
Map 12
Army Group Centre: October - December 1941
22 Wilhelm Bittrich
SS-Division Reich
SS-Kavallerie Brigade
I. SS-Infantry Brigade (MOT.)
U.S.S.R
ARMY GROUP NORTH
ARMY GROUP CENTRE
ARMY GROUP SOUTH
Moscow
Lenino
Istra
Nikolskoje
Rusa
Schelkowka
Mohaisk
Gshatsk
Juchnow
Viazma
Roslawl
Briansk
Orel
Kromny
Russki-Brod
Gluchov
Konotop
Novgorod Seversky
Gomel
Smolensk
Minsk
Toropez
Dubno
Viazma
Daugavpils

due to the lack of men to fill them. *Kompanie's* were at an average of twenty-five men. The *Generals* in this area realized that the capture of Moscow at this time, with the situation as it was, would not be achieved. With that the *SS-Division Reich* moved over to the defensive.

On the 5th of December 1941 the Russian counter offensive began and orders arrived to fall back to better defensive positions on the western side of the Istra River initially, then on the 14th of December they were ordered further west. It was also on this day that the *Waffen-SS* received a further Knight's Cross winner. This was *SS-Oberführer* Wilhelm Bittrich. One week later they moved back as far as the Rusa River. This was the day that Bittrich received word of his Knight's Cross. The *SS-Division Reich* stayed in this position as the third year of the Second World War, 1941, drew to a close.

As previously mentioned, another Knight's Cross was awarded to a soldier of the *Waffen-SS* before the end of 1941, this was Theodor Eicke, but before covering both Bittrich and Eicke in detail, we will outline the actions of the other *Waffen-SS* units within Army Group Centre.

SS-Kavallerie-Brigade

At the end of September 1941 this *Brigade* moved from the Pripjet Marshes area and took up position in Toropez (Toropec), around two hundred and fifty miles north of their previous position. This move was completed by the first half of October and they wasted no time in engaging in action, within this northern extreme of Army Group Centre.

Their initial operations sent elements southwest of Toropez during mid-October, with the task of securing this area against partisan activity. The second half of this month saw them moving eastwards, again securing the main supply routes to Rshev (Rzev). Poor weather in the latter stages of October slowed operations temporarily.

During November and December 1941 elements moved north towards Dubno and also east towards Jetkino. It was within this extended area from Toropez that the *SS-Kavallerie Brigade* operated with success. A noticeable increase in coordinated partisan activity took place in the latter stages of December 1941. At the end of 1941, elements were ordered northeast towards Lake Volga, the pressure from regular Russian forces was increasing.

1. SS-Infantry Brigade (mot.)

Initially operating in the sourthern part of Russia, they were moved north to the Konotop area. They swept this general area for partisans and provided security.

In the middle of November 1941 they were operating northeast of Konotop, around Gluchov (Hluhiv), Putivl (Putyvl) and towards Novgorod (Novhorod), Seversky (Sivers'kij) in the general area between the Desna and Sejou Rivers. These operations continued through to the 9th of December 1941 when they were sent northeast to Kromny (Kromy). They reached their designated area by the 14th of December. During the second half of December 1941 they were operating further east at Russki-Brod.

Wilhelm Bittrich

Date of birth: 26.02.1894

SS Number: 39 177

Born in Wernigerode, his military career began in July 1914. He initially served with one of the mountain units, but within two months he had moved to service in the *German Flying Service*. He served with them for the rest of the war. He ended World War I with the rank of *Leutnant*, in addition he was awarded the Second and First Class Iron Crosses, Wound Badge and Pilots Badge. He then joined the *Freikorps* during the early 1920s, followed by the *Army* in 1923.

His service with the *SS* began at the start of July 1932, receiving promotion to *SS-Sturmführer (SS-Untersturmführer)* the same year. 1934 was a time of movement and change for Bittrich. He served with the *74. Sturm* from early March 1934 and during April he was promoted to *SS-Obersturmführer,* then further still to *SS-Hauptsturmführer* in mid-June. He moved to the fledgling *SS-VT* in late August 1934, serving with the *Hamburg Political Readiness Unit*. This unit was renamed *SS-Regiment 1 'Deutschland'* during September 1935, by then Bittrich was serving in the *2. Kompanie*. He stayed with this *Kompanie* until the start of October 1936, on that date he promoted to *SS-Sturmbannführer* and moved to the command of *Deutschland's, II Battalion*. In late January 1938 he was promoted to *SS-Obersturmbannführer,* followed by another move in May, this time to the newly created *SS-Regiment 3 'Der Führer'*. At the start of June 1939 he was promoted further to *SS-Standartenführer* and began a spell with the *LAH*. It was with the *LAH* that he began actions during the Second World War.

He went with them into Poland as part of their staff. He was awarded the Clasp to the Second Class Iron Cross for his actions; his stint with the *LAH* came to an end on the last day of January 1940. He then moved back to the *SS-VT,* this time with the *SS V Division*. The second half of 1940 would see further recognition and also promotion. In early June he was awarded the Clasp to the First Class Iron Cross, followed at the start of September with promotion to *SS-Oberführer.* Three months later he assumed command of *SS-Regiment Deutschland*. He remained as *Commander* of that *Regiment* until mid-December 1941. He then assumed

A rare signed photograph of Wilhelm Bittrich, following his award of the Knight's Cross. His German Cross in Gold can also be seen. This photograph was signed three months prior to his death in April 1979.

command of the *SS-Division Reich,* after the wounding of Paul Hausser. Previous to this taking place he had been promoted to *SS-Brigadeführer,* on the 19th of October 1941. Five days after that, Paul Hausser had written a recommendation for Bittrich to be awarded the Knight's Cross to the Iron Cross. This was approved on the 14th of December 1941, the day before he took over command of the *Division* and contained the following overview:

> "During the battle for Jelnya his *Regiment* took hill 125.6 on the 22nd of July 1941 and defended this position for two weeks, against continuous attacks by the enemy, until relieved. In addition he distinguished himself on the 13th of October during the attack upon the Moscow protection ring between Gshatsk and Moshaisk. In the early afternoon he determined through reconnaissance that there was a weakly held area near the railway tracks, close to the main road. He recognized that any delay would give the enemy an advantage, Bittrich decided to push ahead. He used the nearby artillery and tanks to soften up the area first. There then followed an attack over the next week, made during difficult weather conditions and having to deal with mounting losses. This initial break into these enemy positions was widened and deepened over the first critical hours of the attack. This situation was made better during the following day and through his quick decision, managed to make this breakthrough a success."

Highlighting the enemy men and material captured, the recommendation lists eight hundred and fifty prisoners, tanks, anti-tank guns, heavy machine guns and other vehicles and weapons.

"The breakthrough, which occurred within twenty-four hours, and the resulting quick taking and opening of the highway are to be credited to the independent decision making of the *Commander* of *SS-Regiment "Deutschland", SS-Brigadeführer* Bittrich."

Moshaisk was occupied four days later and this position was used as the jumping off point for the continued attack against Moscow.

This was not to be Wilhelm Bittrich's only connection to the Knight's Cross, but more details of that in future volumes.

Theodor Eicke

Date of birth: 17.10.1892

SS Number: 2 921

Born in Hamport within the Alsace region, his military career began in 1909. He served with two *Bavarian Regiments* prior to the start of World War I. During that

A formal portrait of Theodore Eicke taken after his award of the Knight's Cross.

war he moved to service with the artillery. He was awarded the Second Class Iron Cross as well as various Bavarian medals during the First World War.

In the inter-war years he pursued a career with the police. This began in 1919 and after various postings his service ended in 1923. Non-military employment followed this until the late 1920s. At the start of December 1928 he joined the *Nazi Party* and entered the *S.A.* At the end of July 1930 he moved to the fledgling *SS* and before the end of that year he had been promoted to *SS-Sturmführer (Untersturmführer)* and was in command of the *147. Sturm*. He was promoted again in mid-November 1931 to *SS-Sturmbannführer.* Further promotion came in 1932 when he moved to the rank of *SS-Oberführer* and was also given command of the *10. Standarte*. He held various postings in the early part of 1933, but by June he took command of the concentration camp at Dachau. 1934 would see him come to prominence during testing times for Adolf Hitler and his rise to power.

During the Night of the Long Knives he was responsible for shooting Ernst Rohm, his former chief from his days with the *S.A.* This was a daunting task for anyone, but his willingness proved exactly how far he would go when under orders. Within two weeks of this occurrence he was promoted to *SS-Gruppenführer* and given control of all concentration camps. From this time until late 1939 he set about training the guards as elite soldiers. He was tasked with forming the *SS-Totenkopf Division,* completed during October 1939.

As has already been highlighted, Eicke and his *SS-Totenkopf Division* took part in the campaign in the west in 1940, but did not participate in the Balkans campaign in 1941. Eicke and his men moved eastwards in June 1941 and became part of Army Group North. Again, details of their battles are contained in the preceding pages, as a quick reminder though, they moved through the Baltic region and then over towards Demjansk. Eicke himself was wounded in early July 1941 and remained away from his *Division* until September. When he returned he led his unit during the crossing of the Lowat River and the difficult battle for Lushno, after which they moved to the defense. He was awarded the Knight's Cross to the Iron Cross on the 26th of December 1941. His file does not contain his recommendation, so it is difficult to determine the exact actions that resulted in this award. However, the advances made by his *Division,* whilst he was in command, all contributed to the successful advances of Hitler's troops. His *Division* also made the furthest eastwards advance at that time within Army Group North. It is not known who penned the award, but it would have been a senior *Commander* to Eicke and as we have seen up to now, any award of the Knight's Cross was not decided upon lightly.

This would not be his only connection to this medal, but more of that in later chapters.

Army Group South

Leibstandarte Adolf Hitler

We have covered the various fighting *SS* formations within Army Group North and Army Group Centre up to the end of 1941, now we will finish this chapter by covering those units fighting in the southern area of operations.

In mid-November 1941 the *LAH* were preparing for their all important assault upon Rostov on Don, along with the *III Panzer Korps*. The city of Rostov is a vital communications and traffic centre for the Caucasus. It had immense value to the Russians and a significant target for the Germans. The attack began on the 17th of November after an initial delay due to heavy fog conditions. The German artillery signaled the start of the attack, followed soon after by a replying attack by the Russian artillery. It was during this attack that Gerd Pleiss was heavily wounded by an artillery shell fragment and died the same day. If you recall, Pleiss was awarded the Knight's Cross to the Iron Cross during the Balkan campaign earlier that same year. The *Waffen-SS* had lost another hero, recognized at the highest level for his bravery.

One of Pleiss' *Kameraden* at that time was future Knight's Cross holder, Heinrich Springer. In correspondence with the author, Springer made mention of the death of Pleiss. He stated that the death of any *Kompanie Commander* was difficult for the men of the *Kompanie*. It had the effect of destroying the 'soul of the *Kompanie'*, something that they would all have difficulty recovering from. However, they had to do just that, as the objective of Rostov would not wait.

The push towards Rostov continued over the next couple of days with the *LAH* taking control of enemy tank ditches and captured Ssultan Ssaly. It was noted that the enemy resistance stiffened as the *LAH* got closer to their main objective. As they got to the outskirts of the city, the orders were issued for the attack itself. The capturing of the large bridge spanning the Don River intact was essential. This important task was given to *SS-Hauptsturmführer* Heinrich Springer and his *3. Kompanie*.

They began their assault during the morning of the 20th of November and after taking the airstrip they moved through the city towards the bridge. Using a lot of luck, a bit of disguise and taking advantage of the extreme confusion on the side of the enemy, Springer successfully led his men across the bridge, where they took control of it and the immediate area (Knight's Cross action covered in the next chapter). They were however, unable to keep control due to the fact that there were not enough additional troops in the area of the bridge. They were orderd back to the northern bank and after doing so, the survivors watched as their prize was blown up by the enemy. It was not all bad news however, as by the end of the next day Rostov had fallen to the Germans.

Although they did not know it at the time, the objective of Rostov on Don represented the furthest eastwardly point reached by the men of the *Leibstandarte Adolf Hitler* during the entire war. Although they had reached it, they could not hold it. Due to the threat of being cut-off by enemy forces in this surrounding area, orders were given for the *LAH* to move back across the Mius River. These moves took place at the start of December with the final positions being on the Ssambek River. The fighting had not been in vain though and the men of the *LAH* could take pride in the fact that they had contributed to the capture of over one hundred and thirty thousand enemy troops, around one and half thousand tanks, two thousand artillery pieces, nine armoured trains and over one hundred planes. They would see out the rest of 1941 in their new positions on the Ssambek River.

The very last day of the year would see a high point for the men of the *LAH*. The first *Waffen-SS* soldier to receive the Knight's Cross to the Iron Cross was recognized further for his contribution to the war effort. This person was Josef 'Sepp' Dietrich, who, on the 31st of December 1941, became the first *Waffen-SS* recipient of the Knight's Cross with Oakleaves. Before giving an overview of Dietrich's successes, we will list the actions of the other *SS* unit fighting in the south at that time.

SS-Division Wiking

This *Division* was last covered as they where in the Astachowo area, north of Rostov on Don, in mid-November. Like the rest of their German *Kameraden*, they now had the added difficulty of the worsening Russian weather. As the *LAH* and the *III Panzer Korps* pushed in towards Rostov, *Wiking,* and the rest of the *XIV Panzer Korps,* were having to contend with a Russian attack. This attack continued over the next few days and all available units were pushed against this enemy threat, as it threatened the success of the capture of Rostov. *SS-Regiment Nordland* came under extreme pressure around Astachowo. The *Commander* of this *Regiment*, Fritz von Scholz, would be awarded the Knight's Cross to the Iron Cross in early 1942 for these successful actions (details to follow).

On the same day that the *LAH* took the bridge at Rostov, further north, the enemy pressure became so great that *Panzer Gruppe 1* gave orders to withdraw back towards the Tusloff River area. This would shorten the defensive sector and help protect the units fighting at Rostov. They initially held this area against the heavy enemy attacks, *SS-Division Wiking* where at the point of this defense and delivered heavy losses on the enemy. These positions around the Tusloff River were deemed ineffective, so the orders were passed down for a further withdrawal behind the Mius River, west of Taganrog. This move started at the beginning of December 1941. From then until the end of 1941, *Wiking* took up position between

Alexejewka and Uspenskaja, Bischlerowka and Jassinowskij. This is the 'triangle' that exists between the Mius and Krynka Rivers. In the early part of December the enemy tried to penetrate these positions, but was beaten back. Further enemy attacks were launched, but none were successful. In these positions, dealing with extreme cold weather and harassing enemy attacks, the *Wiking Division* seen out the end of their first year in combat

Joseph 'Sepp' Dietrich
Date of birth: 28.05.1892
SS Number: 1 177
Although covered in greater detail earlier in this volume, a brief overview of what he had achieved by the *LAH's* entry into Russia is worthwhile.

In the early part of his life he had served in the *German Army*, fighting during World War I and receiving awards for bravery. Serving in the *Freikorps* after the war, he was also a very early supporter of Adolf Hitler and took part in many of their battles as they struggled for power. Leading Hitler's personal protection squad from 1933, holding the rank of *SS-Gruppenführer,* he grew this unit and raised his own level of importance in the years up to 1939, being present at all of the important occurrences in those formative years.

Leading his men into the start of the Second World War, he received further recognition for his skills and abilities. In 1940 he became the first recipient within the *Waffen-SS* of the Knight's Cross to the Iron Cross. He would end 1941 as the first *Waffen-SS* recipient of the Knight's Cross with Oakleaves. So let us give an overview of the actions that led to this higher award.

The recommendation for his Oakleaves to his existing Knight's Cross does not exist on his file and in various sources that detail Dietrich's history, no specific details focus on why he received this high award. The only indication is the words contained within a telegram sent to Dietrich by Adolf Hitler, received by Dietrich on the 6th of January 1942, which read,

> 'To *Obergruppenführer* Sepp Dietrich, *Commander* of the *LSSAH*.
> With thanks for your solemn vows for the New Year, I send my heartfelt wishes to you and my valiant *Leibstandarte*.
>
> My awarding you the *Eichenlaub* (Oakleaves) is the outward expression of my pride in your accomplishments and those of my *Leibstandarte*.
> Signed Adolf Hitler'

So, what had Dietrich and his *Leibstandarte* achieved? Bearing in mind that he received the Knight's Cross during the summer of 1940, it is best to give a brief overview of what had taken place since then.

The formal portrait photograph taken of Sepp Dietrich, taken to mark his award of the Oakleaves to his existing Knight's Cross – the first to a soldier of the Waffen-SS.

Greece 1941 – starting on the 8th of April, they had advanced across the Greek border to Florina, Nikki, Vevi and then captured the Klidi Pass, the Klisura Pass and carried on southwards. Zig-zagging west to east and back, they crossed the Gulf of Patras into Olympia, then onto the capital. Sepp Dietrich himself took the initial Greek surrender and all of this was accomplished within a three-week period.

Into Russia in mid-1941 within Army Group South, they initially went east towards Shitomir then south to Uman, southeast to Perekop at the entrance to the Crimea. From there northeast to Berdjansk, Mariupol and Taganrog, ending up at the prize of Rostov by the end of 1941. By then they had advanced around 750 miles, fought against dozens of enemy divisions and played their part in the capture of almost one hundred and fifty thousand enemy troops, along with thousands of tanks and guns.

Although Hitler was incensed at his *General's* decision to retreat to better positions, he was right to feel proud of Sepp Dietrich and his *Leibstandart*e. Hitler's award of the Knight's Cross with Oakleaves to Sepp Dietrich at the end of 1941 was a fitting level of recognition for the achievements of the *Leibstandarte* with Dietrich at their head.

Summary of Operation Barbarossa in 1941

The expectation of a quick victory had been in every German soldier's mind as they crossed the eastern borders in the summer of 1941. Now that most of them had been stopped and in a lot of cases driven back to previous held positions, as they hovelled in makeshift bunkers braving the harsh Russian winter, what thoughts were on their minds then? It can be determined from personal accounts that they had tasted what fighting the Russians meant and that this new enemy was indeed a very tough and resolute opponent. Although they still had faith in their ultimate victory over the Soviet Union, they now knew that this would not occur in 1941.

How did things stand at the end of this year? In the north Leningrad was surrounded and cut-off, in the central region the outskirts of Moscow had been penetrated and on the southern coast the Rostov bridge had been taken. The Germans were overstretched, under resourced and ill equipped to continue offensive operations. The immediate focus was on survival in this austere location and trying to rest as best they could. On top of all of this, the men of the *Waffen-SS* seen out the end of this third year of combat in the knowledge that a new enemy had joined the fight against them, this new enemy was the United States of America. Although this would have been a worrying development for them, it would be some time yet before they would face each other on the battlefield. The enemy thousands of miles away did not concern them much, the enemy thousands of feet away did.

The end of 1941 in Russia was the third year of combat for the men of the *Waffen-SS* and their *Heer, Luftwaffe* and *Kreigsmarine Kameraden*, in what was termed the Second World War. By this stage twenty three *Waffen-SS* soldiers had been recognized for their achievements and one of them (Dietrich) had been been recognized twice. Fifteen of these awards for bravery had occurred since the start of Operation Barbarossa, only six months earlier. This was an indication of the intensity of the battles that they had endured to date, how different the war in Russia was compared to previous operations and also a portent of what lay ahead. The soldiers of the *Waffen-SS* had displayed fantastic feats of bravery and heroism, at a cost to some of them of their lives. They had gathered vital experience and knowledge of how the Russian soldier fought in the last half-year. This knowledge would serve them well in the coming months and years and give them many further chances to show their skills and abilities as one of the best fighting forces the world has ever seen. But that was far away then and unknown to these soldiers, they seen the Christmas of 1941 far away from home, in a hostile place, facing a hostile enemy, with only letters and photos of loved ones to keep them focused.

CHAPTER SEVEN

RUSSIA - JANUARY TO APRIL 1942

New Year 1942

How did the fighting soldiers of the *Waffen-SS* see in the fourth year of the war? The same way they ended 1941, trying to deal with the privations of Russia. As the Germans were forced back in December, Hitler had stepped in personally and forebade any further retreat backwards. This order helped to stabilize the front and the immediate focus was to wait it out until favorable offensive conditions returned.

We will resume our focus exactly where we ended the previous chapter, within Army Group South, as *Waffen-SS* soldiers in this region were the next to receive the Knight's Cross. The first recipient of 1942 was *SS-Hauptsturmführer* Heinrich Springer. If you recall, he was responsible for leading his *Kompanie* in the capture of the bridge at Rostov back in November, before covering his actions in more detail, we will give an overview the two *Waffen-SS Divisions* fighting within Army Group South.

Army Group South

LAH

On the same day that Dietrich received his telegram from Adolf Hitler, they were contending with harassing artillery fire as well as extreme cold. This continued throughout the remainder of January. Back on the 12th, in a world away from

Russia, Springer received news of the fact that he was to be awarded the Knight's Cross to the Iron Cross. Before covering this award in detail, a brief overview of their neighbouring *Waffen-SS Division* fighting in this area.

SS-Division Wiking

Like their *LAH Kameraden*, they seen in 1942 under extreme cold and harassing enemy artillery fire. January would be a month of highs and lows for these men. On the 18th two of the soldiers from this *Division* were awarded the Knight's Cross to the Iron Cross, details of these to follow shortly. It was also on this day that the Russians opened a major offensive in this area, which affected *SS-Division Wiking* as they had to send troops further south to help the *III Panzer Korps* defend their area.

We will now detail the three new awards of the Knight's Cross to the Iron Cross.

Heinrich Springer

Date of birth: 03.11.1914

SS Number: 291 700

Born in Kiel, Heinrich Springer joined the *Hitler Youth* at the start of May 1931. He then moved to the *Allgemeine-SS* on the 1st of June 1936; he was placed with the *9./50 Sturm*. He spent a spell with the *R.A.D.* from April to October 1937 and then moved to the *SS-Germania Standarte* at the start of November, with the rank of *SS-Sturmmann*. He took part in the annexation of Austria in 1938 and then on the 15th of November he began his officer training at the Bad Tolz *SS-Junkerschule*, which lasted until mid-August 1939, leaving with the rank of *SS-Standartenoberjunker*. He was assigned to the *LAH* at the start of November and then on the 9th of November 1939 he was promoted to *SS-Untersturmführer*.

He did not take part in the actions in Poland, but he did go west in 1940 with the *Leibstandarte* in May. He received the Second Class Iron Cross whilst fighting near Dunkirk on the 8th of June 1940. He was wounded for the first time on the 10th of June (thigh injury) and again on the 21st of June (hand injury). He did not receive the Black Wound Badge until the 3rd of October 1940, when he also received the Infantry Assault Badge in Bronze. Just prior to this, on the 1st of September, he became the *Adjutant* for the *Leibstandarte's*, *I Battalion*. His next change came on the 9th of November 1940 when he was promoted to *SS-Obersturmführer.*

He went eastwards into Russia in mid-1941, still holding the position of *Battalion Adjutant*. It was whilst in the early stages of Barbarossa that he managed a link up with the then cut-off *III Panzer Korps*. For this action he received the

An autographed photograph of SS-Hauptsturmführer Heinrich Springer, taken on the day he was presented with the Knight's Cross by Sepp Dietrich in Lichterfelde, Berlin.

First Class Iron Cross on the 12th of July 1941. At the start of August, Springer took over command of the *Leibstandarte's, 3. Kompanie*. It was at the head of this *Kompanie* that Springer would receive the Knight's Cross.

As has been highlighted previously, the attack towards the city of Rostov on the Don River began on the 17th of November. It took three days to reach the objective and during the advance, Springer was told face to face by Dietrich that he had been promoted to *SS-Hauptsturmführer.* The day after this promotion Springer and his *Kompanie* reached Rostov itself. He had been given the task of capturing the bridge over the river by his *Battalion Commander,* Fritz Witt. For this task, Springer had the support of a group of *Pioneers* from the *2. Kompanie/ Pioneer Battalion* and a signals communication group. They all wore captured Russian clothes and used captured Russian weapons.

Springer recalled that on the 20th of November 1941, the city was in mayhem with large amounts of Russian soldiers and civilians moving towards the bridge. The *LAH* advance had been fast and there were guards standing at some of the official buildings in a relaxed stance. As the *3. Kompanie* moved deeper into the city, intensive house to house fighting broke out. Heinrich Springer almost lost his life during this advance, but was saved by one of his *3. Kompanie Kameraden.* They all carried on and advanced to a position where they could look down on the large bridge below. This bridge was thronging with large groups of civilians and supply trains.

The *3. Kompanie* and the *Pioneers* made it to the railway station where a train was destroyed. The accompanying *Pioneers* also managed to stop a convoy of Russian trucks, which blocked the bridge; the fighting continued into the evening. It was during the evening that the *3. Kompanie* moved onto the bridge from the direction of the city. What lay in front of them was a daunting task. The bridge itself was around 1,650 feet wide and they discovered that it had been prepared for demolition by the Russians. All around them were enemy soldiers and the bulk of the rest of the *LAH* were still fighting outside the city. A Russian train full of soldiers came out of the city and attempted to make it across. *SS-Hauptsturmführer* Springer saw the opportunity to turn this situation to their advantage. He gave the order for all of his men to open fire on the train. The hail of fire punctured the engine and the steam gushed out of the multitude of holes. The loss of pressure brought the train to a halt. The *3. Kompanie* and the *2. Kompanie, Pioneers* quickly advanced across the bridge using the ensuing confusion as their cover. The *Pioneers* concentrated on removing the wires to the demolition charges. The Russians were not expecting any Germans to be this far forward and the *3. Kompanie* managed to get to the opposite end of the bridge and overpower the bridge guard unit positioned there. The *3. Kompanie* managed all of this without losses.

Heinrich Springer and his *3. Kompanie* searched for the bridge guards and came across some in a large red house on the south bank. Entering this house they began a search. Springer came across thirty Russian soldiers eating a meal. They took them prisoner and sent them to the north end of the bridge. With this, the *3. Kompanie*, under *SS-Hauptsturmführer* Heinrich Springer, achieved their assigned objective; the capture of the bridge at the gate to the Caucasus. The drama and action did not end there though.

With the bridge captured, they set up a small bridgehead, but they were coming under increasing pressure from the enemy. The losses to the *3. Kompanie* were starting and worse was to come. They became temporarily cut-off, became engaged in hand to hand fighting and were in urgent need of help. In the early hours of the 21st of November orders were given to abandon the bridgehead. This was a painful order for the men of the *3. Kompanie* but they adhered and withdrew under the relative safety of darkness. The Russians wasted no time in re-linking the demolition charges and destroying the bridge. The hard won objective was sent to the bottom of the Don River. The *LAH* eventually took the rest of the city during the course of the day. It was on this same day that Springer was wounded for the fifth-time (resulting in the award of the Gold Wound Badge), a wound that resulted in him having to be evacuated back to Germany.

It was whilst recovering in hospital in Germany on the 12th of January 1942 that Heinrich Springer was awarded the Knight's Cross to the Iron Cross for his capture of the bridge over the Don River at Rostov. He first heard this on radio and then seen it in the newspapers. He actually received the medal itself on the 23rd of January at 11.00 a.m. from the hand of Sepp Dietrich. Springer had just arrived at Lichterfelde and taken off his coat when Dietrich met him. Springer still had his cap and gloves under his arm. Dietrich informed him that he had something nice for him – he then placed the Knight's Cross to the Iron Cross around Springer's neck, followed by firmly shaking his hand. Springer's award was the only Knight's Cross given to a member of the *LAH* during 1942.

Heinrich Springer stated that he was deeply honoured to receive this high award from the hand of Sepp Dietrich, someone who all of the soldiers of the *LAH* looked up to. No doubt Dietrich was pleased to personally award the Knight's Cross to Springer, the fifth man of his beloved *LAH* to receive this award, besides himself.

Like the rest of the early *LAH* Knight's Cross winners, Springer's recommendation does not survive on his file. Springer himself stated that, "This high honour was at the same time an appreciation of the achievements of my *3. Kompanie*." After having something to eat a photo session followed. This was done on the terrace of the stairway leading to the garden within Lichterfelde.

He also received the Russian Front Medal in May 1942, along with other soldiers of the *German Armed Forces*. It was on the 1st of June 1942 that *SS-Hauptsturmführer* Springer was given command of the *1. Kompanie, 1st Regiment, LSSAH*. He was promoted to *SS-Sturmbannführer* in June 1943 and he would also see service with the *12th SS Panzer Division 'Hitler Jugend'* as the *Divisional Adjutant*. Later he would serve as the *First Ordnance Officer* of *Field Marshall* Model's Army Group B, where he would be present during the *Allied* 'Market Garden' Operation. He also took part in the fighting in the Ardennes at the end of 1944. This brave and highly respected SS Officer survived the war, finally sucumming to his long-term illness on the 27th October 2007.

Helmut Pfortner
Date of birth: 22.04.1913
SS Number: 123 011
Born in Beverungen, he joined the *S.A.* in January 1932, staying there until the 17th of June 1933 when he transferred to the *SS*. He initially served with the *55. Standarte*, but by late April 1935 he was with the *SS-Regiment Germania*. On the 9th of November 1936 he was promoted to the rank of *SS-Unterscharführer* and exactly two years later moved to the rank of *SS-Scharführer*. He fought in Poland and also in the western campaign in the first half of 1940. By that time he had been awarded the Second and First Classes of the Iron Cross, the Infantry Assault Badge and the Wound Badge in Silver. He went to the *SS* Officer training school at Bad Tolz between late 1940 and early 1941. He went into this school with the rank of *SS-Oberscharführer* but not long after leaving there he was promoted to *SS-Untersturmführer*. By the start of April 1941 he was holding that rank and was back serving within the *Germania Regiment*, now part of the *SS-Wiking Division*. He was serving as a *Platoon Commander* with *Germania's, 2. Kompanie* on the 18th of July 1941, it was on that day that he was involved in actions that resulted in his nomination for the award of the Knight's Cross to the Iron Cross. It contained the following:

> "On the 18th of July the *2. Kompanie* took a section of Saalischy that was hostile to *Westland*. Helmut Pfortner was part of the lead group. On one of the flanks was situated the *SS-Pioneers*. They observed an enemy artillery battery raining down fire upon their *Kameraden*. Disregarding this fire, Pfortner decided to send two motorcycles against this enemy position. They raced towards the guns under fire, then, when they got close enough they dismounted quickly. They opened fire upon with their machine pistols and in close combat they overran this enemy battery. Most of the enemy was killed

A pleased Helmut Pfortner photographed after the award of his Knight's Cross. He is seen here with the rank of SS-Obersturmführer, but the actions that resulted in this award were conducted whilst holding the rank of SS-Untersturmführer.

> in their positions and the remainder fled the area. This decisive action was critical for the further advance of the *Battalion*."

Oberkamp wrote this first part of the recommendation, but Steiner also added:

> "Helmut Pfortner is well known as the bravest officer in the *Division*. After outstanding honour in Poland and the west (*SS-Division Reich)* he repeatedly proved himself in the east, he proved through his deeds on the 18th of July he is worthy of the high honour of the Knight's Cross to the Iron Cross.
>
> He led a group of twenty-two men into the city of Toren, holding a population of 80,000. The neighbouring *Regiment* was attacked and could advance no further. In a surprise attack he penetrated the city and advanced into it. He disregarded the heavy hostile fire and was engaged in close combat also. Before Snjawa, they were successful, against the heaviest of enemy fire, in destroying a preliminary bridge used by the Russians to transport ammunition and other supplies. They pushed on towards Krementschug where Pfortner attacked bunker positions with his twenty-two men, fighting against 180 enemy. This created a basis for the successful battles over the next following days. Under the most difficult circumstances they succeeded in probing the enemy positions. The main bridge was unuseable, but they erected a pontoon bridge through a swamp with high reeds growing there. Out of these reeds there came 100 enemy prisoners with 100 horses. After capturing the enemy battery, Pfortner crossed a river in a *Stormboat* at Dnjeprinsel, near Krementschug, where he was heavily wounded."

In late October the same year he was serving with the *Replacement Battalion* within that *Regiment* (after recovering from his wounds). On the 9th of November 1941 he was promoted to *SS-Obersturmführer* and later the same month he was awarded the German Cross in Gold. The recommendation for the Knight's Cross to the Iron Cross for Helmut Proftner was approved on the 18th of January 1942. This made Helmut Pfortner the first, but certainly not the last, soldier of the *SS-Wiking Division* to be awarded the Knight's Cross. On the 9th of November 1942 he was promoted once more to the rank of *SS-Hauptsturmführer*. He was killed on the 28th of February 1943 in Barwendkowo, Russia. At that time he was the *Commander* of *Germania's, 6. Kompanie*.

Fritz von Scholz
Date of birth: 09.12.1896
SS Number: 135 638
Born in Pilsen, Bohemia, his military service began in the *Austrian Army* from August 1914. He served in various *Artillery Regiments* throughout World War I and into 1919. He rose to the rank of *Oberleutnant* and was awarded the Austrian bravery and service medals as well as the Second and First Classes of the Iron Cross. In 1921 he was fighting with the *Freikorps,* he also had a career as a chemical engineer between the wars.

He was within the ranks of the *S.A.* in 1932 and then the following year, on the 10th of June 1933, he joined the *SS* and served as an officer candidate with the *37. Standarte*. During the political changes within Austria around that time, von Scholz moved to Germany. By late August 1934 he had obtained the rank of *SS-Untersturmführer* and by January 1935 he had been promoted further to *SS-Obersturmführer,* serving within *SS-Regiment Deutschland*. By mid-May of 1935 he was commanding the *8. Kompanie* and by the end of January 1936 he had moved to the rank of *SS-Hauptsturmführer*. On the 1st of April 1938 he was promoted to *SS-Sturmbannführer* and took command of the *II Battalion* within the newly created *SS-Regiment "Der Führer"*. In early January 1939 he took part in a course for commanders in Doberitz.

He entered his second major war with this rank and at the end of January 1940 he was holding the rank of *SS-Obersturmbannführer*. He won the Clasp to the Second Class Iron Cross on the 17th of May 1940, followed by the Clasp to the First Class Iron Cross on the 29th of May. At the start of December 1940 he moved to the *SS-Regiment Westland*. On the 30th of January 1941 he was promoted to *SS-Standartenführer* and in the same year, at the start of October, he was promoted further to *SS-Oberführer* – this new promotion came with a move to the role of commanding *SS-Regiment Nordland*. He went with this *Regiment* into Russia in mid-1941.

On the 29th of November 1941 he was awarded the German Cross in Gold for actions fighting with his *Regiment* during the battles in November 1941. For these same actions he was recommended again, only this time for the Knight's Cross to the Iron Cross by his *Divisional Commander*, Felix Steiner. This recommendation contained the following information:

> '*SS-Oberführer* von Scholz deeply influenced, through his personal ruthless actions, the development of the combat situations in the several assignments given to his combat group. In the battles north of Rostov from November 17-20 1941 *Kampfgruppe von Scholz* had to cover the flanks of the

SS-Oberführer Fritz von Scholz pictured after his award of the Knight's Cross to the Iron Cross for actions in southern Russia in 1941, actual award was made in early 1942.

1. Panzer Army in decisive positions and had to resist against heavy enemy attacks.

From midday on November the 17th until the evening of November the 20th, five Russian Divisions, supported by a tank brigade, tried to overrun *Kampfgruppe von Scholz*. They had to face these systematically prepared and operatively significant attacks in focal points along a twenty-four kilometre wide front, absorbing uninterrupted massive attacks in consecutive waves. The enemy was under the constant support of heavy artillery and the heavier tanks. Enemy support increased daily with rocket launchers, bombers and low level attack aircraft.

This *Kampfgruppe* halted massive enemy attacks, attempting to destroy the advance on Rostov by *1. Panzer Army*. Fritz von Scholz's personal intervention and direction allowed his *Kampfgruppe* to hold out for four days against a huge superior force. He was to be seen in the midst of the heavy fighting throughout this time. Successes at Dobropolje on the 18th of November, and Tuslov for his *Regiment Nordland* were amongst their achievements. This was followed by November the 20th, successful disengagement from the enemy – after sustaining repeated attacks from rocket launchers, tanks and infantry. Whilst moving back the following day he led another attack against pursuing enemy forces that led to the capture of four hundred prisoners.'

(Author's note: the same day the Heinrich Springer from the *LAH* captured the bridge over the River Don within Rostov itself).

Although unusual to be awarded twice for the same actions, the significance of his achievements during a testing and critical time for the *German Army* is without question. The award of the Knight's Cross to the Iron Cross for Fritz von Scholz was approved on the 18th of January 1942. He became the second person within the *SS-Wiking Division* to receive this high honour. It would however, not be von Scholz's last association with the various grades of this award, but more detail of that will follow in future volumes.

Army Group Centre

SS-Division Reich

After getting close to Moscow, within ten miles, towards the end of 1941, they had to retreat back to their positions at Rusa by the end of that year. This is where they stayed as the New Year of 1942 began.

Besides dealing with extreme cold, at the end of the first week in January, they had to contend with a fresh Russian offensive that made gains on both sides of Moscow, to the west. On top of all of this, they were given a new *Divisonal Commander* in the shape of *SS-Brigadeführer* Matthias Kleinheisterkamp, after Bittrich was ordered elsewhere.

Due to the danger posed by the Russian advances, especially further north, *SS-Division Reich* where ordered further westwards in mid-January 1942, taking up positions slightly north and southwest of Viazma. They were to hold the line further north around Rshew and prevent the crushing of Army Group Centre. The new Army Group Centre *Commander*, Walter Model, ordered an attack. This attack began at the end of the third week of January 1942. This involved *SS-Division Reich* moving northwards towards Rshew.

The *Motorcycle Battalion* led the attack, but within a few hours of day one they had suffered over fifty-percent casualties. The following day *SS-Regiment Deutschland* also suffered heavy losses as they tried to advance. As these elements were dealing with their losses *SS-Regiment Der Führer* were ordered further north to Rshew itself. There, the Army Group Centre *Commander* himself, ordered the *Der Führer Commander*, *SS-Obersturmbannführer* Otto Kumm, to hold this area at all costs. Kumm took his 650 men and went forwards. As *Der Führer* moved north, *Deutschland* continued their own battle with the Soviets. On the 25th of January they were fighting between Sytschewka (Sycovka) and Rshew (Rzev). This was the same day that Otto Kumm and his *Regiment* reached their new positions on the Volga River, northwest of Rshew.

For the remainder of January both elements fought in their respective areas, *Der Führer* were dealing with another major Russian offensive further northwest – therefore placed on the defensive – launched by over a dozen strong enemy formations attacking straight at the positions held by Kumm and his men. The main element of the *Division* moving eastwards of their starting positions into the attack, these offensive actions succeeded in halting the enemy and forcing him to cease or diminish his offensive actions in that area for the time being. The main element of *SS-Division Reich* moved slightly westwards and into a quieter area at the start of February.

Their *Kameraden* from *Der Führer* could not be in a more different situation, further northwest. As February opened, they continued to contend with enemy attacks. This increased in intensity throughout the first week of February, causing losses to the men of *Der Führer*. These attacks were from tanks and infantry and resulted in the complete loss of some of *Der Führer's Kompanies* altogether! Additional *Army* units had been pushed into this area, but the strength of the enemy continued to soak up these additional troops, with no real overall change in the situation. This section of the front was in danger of being lost to the enemy. To help further, elements of *SS-Regiment Deutschland* were sent to this area to help at the start of the second week of February. Other elements of *SS-Division Reich* were also sent northwest in the following days.

The heavy intensive and costly fighting against tanks, artillery, aerial and infantry attacks continued into the middle of February. The situation flowed back and forth, causing continued heavy losses to both sides. The men of *SS-Division Reich* and especially *Der Führer* held out and by doing so they affected a defeat upon the enemy in this critical sector of the Russian Front at that time. The climax of this battle came on the 17th of February, a day which seen the control move to the Germans – what was left of them! This was the same day that *SS-Obersturmbannführer* Otto Kumm received notification that he had been awarded the Knight's Cross for his recent actions, but more detail of that shortly.

Dozens of destroyed enemy tanks littered the area and it was determined that the Russians lost around 30,000 men, along with hundreds of heavy guns. *SS-Regiment Der Führer* lost around 25% dead and 70% wounded. Only 5%, or thirty-five men, were left fighting fit at the conclusion of this battle. This action helped to save the situation for the Army Group itself, due to the actions of the soldiers contained within it. Otto Kumm was told to hold at all costs and that is exactly what he and his men did.

After receiving permission direct from Adolf Hitler, the remnants of *Der Führer* were moved to Germany for a re-fit.

Otto Kumm was not the only person awarded the Knight's Cross for these battles around Rshew. *SS-Brigadeführer* Matthias Kleinheisterkamp would also receive this award for the overall performance of his *Division*. He did not however, receive his award until the end of March 1942, also *SS-Standartenführer* Hermann Fegelein in early March; again, details of those awards will follow later.

SS-Kavallerie-Brigade

If you recall, this *Brigade* were centered on Toropez, but operating to the northeast near Lake Volga. This is where they found themselves as the Russians opened their major offensive to defeat the Germans in the Rshew area. Like their *Kameraden* from *SS-Division Reich*, they were also under the command of the *9. Armee*. Little did they know it then, but very soon this security unit would find itself fighting against front line, fresh and well equipped Russian formations. Also like *SS-Division Reich*, they would suffer many losses in this early part of 1942.

At the start of 1942 they moved further east to an area north west of Rshew. Increased enemy activity was noted prior to their major push, which started in the first week of 1942. The *Brigade's, Reconnaissance Unit* bore the brunt of the attack and despite some spirited actions they were finally forced to fall back. They arrived back in Toropez one week later, after loosing 400 men out of around 600! But the trouble for the *SS-Kavallerie Brigade* did not end there.

The two *Regiments* from the *Brigade* were ordered closer to Rshew, finally ending up to the west in an area between Rshew and Molodoy-Tud. By the end of the first week of Janaury they were having their first battles with the Russians in this area. For the next two weeks this *Brigade* fought a difficult series of engagements in this area. During this time Walter Model took over the *9. Armee* and became responsible for stabilizing the front in this area at this extremely critical time. In atrocious weather conditions the Germans made attacks into the strong Russian forces and succeeded in forming another enemy pocket. In the third week of January elements of the *SS-Kavallerie-Brigade* linked with elements of *SS-Regiment Der Führer* who were fighting to their left. This link was at Ssolomina on the west bank of the River Volga and formed the boundary line between the two units.

During the remainder of January and into February 1942, the *SS-Kavallerie-Brigade* continued to strengthen its positions in this area against the enemy trapped inside the pocket. These enemy troops were trying to break out and fresh enemy attacks from outside the pocket were being dealt with too. The *Brigade* had moved slightly to the south at this stage. During the first half of February they fought further difficult battles, most notably around Tschertolino (These battles resulted in the award of the Knight's Cross to Hermann Fegelein and will be detailed later). They were taking place at the same time as Otto Kumm's Knight's Cross actions.

We will return to the actions of this *Brigade* later, but for now, a quick overview of the *1. SS-Infantry Brigade (mot.)* and the *4. SS-Totenkopf-Standarte*, before turning further to the actions within Army Group North.

1. SS-Infantry Brigade (mot.)

Life did not change much for this *Brigade* during January and into February 1942. They continued in their anti-partisan sweeps in the area south and east of Orel.

4. SS-Totenkopf-Standarte

This unit was previously part of the *2. SS-Infantry Brigade (mot.)*, but upon their return to Russia, they were sent to an area near Juchnow, within Army Group Centre. They fought in actions that resulted in their leader, Hinrich Schuldt, being awarded the Knight's Cross to the Iron Cross and this will be detailed later on.

Army Group North

SS-Totenkopf Division

This *Division* was positioned southeast of Leningrad at the start of 1942, on the southern edge of Army Group North – whilst their *SS Kameraden* from *Der Führer* and the *SS-Kavallerie-Brigade* were positioned on the northern part of Army Group Centre, around 100 miles apart from each other. The battles of late-1941 had reduced *Totenkopf's* strength considerably and in the midst of dealing with this situation and the extreme Russian weather, they were about to be hit very hard by a major Russian offensive.

This offensive started on the 8th of January 1942, south of Lake Ilhmen and north west of *Totenkopf's* positions. The Russian's initial target was Staraja-Russa, vital to the Germans. German formations were rushed towards this objective to aid in its' defence. These included elements of *Totenkopf's, Aufklarungs Abteilung, Artillery Regiment, Motorcycle Infantry Battalion* and the *Pioneer Battalion*. This newly formed *Kampfgruppe* ran into advancing Russians enroute to Staraja-Russa, but the *SS* men reached it first and helped to recapture it. The massive enemy forces surrounded this city, but it remained in German hands despite extreme pressure. The *Totenkopf* elements listed above helped to keep the city in German hands throughout the rest of January 1942. No rearwards movement was permitted by Hitler at this time.

A further *Kampfgruppe* was formed under the overall command of *Totenkopf's Divisional Commander*, Theodore Eicke. They were positioned further southeast of Staraja-Russa, around Salutschje near the Pola River. The third *Kampfgruppe* made up from *Totenkopf* troops – *SS-Totenkopf Regiment 1* – was further east of there, around Lushno, north of Demjansk itself and was under the control of Max Simon. These *Kampfgruppes* stood firm against the Russian tidal wave that engulfed this area at that time. The Russians did surround the Germans and formed a large pocket, which became known as the Demjansk Pocket. One soldier within Max Simon's group during January was *SS-Oberscharführer* Ludwig Kochle. He conducted successful actions during this time that resulted in him being awarded the Knight's Cross to the Iron Cross (details to follow).

The fighting within the Staraja-Russa area in January and February 1942 was very intense. One element, the *Kradschutzen Battalion*, under *SS-Sturmbannführer* Franz Kleffner, achieved considerable success around Wassiljeschtschina & Bjakowo, just southeast of Staraja-Russa (These actions resulted in the award of the Knight's Cross to Kleffner and will be covered in detail later). The *Commander* of the *Kampfgruppe* in this area, *SS-Sturmbannführer* Karl Ullrich, achieved his own successes against enemy tank and infantry attacks around Lipowitzi and more notably at Kobylkina and Korowitschina, close to the Lowat River. *SS-Hauptsturmführer* Max Seela was also part of this *Kampfgruppe*. (Karl Ullrich and Max Seela received the Knight's Cross for their actions in these battles, full detail to follow later). Ullrich's *Kampfgruppe* broke out of this area on the 21st of February and returned to the area held by Eicke, further southeast. They reached Eicke and his men two days later, by this time they were one-third of their original strength!

Earlier in February, the 8th, the pocket around Demjansk had been closed and survival for those inside became the chief objective. The two *Kampfgruppes* of *Totenkopf,* (Eicke and Simon), where at the western and eastern extremes of this pocket area. Ullrich's remnants were a welcome addition to the men of Eicke's *Kampfgruppe* from the 23rd of February.

Another Knight's Cross related occurrence took place in early February 1942. That was the actions of the then, *SS-Standartenführer* Hermann Priess. He was the *Commander* of *Totenkopf's, Artillery Regiment* at the time and was caught up in the Demjansk fighting. His Knight's Cross recommendation was not approved until late April 1943, so the full details of the actions will follow in Volume 2. He would in fact, be the last *Totenkopf* soldier to receive the Knight's Cross for the intensive fighting that took place in the area around Demjansk.

We will leave *Totenkopf* within the Demjansk Pocket for the time being and cover the *Polizei Division,* the *2. SS-Infantry Brigade (mot.)* and the *SS-Legion Niederlande,* before turning south to Army Group South.

Polizei Division

We last covered this *Division* in the Pushkin area on the outskirts of Leningrad and as with the rest of the *Waffen-SS* units, nothing much changed for them as 1941 turned into 1942. However, just before the middle of January 1942 the Russians hit this area in strength, in order to relieve Leningrad. Just like in other areas of the Soviet Union, the enemy was using the weather and its' available reserves to hit the Germans. Survival was at stake for both sides and the price they would pay for this was about the rise considerably!

The Soviets achieved their first breakthrough around seventy miles southeast of Pushkin, on the Wolchow River, between the 10th and 13th of January 1942. This new threat directly north of Lake Ilmen was repeated south of that lake for the *Totenkopf* men, as covered in preceeding pages. Extreme pressure in multiple places gave no chance to move forces around and help. These were dangerous and critical times.

Towards the end of the third week *Polizei* were moved southeast towards Ljuban and into Tschudowo (Cudovo), north of the enemy penetration. Final positions were at Mostki and Ljubino Pole, where during the third week in January 1942, *Polizei* engaged enemy forces to the south, west and east of those positions. Elements became cut-off by the masses of attacking enemy troops and remained cut-off until the end of the first week in February, a total of ten days.

One of these elements was the *I Battalion* of the *Polizei Schutzen Regiment 2* under the command of *SS-Sturmbannführer* Rudolf Pannier. His heroic and successful defense at that time resulted in the later award of the Knight's Cross (details will follow later). This units' defense and that of nearby *Heer* units succeeded in stopping the Russian success in that area – a situation that the Germans wished to exploit.

No sooner had they dealt with this situation, than a further enemy threat loomed on the horizon. The Russians were keen to take this area and applied further pressure around this area as the middle of February 1942 beckoned. The enemy forced the evacuation of Ljubino Pole. The Russians were gaining control of more and more ground in this area south of Tschudowo (Cudovo).

2. SS-Infantry Brigade (mot.)

In the first six weeks of 1942 this *Brigade* was busy dealing with intense enemy pressure in the area between Novgorod and Tossno, along with *SS-Legion Flandern*. There is limited detail about these smaller *SS* units at this time.

SS-Legion Niederlande

They were moved from Ayrs in East Prussia in late January 1942, traveling through Latvia on the way. They were led at that time by *SS-Oberführer* Reich and their final destination was at Selo Gora, between Tschudowo and Novgorod. At the start of February they became engaged in their first fighting against the Soviets. This was in the same general area as *Polizei,* placing them within the Wolchow area.

We will leave the *SS* troops fighting within Army Group North, detail three Knight's Crosses awarded in mid-February 1942 and then move south to Army Group South.

Otto Kumm

Date of birth: 01.10.1909

SS Number: 18 727

Born in Hamburg, his connections to Adolf Hitler and his various organizations began at the age of 21 when he joined the *S.A*. At the start of December 1931 he moved to the fledgling *SS*. In the early 1930s he served with the *28. Standarte*

Otto Kumm photographed after his presentation of his Knight's Cross, then holding the rank of SS-Obersturmbannführer. His collar patches are not the usual officers quality.

and the *9. Standarte*. In August 1934 he moved to the *Hamburg Political Readiness Detachment*. By that time he had been promoted from *SS-Sturmführer* (*Untersturmführer*) to *SS-Obersturmführer.*

The mid-1930s would see Kumm being promoted further and also changing commands. By mid-September 1936 he was holding the rank of *SS-Hauptsturmführer,* three months later he moved to *SS-Regiment Deutschland*, serving as *Commander* for various *Kompanies*. He then moved to the newly created *SS-Regiment Der Führer* in May 1938, again as a *Kompanie Commander*. He took part in the marches into Austria and the Sudetenland prior to the start of World War II.

With *SS-Regiment Der Führer* he took part in the campaign in the west in 1940. During that campaign he won the Second Class Iron Cross on the 29th of May, the First Class Iron Cross on the 4th of June and the Black Wound Badge on the 8th of June. On the same day as winning his First Class Iron Cross, he moved to command of *Der Führer's, III Battalion*. Promoted to *SS-Sturmbannführer* at the start of September 1940 and ending the year with the award of the Infantry Assault Badge in mid-December 1940. He went with *Der Führer* into Russia in the summer of 1941 and by the 11th of July he had taken over command of the whole *Regiment*. At the start of October he was promoted to the rank of *SS-Obersturmbannführer.* He led his *Regiment* during the early difficult battles of Barbarossa in 1941, enduring many losses to his men. These battles were nothing in comparison to what he would have to contend with at the start of 1942. By the end of 1941 he had been awarded the German Cross in Gold.

His *Regiment* was sent to the Rshew area – despite being below strength. Here they were ordered to hold the line at all costs, as has been highlighted earlier. Otto Kumm accomplished this order, but at a very high cost. When they were relieved towards the end of February 1942, he stood with only thirty-five men outside the command post of Walter Model. Recognising his accomplishments, Model had already recommended Otto Kumm for the Knight's Cross to the Iron Cross. The details of that recommendation contained the following information:

> "Through a daring attack on January 22nd 1942 Kumm took the dominating hilly territory north of Jachino-Kelpenino. He closed the break through gap of the enemy west of Rshew, proving himself in an outstanding manner during the following heavy defensive combat with his organization and execution of the defense. During the enemy breakthrough attempts of February 7th and 8th west of Rshew, executed by strong infantry and armour forces after artillery and aerial bombing preparation, Kumm succeeded after numerous enemy penetrations, in preventing a full breakthrough. He led

> operations with continuous personal decisions, especially with the holding of the Regimental Command Post and occupying Ojengina with parts of *Der Führer*. During the above mentioned defensive actions alone, two dozen tanks were destroyed under his personal leadership. He prevented, decisive for the overall situation, contact between the enemy assault force and the tenaciously holding enemy troops encircled in Kantschalowo. His personal imperturbable bearing during the heavy artillery fire and continuous tank attacks, again and again gave the troops new fighting spirit with confidence in victory."

The above recommendation was approved on the 16th of February 1942, the day before the battle reached its' climax. The part played by Otto Kumm is well highlighted above and the significance of this *Regiment's* actions cannot be underestimated. They held the line against everything the enemy threw at them. Walter Model personally presented the Knight's Cross to Otto Kumm as he arrived at Model's Headquarters with his thirty-five survivors.

This would not end Otto Kumm's connection the Knight's Cross or its various grades, but details of that will follow in future volumes.

Franz Kleffner

Date of birth: 02.06.1907

SS Number: 7 939

Born in Altena/Westfalen, he entered the *Allgemeine-SS* on the 15th of December 1930, serving with the *20. Standarte*. By the 15th of February 1934 he was holding the rank of *SS-Obertruppführer (SS-Hauptscharführer)*, serving within *SS-Regiment Deutschland*. He finished an officer's course at Braunschweig in early 1935 and by the 20th of April the same year he was holding the rank of *SS-Untersturmführer*. By mid-September 1935 he had risen to the rank of *SS-Obersturmführer*, followed by *SS-Hauptsturmführer* on the 9th of November 1936. He remained at the Officers School in Braunschweig until the 25th of January 1938 when he moved to the *1. Totenkopf Standarte*. This was quickly followed by a move to the *4. Totenkopf Standarte* at the start of July 1938. During 1938 he took part in the march into Austria and also the Sudetenland. By early September 1939 he was serving as the *13. Kompanie Commander* within the newly created *SS-Totenkopf Division*. He went west with his *Division* in 1940 and on the 22nd of June 1940 was awarded the Second Class Iron Cross. He then moved east into Russia during mid-1941 and on the 13th of July 1941 was awarded the First Class Iron Cross. By the end of October 1941 he was commanding *Totenkopf's, Kradschutzen Battalion*. On the 30th of January 1942 he was promoted to *SS-Sturmbannführer* and then on the 17th of February he was recommended for the

Franz Kleffner pictured after his award of the Knight's Cross to the Iron Cross.

Knight's Cross to the Iron Cross by the Army Group North *Commander*, Kuchler. This recommendation was short and to the point:

> 'As leader of a *Kampfgruppe* in Bjakowo he fought under his exemplary brave use of his skills and with his mixed force. They fought decisively for two weeks against superior enemy forces.
>
> They were attacked repeatedly with heavy tanks, they beat off all attacks and caused considerable losses to the enemy in men and material.'
>
> (Signed) Hansen, *General der Artillery, Commander X Armee Korps*

This recommendation was approved two days later (along with the one for Karl Ullrich). He was awarded the Infantry Assault Badge on the 12th of June 1942, followed by the Russian Front Medal on the 24th of August. By the start of February 1943 he was holding the rank of *SS-Obersturmbannführer* and was commanding the *I Battalion* within *SS-Panzer-Regiment 10, SS Frundsberg Division*. He was killed on the 16th of March 1945 in Hungary, at Sakarestics, whilst commanding *SS-Regiment 6 'Theodore Eicke'*.

Karl Ullrich

Date of birth:01.12.1910

SS Number: 31 438

Born in Saargrund, Ullrich first served in the *S.A.* from the 18th September 1931 until the 1st of April 1932, this was the same day as moving to the *Allgemeine-SS*, serving with the *56. SS-Standarte*. By early January 1934 he was serving with the *SS-Regiment Deutschland*. He attended the Officers School at Braunschweig from late April 1935 until February 1936. It is interesting to note that whilst doing all of this, he still found time to spend a three-month stint with the *Army* from June 1933 and also a six-month spell with the police in the first half of 1934. At the start of April 1936 he was holding the rank of *SS-Standartenoberjunker,* but by the 20th of the same month he was promoted to *SS-Untersturmführer* and was serving in the *Pioneer Replacement Battalion*. A further promotion to *SS-Obersturmführer* came on the 12th of September 1937 and by late April 1938 he was the *Commander* of the *3. Kompanie* within the above named *Battalion*. On the 9th of November 1938 he was promoted further to the rank of *SS-Hauptsturmführer.* Prior to the outbreak of World War II he earned the Austrian and Czech Medals.

He fought in Poland during 1939 and also entered the western campaign in 1940 with the *SS V Division*. It was with this unit that he earned the Second Class Iron Cross on the 18th of May 1940, followed by the First Class Iron Cross on the 1st of August the same year. On the 9th of November 1941 he was promoted

A photo of Karl Ullrich taken after his award of the Knight's Cross. It also shows him as an SS-Obersturmbannführer, he was an SS-Sturmbannführer at the time of his action that resulted in this award.

to *SS-Sturmbannführer* and by this time he was the *Commander* of the *Pioneer Battalion*, with the *Totenkopf Division*. It was with this *Battalion* that he found himself in the early part of 1942 as the Demjansk Pocket was being formed.

On the 17th of February 1942 *General der Artillerie* Hansen, who was also the *Commander* of the *X Army Korps*, wrote a short recommendation for the Knight's Cross to the Iron Cross. It contained the following information:

> '*SS-Sturmbannführer* Ullrich, *Commander* of the *Kampfgruppe* at Koblykino, fought with his own exemplary bravery and battled for more than two weeks with weak gathered units in decisive positions against an often superior opponent. Being encircled himself several times, he has so far repelled all of the attacks even against heavy tanks, inflicting on the enemy severe losses in both men and material.'

This brief, but effective, recommendation was approved two days later on the 19th of February 1942. Ullrich himself did not break out of this area until the 21st, when he made it to Eicke's territory, as highlighted previously.

This would not be Karl Ullrich's only connection to the Knight's Cross to the Iron Cross, but details of that will follow in later volumes.

Army Group South

SS-Wiking Division

We last briefly covered *Wiking* in the first half of January 1942, up to the award of Pfortner and von Scholz's Knight's Crosses. They were still in their positions west of the Mius River, north of Taganrog. They remained there during the early stages of 1942. On the 18th of March 1942 the third person within this *Division* was approved for the award of the Knight's Cross to the Iron Cross, this was Karl Schalmelcher.

LAH

Their situation remained largely un-changed throughout February and March 1942. The cold and the sporadic enemy fire were their main issues.

Army Group North

Polizei

In the second half of February, *Polizei* were moved from those positions south of Tschudowo (Cudovo) to an area to the northwest, south of Ljuban. Their former positions were taken over by the *V Battalion LAH* and the *SS-Norwegian Battalion*. The enemy pressure did not relent at all during this time and all units were under severe threat of being surrounded and annihilated.

Totenkopf

We last covered them towards the end of February as the enemy ring around the Demjansk Pocket was closed. Two main elements had been formed, one *Kampfgruppe* under Theodore Eicke was in the western part; the other *Kampfgruppe* under Max Simon was in the eastern part.

The importance of holding this area against the masses of enemy troops was not lost on the men of the *Totenkopf Division*. The Russians put in countless repeated attacks, but the *SS* men held out against this intense enemy pressure, alongside enduring the extreme cold weather prevailant at that time.

Before February had ended, an *SS-Oberscharführer* from the *Artillery Regiment's, 8. Kompanie* distinguished himself. His name was Ernst Staudle and his brave actions took place on the 26th of February 1942. They would result in the award of the Knight's Cross, but more details of that later.

Although they held, the cost was high with many dead and wounded. One focus point of the fighting at this time was around the town of Bjakowo, southeast of Staraja-Russa. Throughout the early part of March the hellish fighting raged all around this focus point. Enemy tank and infantry attacks were suffered and the losses to the Germans mounted. *SS-Obersturmführer* Erwin Meierdress was wounded and evacuated by light aircraft. The *SS* troops held out against this until the 17th of March 1942, without aerial or heavy weapons support. At the end of this, only thirteen fit men and fifty wounded came out. They had been cut-off since the 9th of February 1942. Meierdress's determined defense resulted in the award of the Knight's Cross to the Iron Cross on the 13th of March 1942, this will be detailed later on.

One soldier who was serving under Meierdress during this critical time in Bjakowo was *SS-Unterscharführer* Hans Meguscher. He recalled this very intense fighting and pressure exerted by the Russians. As Meierdress was being loaded onto the Feisler Storch, he called Hans over to him. Meierdress removed his own First Class Iron Cross and pinned it onto Hans' tunic (later officially recommending him for this award). *SS-Untersturmführer* Wissebach took over from Meierdress, but he was also wounded and unable to remain in command. Losses in dead and wounded continued to mount for the handful of survivors, fighting against enemy troops who had tank support. The orders came through for the town to be evacuated. The remaining thirteen men broke out on the 17th of March, taking with them fifty wounded *Kameraden*. They successfully reached the main group of the *Division*. The person who led this successful breakout was the above mentioned *SS-Unterscharführer* Hans Meguscher. When the Russians finally entered Bjakowo they found only dead Germans and hundreds of their own dead comrades. Hans Meguscher ended the war as an *SS-Untersturmführer.*

Further to the east, Max Simon was also fighting hard. During the whole of March his men held control of this area, including the important airfield at Demjansk, against superior strength enemy troops. We will leave *Totenkopf* for now and cover other *SS* troops within Army Group North.

SS-Legion Niederlande

They continued their fighting in the Selo Gora area, losses to them mounted during February and March 1942. It was also around this time that *Niederlande* became incorporated into the *2. SS-Infantry-Brigade (mot.),* alongside the other foreign legions.

Army Group Centre

SS-Kavallerie-Brigade

During the second half of February 1942 they moved southwest of Olenino, towards Gusevo, to help defeat the enemy in that area. They were engaged in tough battles with the Russians on into March. It was during this time that Fegelein went to Poland, with *SS-Sturmbannführer* Gustav Lombard taking over command of the *Brigade*. During the rest of March they continued to fight and endure further losses.

SS-Division Reich

The rest of *SS-Division Reich* initially moved slightly west during the remainder of February. They were re-oragnised into *Kampfgruppe Reich* and then during March they were placed into the fight once more. Kleinheisterkamp was recalled at the end of February and *SS-Standartenführer* Werner Ostendorf took over command. Their new positions were southeast of Olenino, west of Rshew. The enemy was improving a breakthrough they had achieved further west. Throughout March *Kampfgruppe Reich* fought against elements of the enemy who were attempting to expand this penetration. This additional fighting was costly to the *Kampfgruppe*, but they held the overall area – despite the see saw actions of capturing villages and then loosing them again. This particular part of hell for the remnants of the *SS-Division Reich* came to an end on the last day of March 1942.

We will now detail the awards of some Knight's Crosses before proceeding with more fighting.

Ludwig Kochle
Date of birth: 28.01.1921
SS Number: Unknown
Born in Nofels, Austria, he entered the *SS* in 1938, aged seventeen. After one year's training he fought in Poland and also the western campaign in 1940, he was an *MG-Schutze*. By 1940 he had reached the rank of *SS-Unterscharführer* and *Zug Commander*. He went east with *Totenkopf* in June 1941. He proved himself during the march forward into Russia as part of Army Group North. His coldblooded determination was noted and by the end of 1941 he was *SS-Oberscharführer* and holder of the Iron Cross Second Class, 28th July 1941 and the First Class Iron Cross on the 17th of November 1941.

During the early stages of the Demjansk Pocket battles in January he withstood over thirty attacks along with a group of 100 *SS Kameraden*. His courage was well known and he was mentioned in the daily orders. He was regarded as an exemplary leader.

In 1942 during the cut-off in Demjansk he successfully led his men into the flank of one enemy position threatening them, it was a bold action. This bold and brave *SS-Oberscharführer,* leading a group within the *5. Kompanie,* destroyed six enemy bunkers using hand grenades, on top of this a machine-gun position and also the enemy troop garrison. They then held this position despite repeated enemy counter attacks. He was indeed an excellent example of a fearless soldier of the *Waffen-SS*. This successful and important action earned him the Knight's Cross to the Iron Cross. The recommendation does not survive, so it is not known who wrote it or when it was written. The approval came through on the 28th of February 1942.

One man who was fighting within Kochle's *Zug* at that time was *SS-Sturmmann* Adolf Schaaf. He was performing the role of *Melder,* or messenger and spent his time relaying messages between this group and the *Regiment*. On one such trip between the front line fighting and the *Regiment*, he came across a dead *Kameraden* who had four machine-gun ammunition boxes in his hands. Adolf knew that his *Zug Führer,* Kochle, and his men were almost out of ammunition. He lifted the

The only known photograph of SS-Oberscharführer Ludwig Kochle, taken after his award of the Knight's Cross at the end of February 1942 and prior to his death in June 1942.

boxes and took them onto Kochle, before then continuing with his original task of reporting to the *Regiment*. This additional ammunition helped Kochle and his men to hold out longer against the Russians and inflict further casualties upon the enemy. Adolf Schaaf earned the Second Class Iron Cross for this. He was wounded in early March 1942 and had to leave the front line. He later served in *Panzer Brigade Gross,* under Knight's Cross holder Martin Gross. He finished the war fighting near Hannover with another Knight's Cross holder, Karl Nicolussi-Leck. Adolf Schaafs himself was holding the rank of *SS-Untersturmführer* at the time. In 2007 he recalled the bravery and fighting skills of Ludwig Kochle during those dark and difficult days in January 1942, fighting between Staraja-Russa and Lushno and how these skills helped to stabilize the German lines.

Unfortunately, Ludwig Kochle died during an artillery attack southwest of Lake Ilhmen on June the 9th 1942. Besides the Knight's Cross, he is known to have been awarded the Infantry Assault Badge and the Black Wound Badge, although the dates of these awards are not known.

Karl Schlamelcher

Date of birth: 21.09.1912

SS Number: 266 435

Born in the Harz region of Germany, he initially served in the police from 1930 where he rose through the ranks. In 1935 he joined the *SS* and initially served in the *III Battalion, SS-Regiment Germania*. By November the same year he was holding the rank of *SS-Untersturmführer.* By mid-1939 this he has risen to the rank of *SS-Hauptsturmführer.* It was during this year that he moved to the *Artillery Regiment* of the *SS V Division*, staying there into early 1940, where he served as the *Battalion Adjutant*. After attending a course at Juterbog for battalion commanders, he transferred to the *SS-Division Wiking,* where he took command of the *III Battalion,* within their *Artillery Regiment*.

He went with this *Regiment* into Russia in 1941 and it was with this unit that he engaged in the actions that resulted in the award of the Knight's Cross. An overview of these actions is as follows.

On the 3rd of July 1941 a combat group of *SS-Division Wiking* ran into a strong enemy column that was protected by many tanks. *SS-Sturmbannführer* Schlamelcher's *III Artillery Battalion,* re-inforced with heavy weapons, went into action immediately. They went into the attack and fired over sights, in unprotected positions. They quickly destroyed seventeen enemy tanks, one-hundred and forty-four trucks and over six-hundred enemy troops. A further twenty-seven tanks and a battery of 12cm guns were captured intact. The threat from the enemy was quickly removed.

Karl Schlamelcher photographed after his award of the Knight's Cross.

Three weeks later, the 23rd and the 24th of July, he used his artillery with great effect and success. He was in the front line, again exposed and firing in open positions. Five enemy batteries were destroyed at the same time. The enemy launched violent counter-attacks, smashed with strong artillery support from the *III Battalion* of the *Artillery Regiment*, under Schlamelcher. The artillery batteries helped to influence the outcome of a battle for a key road junction and bridgehead, whose quick control was made with its' artillery fire.

The successful, brave and resolute uses of the artillery by this *Commander* resulted in the award of the Knight's Cross to the Iron Cross on the 1st of March 1942.

In later battles he received a serious head wound caused by an enemy bullet that removed him from front-line service. He was promoted to *SS-Obersturmbannführer* in 1943. He then commanded an artillery school at Beneschau. Further promotion came in February 1945 to the rank of *SS-Standartenführer*, before the end of the war he was placed in command of the *Artillery Regiment 31* in April 1945. He survived the war, but died in 28th June 1948 in Bad Pyrmont. The severe head wound he suffered during the war resulted in his eventual death.

Hermann Fegelein
Date of birth: 30.10.1906
SS Number: 66 680
Born in Ansbach, he moved to Munich with his family in 1912, and was introduced to riding from an early age. He served in a machine-gun unit during 1925 and 1926, within a *Cavalry Regiment*. The following year he joined the police in Bavaria, staying with them until 1929.

His service with the *SS* began in mid-May 1933 and less than one month later he was holding the rank of *SS-Sturmführer (SS-Untersturmführer)*. He became the *Adjutant* to the *Riding Leader* of *SS-Group South*. In July 1934 he took command of the *15. Reiter Standarte,* just prior to this, in April, he became an *SS-Obersturmführer.* Another quick promotion to *SS-Hauptsturmführer* followed in November the same year. By this time he was *Commander* of the *SS* Cavalry, Greater Area South. In 1936 he was promoted further to *SS-Sturmbannführer* and also given command of the *SS* Main Riding School. 1937 would see him promoted to *SS-Obersturmbannführer,* and further still to *SS-Standartenführer.* He was an accomplished rider and the school he commanded became a show piece of the Third Reich.

As the war beckoned he moved to *Commanding Officer* of the newly created *SS-Totenkopf Reiter Standarte*. The actions of this unit and its' subsequent expansions and renaming have been covered in preceding chapters. The

Hermann Fegelein pictured as an SS-Standartenführer and after his award of the Knight's Cross to the Iron Cross.

performance of those various units resulted in the award of the Second Class Iron Cross in mid-December 1940, and the First Class Iron Cross towards the end of June the following year. This was taken further on the 2nd of March 1942 when he was awarded the Knight's Cross to the Iron Cross. The recommendation, written by *XXIII Army Korps Commander*, *General* Albrecht Schubert, contained the following information:

> 'Since January the 25th 1942, the *SS-Kavallerie Brigade* was located on the southwest front of the *XXIII Army Korps*. Their task was to prevent the advance of strong enemy forces that had breached the gap west of Rshew, towards the south. The *Brigade* foiled all attempts of the enemy, inspite of heavy casualties. Not only did they defeat all enemy efforts, but also led the main offensive attacks. In addition, they led the encircling and annihilation attacks which lasted for days.
>
> During all the defensive and offensive fighting, the personal unshakability, exemplary bravery and constant desire to attack of the *Brigade Commanding Officer* were shown. He was able to complete his assignments with endless attack operations during which, he rallied his men behind him.
>
> On February the 5th 1942 the *Brigade* attacked a strong enemy group northwest of Tschertolino on the personal decision of the *Brigade Commanding Officer*. The attack was carried out under his personal leadership with a tremendous swing in a bold advance, in spite of the most difficult terrain and weather conditions, against a vastly superior enemy in possession of strongly fortified positions.
>
> The enemy lost 1,800 dead and tons of material, while we suffered minimal casualties. The resulting shortening of the front freed stronger forces and the *SS-Kavallerie Brigade* succeeded in tightening the ring around the encircled enemy southwest of Rshew in a bold attack. The route to the village of Jersowo, which was taken on February 14th 1942 after heavy fighting, which teetered back and forth, completed the challenge for the destruction of the surrounded enemy group.
>
> *SS-Standartenführer* Fegelein was able to completely defeat these strong enemy forces with his enthusiastic decision making and full tempered leadership. His personal bravery and readiness for action enabled the cleansing of the situation southwest of Rshew.'

As highlighted above, this recommendation was approved in early March 1942 and with this, Fegelein became the first Knight's Cross holder for *SS Kavallerie* troops. This would be the first of many to formations raised as 'second-line' or 'rear-line' units. He became the 32nd *Waffen-SS* soldier to be awarded the Knight's Cross to the Iron Cross.

Matthias Kleinheisterkamp
Date of birth: 22.06.1893
SS Number: 132 399
Born in Elberfeld, Kleinheisterkamp's military service seen him fight throughout the First World War from 1914 to 1918. During that time he was awarded both classes of the Iron Cross, as well as the Wound Badge. He reached the rank of *Leutnant*, served as a *Platoon Leader, Battalion* and *Regimental Adjutant* and also as a *Kompanie Commander*. After the war he stayed in the *Army* until 1919, he then moved to the *Reichsheer* from 1921 to 1934. He fought with the *Freikorps* during this time and also by 1929 he had reached the rank of *Hauptmann*.

At the start of November 1933 he joined the *SS,* quickly becoming an *NCO* in early 1934. On the 12th of April the same year he had obtained the rank of *SS-Sturmführer (SS-Untersturmführer)*. Rapid promotion followed and by the 17th of June 1934 he was an *SS-Obersturmführer,* then *SS-Hauptsturmführer* on the 20th of April 1935 and by the start of June 1935 he had risen to *SS-Sturmbannführer.* Just under one year later, 1st of April 1936, he moved to the Staff Inspectorate of the *SS-VT,* staying there until the end of May 1938. By then he had risen to the rank of *SS-Obersturmbannführer,* obtained on the 20th of April 1937. After leaving the *SS-VT* role, he went to the staff of *SS-Regiment Deutschland,* but by the start of December the same year he was serving as the *III Battalion Commander*. It was with this unit that he entered the Second World War.

He stayed with the *III Battalion, Deutschland* until the early part of June 1940 when he moved to the *Totenkopf Division*. He was awarded both Clasps to the Iron Cross, (13th of September 1939 and 2nd of October 1939 respectively), for actions in Poland. During his time with *Deutschland* he was recommended for the Knight's Cross by Paul Hausser on the 18th of July, but this was rejected. Just prior to moving to *Totenkopf*, on the 18th of May 1940, he was promoted to *SS-Standartenführer.* He initially served as a *Battalion Commander* within the *SS-Infantry Regiment 3,* but soon took over this *Regiment* in July, when the previous commander was killed. One year later he was promoted to *SS-Oberführer,* the same month that he was recommended a second time for the Knight's Cross by Eicke on the 6th of July 1941, also rejected. On the 9th of November 1941 he obtained the rank of *SS-Brigadeführer und Generalmajor der Waffen-SS*. At the end of 1941 he assumed command of *SS-Division Reich* and it was with this *Division* that he would finally be awarded the Knight's Cross.

Matthias Kleinheisterkamp photographed after he was finally awarded the Knight's Cross in 1942 for leading SS-Division Reich. He already had two recommendations rejected!

This third recommendation was written on the 17th of March 1942 by *General* von Vietinghoff, the *Commander* of the *XXXXVI Panzer Korps*. Although this was a short recommendation, it proved enough; it contained the following information:

> 'From January the 10th to March the 15th eradicated again and again the enemy threat in their area. He is a dependable leader and was in the lead during each situation. I recommend him for the Knight's Cross to the Iron Cross. The situation in this area at that time, ended well and it is to be fully credited to the role of this *Divisional Commander*.'

This recommendation was approved on the 31st of March 1942 and would not be Kleinheisterkamp's only association with the Knight's Cross or its' various grades, but more of that in later volumes.

Erwin Meierdress
Date of Birth: 11.12.1916
SS Number: 265 243
Born in Wesel, he first served with the *Hitler Youth* from mid-February 1933 until the start of August 1934. He followed this by joining the *SS* on the 1st of August – straight from the *Hitler Youth*, serving initially with the *LAH*. From the start of April 1938 until the start of February 1939 Meierdress went to the *SS* Officer's School at Braunschweig. He became an *SS-Untersturmführer* on the 20th of April the same year. By June he was serving with the *13. Kompanie, SS-Regiment Der Führer,* but by September the same year he had moved to the *4. Kompanie, Artillery Regiment 2*. He fought with this unit in Poland and earned the Second Class Iron Cross on the 15th of November 1939. In May 1940 he was holding the post of *Adjutant, I Battalion, Artillery Regiment 3,* and went west with this *Battalion* during May and June. On the 9th of November 1940 he was promoted to *SS-Obersturmführer.* He went east with *Totenkopf* in 1941 and by January 1942 was caught up in the intense fighting near Staraja-Russa. It was during this fighting that he conducted actions which resulted in the later award of the Knight's Cross to the Iron Cross, he had recently been awarded the First Class Iron Cross on the 15th of January 1942.

The recommendation was written by Theodore Eicke on the 1st of March 1942 and read as follows:

> 'During the Russian breakthrough of our lines southeast of Staraja Russa in January 1942, *SS-Obersturmführer* Meierdress was fighting within

Erwin Meierdress photographed after he was awarded the Knight's Cross, he is seen here, in hospital, still recovering from the wounds he received in the Demjansk pocket.

Kampfgruppe Bochmann, first used to maintain positions in the northeast and then the southeast of Staraja Russa. Through numerous resolute actions, it fought hard against enemy paratroopers and inflicted heavy losses on them. After most of the *Kampfgruppe* Officers had been put out of action, *SS-Obersturmführer* Meierdress gathered the rest of the group and defended Bjakowo, on the road to Staraja Russa, within the Demjansk Pocket.

Since the end of January 1942, Meierdress defended this area on all sides during courageous battles against a very strong enemy. The Russians penetrated with tanks and infantry into this place. As an example of a courageous fighter to his men, *SS-Obersturmführer* Meierdress succeeded in throwing the enemy out of this town.

The defenders of Bjakowo stood firm under their leader. The holding of this place is of decisive importance to the fortress of Demjansk. The taking of this place by the enemy would have allowed them to connect with Gortschizy in the south and their own troops.

In recognition of this hero and his courageous fight and its' connected success, I ask that *SS-Obersturmführer* Erwin Meierdress be given the Knight's Cross to the Iron Cross.'

To summarise how costly the fighting had been, 120 men had went into this area, with only thirteen fit men and fifty wounded men coming out. They had fought their way out using grenades and mortars and they left 200 dead enemy troops behind them. They had initially fought in the west, north and northeast but later on they fought in the east. They inflicted a further 150 dead upon the enemy at a cost of one dead and seven wounded to their own numbers. By the time Meierdress was wounded and evacuated, there were a total of thirty wounded.

This recommendation was approved on the 13th of March 1942 and would not be his only association with this medal and its' grades, details of his later awards will follow in future volumes.

Army Group North

Totenkopf

We last covered them at the end of March as the enemy tightened their hold around Demjansk. Within this area, the two main elements under Eicke and Simon were battling hard to resist the strong Russian forces.

As previously highlighted, Max Simon was fighting hard around the important airfield at Demjansk, which they held until the 21st of April 1942 when they were relieved. It was at this time that friendly troops finally broke into the Demjansk Pocket.

The intense fighting had placed a heavy burden upon all of the German troops inside, which included the *SS Totenkopf* men. Total casualties were just over 12,000, with around 30,000 enemy casualties. Many acts of bravery were witnessed and some of these were recognized throughout April for the men of the *Totenkopf Division*.

The first of these was the award of the Knight's Cross to Ernst Staudle, on the 10th of April. Theodore Eicke's Oakleaves to the Knight's Cross – the second such award to a soldier of the *Waffen-SS* – followed on the 20th of April. The final award in April for a *Totenkopf* soldier came one day later, on the 21st of April, when Wilfred Richter was awarded his Knight's Cross for actions around Kalitkino. This was the same day that the Demjansk Pocket was opened. Further awards of the Knight's Cross to the Iron Cross would follow for actions during this time, but they will be detailed later in this volume.

Polizei

During the second half of February 1942 they were fighting under intense pressure, whilst their *Totenkopf Kameraden* were being closed up with the Demjansk area, to the southeast. This was not the only area of focus for the Russians and they were going all out to defeat the Germans south of Leningrad.

As the enemy pressure increased, the Germans held area constricted further, more units were sent to try and help. These additional units were welcomed by the defenders already in place. One such unit sent from their positions northwest, closer to Leningrad, was *Battalion Dorner,* under the command of *SS-Sturmbannführer* Helmut Dorner.

They conducted a rapid march in poor weather conditions to reach *Kameraden* from the *Heer's, 254. Infantry Division* on the 14th of February. They then conducted attacks against the enemy over the following days. This *Battalion* took Glebowo and Ssawkino. As highlighted above, the *V Battalion LAH* and *SS-Freiwilligen Legion Norwegein* relieved the *Polizei Division* and *Heer Divisions* in this area. This group was known as *Kampfgruppe Jeckeln* and was under the command of *SS-Obergruppenführer und General der Polizei* Friedrich Jeckeln.

On the 24th of February 1942 the *Polizei Divison* officially became known as *SS-Polizei Division*.

Towards the end of February *Battalion Dorner* and other *Polizei* elements were fighting intense battles along the Tossno River and at Krassnaja Gorka, south of Ljuban. The enemy had launched another attempt to take overall control in this area. This fighting stretched along the main highway running west to east and it lasted from the end of February and on into March. Around the 8th and 9th of March a new enemy offensive opened. Dorner and elements remained in the east, whilst the rest of *Polizei* moved to the south towards Motski and Ljubino Pole.

The German attack coincided with an enemy attack around Pogostje. This enemy attack pushed in different directions and put the Germans under intense pressure. It actually delayed the start of the planned German attack, alongside the atrocious weather situation. The western group was not able to finally start their attack until March the 15th. Wunnenberg was the *Commander* of the group in the west. For four days the attack pushed forwards and attained their objective of containing the enemy within a pocket, whilst also controlling their supply routes, linking with the eastern group.

During that time and beyond, the eastern group was fighting alongside *Divisions* of the *Army*, their struggle lasted until the 28th of March, before quietening down slightly.

After the link up with the two elements on the 19th of March 1942, the bulk of the *SS-Polizei Division* moved onto the defensive. A few days later, on the 23rd of March, Russians inside this pocket pushed a new attack to re-open the ring around them. This stage of the fighting had been costly already with around 1,300 casualties. This renewed Russian push achieved a partial breakthrough on the 27th, with *SS-Polizei* and other units fighting there shifting emphasis the following day to contain the opening. A further 'peak' in enemy activity was dealt with around the 7th of April, with more tank assisted attacks launched on the 14th and 15th of April. It must be pointed out that, although the heavy attacks were noticeable, the fighting was almost continuous throughout time from late March and into mid-April.

The Russians were fighting for their very survival, whilst the Germans, including of course *SS-Polizei,* were determined to remove the enemy threat once and for all. The Russians finally managed to open one small corridor from the west on the 21st of April and held it open. Other attempts to replicate this small local success elsewhere were not successful.

Two days later the notification of Wunnenberg's Oakleaves came through. This is a good point to leave the actions of the *SS-Polizei Division* and highlight the other *SS* units fighting within this army group.

2. SS-Infantry Brigade (mot.)

The various elements of the *2. SS-Infantry Brigade (mot.) – Flandern, Niederlande & Norwegian* – were employed in this area throughout the second half of February and through to April, they were not employed as a complete unit, but dispersed where they were needed.

V Battalion LAH

Whilst the bulk of the *LAH* fought within Army Group South, one *Battalion* remained in Berlin. This was known as the *V Battalion*, or *Wach Battalion* and they had existed since mid-1941.

Due to the extreme situations experienced on the Russian Front in the first winter of Barbarossa, any available units were employed where it was felt they would make the most difference. This is how one element of the *LAH* fought at the opposite end of the Soviet Union to their *Kameraden* in the south.

Towards the end of 1941 and into early 1942 the enemy launched their major offensive south of Leningrad with the objective of defeating the Germans in this area and relieving Leningrad. The *V Battalion LAH* where moved from Germany to this area in the last week of February 1942. This *Battalion* of around one thousand men was under the command of *SS-Hauptsturmführer* Hugo Kraas. They were initially positioned south and southwest of Leningrad around Krassnogwardiesk, this unit became part of *Kampfgruppe Jackeln*.

They took over their assigned positions and allowed other units to gain some rest. They took their first losses and contact with the enemy as February passed into March 1942, they remained there until the end of March. They were then ordered closer to, and changed direction to the southeast of, Leningrad, with their final positions being at Mga and its' surrounding areas. These *LAH* men engaged the enemy in and around this area throughout April 1942 also.

Army Group South

SS-Wiking Division

We last covered *Wiking* up to the 1st of March 1942 when Franz Kleffner was awarded the Knight's Cross. So what took place for these men during March and April 1942? They remained in their positions on the west side of the River Mius. No major changes or offensives occurred during these two months.

On the 23rd of April 1942 another *Kameraden* from *Wiking* was awarded the Knight's Cross to the Iron Cross. This was August Dieckmann. He was awarded his Knight's Cross on the same day that *Polizei's* Alfred Wunnenberg received his Knight's Cross with Oakleaves.

Before detailing these two awards, what of the other *SS* units operating within Army Group South?

LAH

No changes or major engagements took place for these men during this time up to the end of April 1942.

1. SS-Infantry Brigade (mot.)

There is very little detail on this particular unit during this early stage of 1942.

Now to detail six *SS* soldiers who were awarded the Knight's Cross in April 1942.

Hinrich Schuldt

Date of Birth: 14.06.1901

SS Number: 242 677

Born in Blankensee, his military service began in 1922 within the *Reichsmarine,* by the time he left the *Navy* in 1928 he had risen to the rank of *Leutnant*. He joined the *S.A.* at the start of February 1932 and stayed there for eighteen months before moving to the *SS* in September 1933, with the rank of *SS-Sturmführer (SS-Untersturmführer)*. By the start of 1935 he had risen to the rank of *SS-Obersturmführer.* Just prior to this, in October 1934, he had been given command of the *LAH's, 3. Kompanie*; staying with this unit until 1938. Inbetween these dates he had been promoted to *SS-Hauptsturmführer,* on the 10th of March 1935. After the *LAH,* he moved to serve within the *I Battalion, SS-Regiment Germania*. It was also during 1938 that he was promoted to *SS-Sturmbannführer,* on the 9th of November, and came after his attendance at a *Battalion Leader's* course in Doberitz. He stayed with *Germania* until June 1939 when he moved to take command of the *I Battalion, SS-Regiment Deutschland*. It was with this unit that he entered the Second World War.

He fought in Poland and earned the Second Class Iron Cross on the 24th of October 1939. By then he had left *Deutschland* and moved to *Germania* once again, staying there until mid-December 1939. He followed this by moving to *Polizei* for a period of just over three months, before moving once again to the *I Battalion, 4. SS-Totenkopf Standarte*. He would stay with this unit as it changed its' name to *SS-Infantrie-Regiment 4,* also as he was promoted again to *SS-Obersturmbannführer* on the 1st of September 1941, whilst he received the First Class Iron Cross in November 1941. Schuldt had commanded this unit from early July 1941, but this was not made official until almost the middle of November the same year.

It was with this unit that he went to the Juchnow area, within Army Group Centre, in late 1941 and early 1942, where he took part in actions that resulted in the award of the Knight's Cross. It is not known who wrote the recommendation or for which actions he received this coveted award, so it is best to give an overview of what his unit done during that time.

As mentioned above, he was the *Commander* of the *SS-Infantrie-Regiment 4,* within the *2. SS-Infantry Brigade (mot.)*, in late 1941. This unit was sent to the

Hinrich Schuldt photographed after his award of the Knight's Cross in April 1942.

Leningrad Front during the final stages of 1941. They were briefly withdrawn, but then sent back into the line close to the *SS Kavallerie Brigade,* within Army Group Centre, between the 18th and the 30th of December. Three thousand men went into the Juchnow area and some of these men had to start fighting straight off the planes they were transported in on, as the Soviets held some of the airfields. They battled against the enemy into late January 1942 within this area, holding a corridor open to the north. Heavy pressure forced the defense to concentrate on Juchnow during late January and into February. The enemy attacks intensified during that time and further ground at Kolodosi was lost, with losses to Schuldts' men mounting all of the time.

After being relieved they moved slightly northwards in early February to help hold more ground. The new area had to be fought for. This was the main battle line running from Juchnow to Viazma. They fought without tank or artillery support and their ineffective anti-tank guns were crushed under the tracks of the Russian T-34s. They fought in this area until March, against heavy enemy attacks, without much rest. They were finally relieved in March and at that time they had only 180 men left standing.

One officer fighting under Schuldt at that time recalled, "The *Regiment* fought superbly, thanks to focused and superior leadership by its' *Commander*. It had compensated for the disadvantages of being employed on its' own, with other formations or on sectors of the front where only pitiful remnants attempted to hang on".

This was an important part of the overall defense against the major Russian offensive launched during that time. In recognition of their part in holding the line, the *SS-Infantrie-Regiment 4 Commander*, *SS-Obersturmbannführer* Hinrich Schuldt, was awarded the Knight's Cross to the Iron Cross on the 4th of April 1942. His *Regiment* was also given the honour of being renamed '*SS-Regiment Langemarck*'. This would not be Hinrich Schuldt's only connection to the grades of the Knight's Cross, but as with others, details of those actions will follow in later volumes.

Ernst Staudle

Date of Birth: 06.06.1913

SS Number: 226 097

Born in Heidenheim, he served in the *Hitler Youth* from October 1931 until the 9th of November 1933, being awarded the Golden Hitler Youth Badge. He then moved to the *Heer* at the start of October 1935 and stayed there until the end of September the following year. His service with the *SS* began in mid-September 1939 when he joined *Totenkopf.*

Ernst Staudle photographed after his promotion to SS-Untersturmführer. The actions that resulted in his Knight's Cross award were done whilst serving as an SS-Oberscharführer.

He went east with them in mid-1941 and on the 23rd of September he was awarded the Second Class Iron Cross. This was followed on the 17th of February 1942 with the award of the First Class Iron Cross. By this time he was holding the rank of *SS-Oberscharführer* and was serving with the *8. Kompanie, Artillery Regiment 3*. In late February 1942 he was fighting within the Demjansk Pocket and his actions at that time resulted in the award of the Knight's Cross to the Iron Cross. The recommendation was written by his *Divisional Commander*, Theodore Eicke, on the 1st of March 1942 and contained the following overview:

> '*SS-Oberscharführer* Staudle was on the night of 26th and 27th of February 1942, fighting near Schumilkino. He was an advance observer, watching the fire of his artillery battery against an enemy attack running from the west, with artillery and mortar support.
>
> In the course of the attack, it succeeded in approaching the village with 50 men. There were only a few weak men to hold this area. These men pushed against the enemy as if fighting in *Battalion* strength and successfully put the Russians to flight.
>
> In this critical situation, and himself suffering from a heavy wound, Staudle ordered the rest of the men to defend against this Russian attack, using their 3.7cm Flak firing at short range.
>
> Through the halting of this attack, affected the Russian plans and they arrived piecemeal in Salutschje.
>
> I ask for the award of the Knight's Cross to the Iron Cross in recognition of his successful and decisive actions.'

This was approved on the 10th of April 1942. Following on from this he was promoted to *SS-Untersturmführer* on the 1st of November 1943 and was serving in the *SS* Artillery School. He was further promoted to *SS-Obersturmführer* on the 21st of June 1944, when he was the *Commander* of the Artillery School in Jaworznow. He survived the war and died on the 11th of July 1946. Besides being awarded the medals listed above, he also won the Black Wound Badge, the Russian Front Medal and the General Assault Badge.

Theodore Eicke
Date of Birth: 17.10.1892
SS Number: 2 921
His exploits up to the award of the Knight's Cross to the Iron Cross are covered in previous chapters. What we will be focusing on now is his award of the Knight's Cross with Oakleaves.

An autographed photo of Theodore Eicke showing his formal portrait; following his award of the Knight's Cross to the Iron Cross with Oakleaves.

Another photograph showing Eicke after his award of the Oakleaves. This probably shows the same Feisler Storch that he was shot down and killed in, in the early 1943.

Since the 3rd of February 1942, Theodore Eicke and his *SS-Totenkopf Division* had been surrounded and cut-off inside the area known as Fortress Demjansk or the Demjansk Pocket. Inside this pocket were *Totenkopf* and five *Divisions* from the *Heer,* all totaling around one hundred thousand men. This pocket was the first of many such 'pocket' battles that the Germans would have to endure. The battle that raged around this area involved three Soviet *Armies*, eighteen *Infantry Divisions* and three *Brigades*. All of this enemy might was unable to smash the will of the German defenders at that time. The battle itself was in two main stages, the first lasting from the 3rd of February until the 21st of March 1942. The second stage came after the corridor was opened and it focused on widening the corridor, this lasted from the 21st of March until the 21st of April 1942. Inside this area there were many acts of bravery, some of which have already been covered and some others will be covered within this volume. In 1943 every soldier that fought within this pocket at that time was issued with the Demjansk Shield in recognition of their struggle and overall bravery. It cannot be under estimated just how important the holding of this area at that time was to the Germans. It is sufficed to say the Germans were not in a position to loose five *Divisions* at that time and in that area.

So, what of Eicke's part in the eventual success? He personally ordered his men within *Totenkopf* to hold or die, and they most certainly complied with this order! They endured the frequent, heavy and unrelenting attacks that produced some outstanding feats of bravery, courage and heroism. Eicke recommended some of his troops for the Knight's Cross, the majority of these were written as the battle was still raging and undecided.

Theodore Eicke and his men held from the start of February until the end of March, when the first corridor was established. They then helped to expand this corridor over the next month or so until success could be well and truly achieved. The preceding pages contain more details of what took place. The award of the Knight's Cross to the Iron Cross with Oakleaves was approved on the 20th of April 1942 and was followed the next day by a promotion to *SS-Obergruppenführer und Generalleutnant der Waffen-SS*. It is not known who wrote the recommendation, when it was written or for what exact actions. It is fair to say that it would have covered some, if not all, of the actions that took place in the almost two month period from February until towards the end of April.

Some quotes may help in understanding the significance of these battles and the defense that was put in by Eicke and his men from *Totenkopf*.

Generaloberst Busch, *Commander* of the *XVI Army*, (written in mid-March 1942).

"A successful defense by Gruppe Eicke, especially the garrison at Bjakowo, has earned the highest recognition due to its' obvious necessity."

General Hansen, *Commander X Armee Korps.*
"What each of you accomplished in battle with this enemy in terms of overcoming the severest weather and arduous terrain belongs to the annals of the greatest feats of German arms. Thanks are first in order for those who gave life and health here on the battlefields south of Lake Ilhmen."

General Graf von Bruckendorff, *Commander* of the *II Armee Korps.*
"Few in number, but iron in your will, you have proven that the trust the Führer and Fatherland have placed in you is well justified in this first offensive of the year."

I feel that these words from high ranking officers give a good view of the importance of Eicke's successes. This award was the second award of the Knight's Cross with Oakleaves to a soldier of the *Waffen-SS*. It is also worth noting that it had been a period of only four months inbetween Eicke's Knight's Cross award and the subsequent award of the Oakleaves.

Eicke was presented his Oakleaves personally by Adolf Hitler and then followed this by a long spell of leave away from his *Division*. He returned with *Totenkopf* to Russia in early 1943 and on the 26th of February 1943 he was killed after his light aircraft was shot down by enemy soldiers. This brought to an end the life of one of the most determined, cold-blooded and fervent supporters of the Third Reich. He was also one of the most controversial commanders within the *Waffen-SS*.

Wilfred Richter
Date of Birth: 09.05.1916
SS Number: 279 192
Born in Pforzheim, he served in the *Hitler Youth* from the start of April 1933 until the 9th of November 1934. He then spent some time in the *R.A.D.* from April until October 1937. His service with the *SS* began in November 1937, joining the *15. Kompanie, SS-Regiment Deutschland*. He went to the *SS* Officer School at Braunschweig from late 1939 until early 1940. He moved to the rank of *SS-Untersturmführer* on the 1st of May 1940, and moved to the *Motorcycle Infantry Replacement Kompanie,* within the *Totenkopf Division*. He stayed there until the 25th of June 1941, when he moved to the *Sturmgeschutze Batterie* within *Totenkopf*. He was awarded the Second Class Iron Cross on the 14th of September

Wilfred Richter photographed after his award of the Knight's Cross to the Iron Cross.

1941 and the First Class Iron Cross on the 22nd of October. A further promotion came at the end of January 1942. It was soon after this that he found himself within the Demjansk Pocket.

On the 19th of April 1942 Theodore Eicke recommended Richter for the Knight's Cross for the following actions:

> '*SS-Obersturmführer* Wilfred Richter was with his *Kompanie*, from the 15th of March 1942, in the town of Kalitkino. They were under enemy artillery, aircraft and tank fire. On the 5th of April in the early morning, they were fighting the Russians in the northern front within *Gruppe Eicke*, at the focus point of Kalitkino. Sixteen T-34s broke in against their defensive positions, supported by an attack from the west and north-west of Kalitkino. Richter and his men only had two *Pak* guns. They engaged the enemy and destroyed ten T-34s as well as infantry losses on the enemy infantry coming from the north of Kalitkino. The enemy took hold and cut them off. Richter gathered the last of his men and pushed against this enemy incursion, despite heavy enemy tanks and infantry fire. They successfully knocked out five T-34s using magnetic teller mines. Their courageous acts gave them success and they pushed into the enemy positions, capturing one enemy tank officer and another enemy soldier.
>
> Throughout the rest of the day they expanded their positions, defended them and remained ready. *SS-Obersturmführer* Richter's dogged determination and heroism was an example again and again to his weak group of men cut-off in this area. Holding out to the last, Kalitkino was held firmly within our control.
>
> The holding of the village lying as a support point two kilometres before the front was of decisive importance. The enemy was to the south and east. Moreover, this cornerstone is important for the start point for us for future attacks.
>
> I recommend *SS-Obersturmführer* Wilfred Richter for the award of the Knight's Cross to the Iron Cross in recognition of his heroism and courage and the successes connected to it.'

The *II Armee Korps Commander*, *General* Graf von Bruckendorff, repeated the above points, once again highlighting Richter's decisive part in holding this area and his personal heroism – repeatedly holding this important town, despite these attacks.

"I recommend the Knight's Cross to the Iron Cross for this brave Officer and it comes with my warmest approval."

Generaloberst Busch further approved this recommendation, as did the Army Group North *Commander*, *Generaloberst* Kuchel. It was approved on the 21st of April 1942, only three days after it was written. Richter had been promoted to *SS-Hauptsturmführer* the day before this.

By July 1943 he was with the *13. Kompanie, Panzer Regiment 3*. By late October the same year he was with the *Panzer Training and Replacement Regiment,* staying there until the 21st of March 1944. He then moved to a spell at the Braunschweig and also the Bad Tolz Officer Schools. By April 1945 he was the *Commander* of the *II Battalion, SS-Panzer-Grenadier Regiment 96,* within the *SS-Division Nibelungen*. He survived the war and died on the 18th of April 1981.

August Dieckmann

Date of Birth: 29.05.1912

SS Number: 183 917

Born in Badenberge, he entered the *SS* on the 4th of November 1933, serving with the *1. Kompanie, 88. SS-Standarte*. By the start of October 1934 he was serving with the *2. Kompanie, SS-Regiment Germania*. On the 24th of April 1935 he began at course at Braunschweig. A series of promotions followed with him holding the rank of *SS-Rottenführer* at the start of June, *SS-Unterscharführer* at the start of July and *SS-Standartenjunker* on the 9th of November. On the 25th of February 1936 he was holding he rank of *SS-Standartenoberjunker* and by the start of April he had moved back to the *Deutschland Regiment*. On the 20th of April 1936 he was promoted to *SS-Untersturmführer* and by the start of October the same year he was serving within the *IV Battalion, SS-Regiment Deutschland*. On the 12th of September 1937 he was holding the rank of *SS-Obersturmführer* and around six-weeks later he moved to the *III Battalion*. At the start of May 1938 he had moved again, this time to the *II Battalion* and also went into Austria. At the end of May 1939 he attended a course for pioneers and on the 1st of September 1939 he received a promotion to *SS-Hauptsturmführer.*

He fought in Poland and the west – where he was commanding the *2. Kompanie* within *Deutschland*. From the start of August 1940 he began a stint as a tactics instructor at Braunschweig. On the 28th of September he received the Second Class Iron Cross, followed by the First Class Iron Cross on the 3rd of May 1941. He went into Russia in mid-1941, receiving a wound on the 22nd of August. By the 2nd of December 1941 he was commanding the *I Battalion, SS-Regiment Germania,* within the *Wiking Division*. On Boxing Day the same year he was promoted to *SS-Sturmbannführer.* He was awarded the German Cross in Gold on the 28th of February 1942 and soon afterwards, on the 21st of April 1942, Felix

August Dieckmann photographed after his Knight's Cross award; like Otto Kumm, he is seen wearing the non-officer type collar patches.

Steiner recommended Dieckmann for the Knight's Cross to the Iron Cross. The recommendation contained the following information:

> '*SS-Sturmbannführer* Dieckmann, the leader of the *I Battalion, Germania* is a very courageous soldier earning the Second Class Iron Cross in Poland and the First Class Iron Cross for actions in combat at Kuzmin and in the defensive battles, very courageous deeds.
>
> On the 6th of August 1941 *SS-Hauptsturmführer* Dieckmann was the *Commander* of *Kampfgruppe Dieckmann (*Reinforced *I Battalion* and reinforced *Kradschutzen Kompanie, SS-Regiment Germania)* and was ordered to secure the advance route and bridgehead around Ssmela, against the north. In the early hours of the morning they moved through far superior forces (*116. Infantry Division* and *Infantry Regiment 692*) using surprise attacks on both sides, attacked by the enemy who tried to remove *Kampfgruppe Dieckmann*. Using his *3. Kompanie* in a counter-attack he breached the enemy ring around Ssmela. *Kampfgruppe Dieckmann* changed a serious situation for the *Division*. They fought on decisively and smashed the enemy and sent them into a retreat.'

Dieckmann's *Regiment Commander*, Oberkamp, also added the following:

> 'The enemy attacked with elements of the *227 Infantry Division* and *116 Infantry Division,* out of the Tscherkassy direction, surprised against the flank, the right wing of the extreme point of the *Panzergruppe 1,* advancing towards Kamenka – Tschigirin. The *Division Wiking* was advancing on Smela before the order by the *Division Wiking* that the foremost *Regimental Combat Group* had arrived already through the *68. Infantry Division* at Korsun, but not as far as Goroditsche. Smela was occupied at this time by the *I Battalion, Germania* and two *Batteries* of the *III Battalion, Artillery Regiment 5*.
>
> Russians with strong, superior artillery supporting their attack came from the north, northwest, southeast and south, moved around the rear of the *I Battalion, Germania. SS-Hauptsturmführer* Dieckmann placed himself in defense at Smela. Unshakeable against air attacks they advanced south and opened a route to the south.
>
> In the action against the enemy south of the Samara, Otscheretino was taken on the 16th of February. Strengthening of that garrison in the village they controlled the situation and the approach. Otscheretino was the controlling, important cornerstone on the right wing of *Gruppe Sanne,* whose possession for the lead in the battle was of decisive importance.

In the afternoon of the 19th of February 1942 a very strong Russian attack accompanied by strong artillery, mortar and eight heavy Russian tanks was launched. After a hard battle they succeeded with tanks and infantry to penetrate the east of the village, advancing together. The anti-tank guns were destroyed by enemy tank rounds. The anti-tank guns remained ineffective. This was the decisive moment in the possession or loss of the village. *SS-Hauptsturmführer* Dieckmann proceeded to take control of one gun battery and directed the fire unwaveringly and leading by example. Dieckmann directed the gun towards the enemy tanks and shot up four of them.

SS-Hauptsturmführer Dieckmann decided to exploit this favourable moment and pushed against and threw the far stronger enemy out of this area. With other troops of the *Battalion* he repulsed on the 20th of February and the night of the 22nd and 23rd, running tank attacks of the enemy. The enemy lost over 300 dead and various weapons, as well as twenty-nine prisoners taken.

Through his good personal example, personal courage and independent decisions, *SS-Hauptsturmführer* Dieckmann held the decisive share of Otscheretino and inflicted bloody losses on the enemy.'

Oberstleutnant Troger, *Commander* of *Gruppe Troger,* approved this proposal and highlight Dieckmann's success fighting the enemy in full view of them and in difficult weather conditions. Defeating superior tank and infantry forces, he led teams with confidence to the successful outcome.

This recommendation was endorsed by *Generalmajor* Sanne, *Commander* of the *100. Light Infantry Divison,* also von Mackensen, *Commander* of the *III Panzer Korps*. Further signed by *Generaloberst* von Kleist, *Commander* of the *I Panzer Armee* and finally signed by *Generalfeldmarschall* Keitel.

It was approved on the 23rd of April 1942 and would not be August Dieckmann's only link with the Knight's Cross to the Iron Cross. But, as with others, details of those further links will follow in later volumes.

Alfred Wunnenberg
Date of Birth: 27.07.1891
SS Number: 405 898
As previously covered, Alfred Wunnenberg had been awarded the Knight's Cross to the Iron Cross in November 1941. Now he was being awarded the Knight's Cross with Oakleaves less than six-months later. Like his Army Group North *Kameraden*, Theodore Eicke, he had endured a difficult and testing time with his *Division* during the first critical part of 1942. What his *Division* had gone through is detailed in the preceding pages.

Alfred Wunnenberg photographed after his award of the Knight's Cross to the Iron Cross with Oakleaves. He is seen wearing his Waffen-SS uniform, after Polizei's incorporation into the Waffen-SS in early 1942.

The recommendation itself does not survive, so it is not known who wrote this or when it was written. What is known is that a teletype message arrived at the headquarters from Adolf Hitler's *Führer Headquarters*, it read as follows:

> "In grateful recognition of your heroic achievements in the struggle for the future of our people. I award you the Knight's Cross to the Iron Cross with Oakleaves as the 91st soldier of the *Wehrmacht*.
>
> Adolf Hitler"

This made Wunnenberg the third *Waffen-SS* soldier to be awarded this high honour. Following this at the start of July he was promoted to *SS-Gruppenführer* and also *Generalleutnant der Polizei* on July the 11th. He was charged with raising the *IV SS Panzer Korps* from June the 1st 1943 and one month later he was promoted further to the rank of *SS-Obergruppenführer und General der Waffen-SS und Polizei*. At the end of August 1943 he was moved to the Main Office of the *Ordnungs Polizei*, remaining in that post until the end of the war.

He survived the war, dying on the 30th of December 1963. He was a very effective and respected officer and career policeman. He witnessed his men as they were transformed from policemen into fighting soldiers and incorporated into the ranks of the *Waffen-SS*. The fighting record of the *Regiment*, and later *Division*, under his command is a testament to his abilities. The award of the Knight's Cross to the Iron Cross with Oakleaves was a fitting recognition of these abilities. This made him the third *Waffen-SS* recipient of this high honour.

SS-Freiwilligen-Division 'Prinz Eugen'

As the majority of existing *Waffen-SS* units were being pounded in Russia in these opening months of 1942, a new *Division* was raised. Back in February 1942, *SS-Brigadeführer* Artur Phelps was assigned the task of raising this new unit using ethnic Germans from Croatia and the Banat region, within Yugoslavia. The official order for the 'birth' of this new unit came on the first day of March 1942. Their title was given as the *Freiwilligen-Gebirgs-Division* and they became the second *Mountain Division* to be raised within the ranks of the *Waffen-SS*. As highlighted above, the members of this new unit were predominantly from the Banat region and their numbers were bulked out with German officers and *NCO*s. On the 1st of April 1942 their name was changed to the title of *SS-Freiwilligen-Divison 'Prinz Eugen'*. This *Division* consisted of two *Regiments*, an *Artillery Regiment*, along with *Reconnaissance, Pioneer* and other *Battalions*.

The were named after the legendary 17th century Knight who helped clear southern Europe of the Turks in the late 1600s and went onto defend the Reich in other important battles. Some of his most important victories took place in the very area that this new *Division* was raised from. '*Prinz Eugen*' would be the first of many *Waffen-SS Divisions* that would be named after famous historical Knights.

We will not cover this unit in too much detail in this volume as the majority of 1942 for them was spent training their men and getting used to the various equipment they would be using in later battles.

CHAPTER EIGHT

THE SPRING THAW - MAY AND JUNE 1942

May 1942 was another period of change for the *Waffen-SS* as they began their transformation to *Panzergrenadier Divisions*. In addition, the raising of the *SS Panzer Korps* also started. However, these changes would not come into full fruition until the start of 1943 when the principle *Waffen-SS* formations returned to the Russian Front, so these changes and their effects will be covered at the start of Volume 2 of this project.

Army Group Centre

SS-Kavallerie-Brigade

In the early part of April 1942 a proposed reorganization was put forward. This was due to the fact that the *SS-Kavallerie-Brigade* was very depleated after the recent difficult battles. This proposal was accepted and parts of the remaining *Brigade* began to move to Warsaw in Poland during mid-April.

The elements that stayed in Russia were formed into *Kampfgruppe Zehender* and they took part in various smaller operations in April and throughout May 1942. The weather changed and the cold climate and heavy snowfalls were replaced by rain and mud, not helping the overall German situation. Towards the end of May 1942 the last remnants of the *SS-Kavallerie-Brigade* were sent to Debica in Poland. The *Brigade* was to be built up to a *Division*. They therefore became the first *Waffen-SS* unit to be removed from the Russian Front in 1942 – but not the last.

SS-Division Reich

Further smaller attacks continued into April for this unit, but this became a quieter month for this ever decreasing group. The Russian's offensive capabilities were halted for the time being. This situation continued into May 1942. A general defensive posture was adapted by both sides, mainly due to the spring thaw, which reduced the roads to 'bottomless morasses'.

At the start of June they left Russia and traveled back to Germany via the Baltic countries. They were the second, but not the last, of the *Waffen-SS* units to be removed from Russia in 1942. With their removal, the *Waffen-SS's* presence within Army Group Centre came to a temporary halt.

We will cover what took place for *SS-Division Reich* during the rest of 1942 later on, but for now we will briefly cover their *SS* neighbors within Army Group North.

Army Group North

SS-Totenkopf Division

We last covered this unit towards the end of April 1942, the 21st to be exact, when the opening of the Demjansk Pocket was achieved. This opening was referred to as the Land Bridge and the Germans welcomed this partial relief and improvement in the overall situation. However, the Soviet enemy was not about to let up and on the 3rd of May a renewed Russian attack started.

This was the same day that *SS-Hauptsturmführer* Georg Bochmann was awarded the Knight's Cross to the Iron Cross – full details of this will follow later.

The Russians had moved new *Divisions* and *Brigades* to the areas north and south of this 'Land Bridge'. They proceeded to unleash a combined artillery and air strike against the Germans, as well as attacks against the edges of the pocket and land bridge itself. The intensity of these attacks was considered to be greater than those experienced during the attacks of the previous two months. The fight for survival raged during May and June 1942.

Back in the early part of May, the 8th, *SS-Sturmbannführer* Otto Baum and *SS-Sturmbannführer* Dr. Eduard Deisenhofer received notification that they were awarded the Knight's Cross to the Iron Cross, as with their two *Kameraden* above, full details of these will follow shortly.

Towards the middle of June Eicke had to go on sick leave and Max Simon took over command of the *Division* temporarily.

On the 28th of June notification of the award of the Knight's Cross to the Iron Cross to *SS-Hauptsturmführer* Otto Kron came through.

We will leave *Totenkopf* for now at the end of June 1942 and cover other *SS* units fighting within this Army Group.

SS-Freikorps Denmark

Danish volunteers into what became known as the *Waffen-SS* had started as early as 1940 and at one stage around two hundred men fought with the *SS-Wiking Division* within Army Group South.

The forming of *SS-Freikorps Denmark* began in earnest in July 1941 after the invasion of the Soviet Union. They were trained in Hamburg and increased in number throughout the rest of that year, finishing with almost 1,200 men by the start of 1942. Christian von Schalburg was the first *Commander*. They were moved to East Prussia for further training in late 1941.

On the 8th of May 1942, the same day as Baum's and Deisenhofer's Knight's Cross awards, they began transport from their training area to the Demjansk area. They were sent there to provide additional resource to stem the flow of Soviet attacks. They were placed under the command of *Totenkopf* and as has been covered, their arrival came in the middle of the renewed Russian attacks in this area.

They took part in the defensive battles in late May and throughout June 1942. The intense battles caused severe loses to this *Battalion*, these losses included von Schalburg and his temporary replacement, *SS-Obersturmbannführer* Hans Albert von Lettow-Vorbeck. *SS-Sturmbannführer* Knud Borge Martinsen assumed command as this *Battalion* withdrew to better defensive positions due to its' losses. Without doubt, a very eventful baptism of fire had been handed to this new unit during May and June 1942!

SS-Polizei Division

This tried and tested *Division* was last covered as Wunnenberg became the third *Waffen-SS* recipient of the Knight's Cross with Oakleaves, on the 23rd of April 1942.

Polizei's struggle around the Wolchow Pocket continued unabated into May 1942. Starting on the 6th of May and lasting until the 26th, various elements of this unit were relieved in the Wolchow area. A partial rebuild with replacements took place at Wyriza as other elements were still fighting northeast at Krassnaja Gorka.

Around the middle of May, the 11th, *SS-Sturmbannführer* Rudolf Pannier and *SS-Sturmbannführer* Helmut Dorner, on the 15th, were awarded the Knight's Cross to the Iron Cross for their earlier actions, full details of these awards will follow.

The final battles to finish the fighting in the Wolchow Pocket began from the 22nd of May 1942 and lasted until the end of June. In that time the *SS-Polizei Division* fought with *Heer Divisions* and destroyed what was left of the Soviet forces contained within that area. On the 27th of June *Polizei* were ordered to a new area. It is estimated that the Russians lost over one-hundred and thirty-thousand dead, wounded and taken prisoner during that long drawn out battle, along with hundreds of guns and tanks.

We will now leave *Polizei* towards the end of June 1942.

2. SS-Infantry-Brigade (mot.)

During May and June 1942 they continued their operations in the Wolchow area, around Selo Gora. The Wolchow Offensive by the Russians had been blunted somewhat and this helped to ease the pressure for the time being.

Army Group South

LAH

Their situation remained unchanged as May began, but towards the end of the month – on the 23rd – elements of the *LAH* began to move to Taganrog and then onto Mariupol. By the end of the month these moves were complete for the majority of the *LAH*.

June saw them take up new positions on the coast around Mariupol, at that time a quieter sector of the Russian Front. On the 17th of June 1942 the *V Battalion* moved into this area from their previous positions near Leningrad. No further major occurrences took place during the remainder of June 1942.

SS-Wiking Division

They remained in their positions during the months of May and June 1942. Their focus was on training and improving their general situation. One noticeable change was the arrival of an integral *Panzer Abteilung*, making *Wiking* the first *Waffen-SS* formation to receive the addition of a tank unit at the front lines.

1. SS-Infantry Brigade (mot.)

There is no precise detail on this unit during this time.

We will now cover the details of some of the recent Knight's Cross recipients.

Georg Bochmann
Date of Birth: 18.09.1913
SS Number: 122 362
Born in Albenau, he served in the *Hitler Youth* between the 1st of October 1930 and the 2nd of May 1933, he had joined the *SS* on the 14th of March the same year, serving with the *2. Kompanie, 7. SS-Standarte*. From 1933 through to 1936 he rose up through the ranks and by the 20th of April 1936 he had attained the rank of *SS-Untersturmführer.* He served within various *Kompanies* within the *Totenkopf Sturmbann 'Sachsen'*, staying there until he had reached the rank of *SS-Obersturmführer* on the 20th of April 1937, he then moved to *Totenkopf Sturmbann 'Oberbayern'*. He also attended various training courses prior to the war and on the 26th of August 1939 he moved to the rank of *SS-Hauptsturmführer.*

He continued his attendance at various training courses after the outbreak of World War II. He was awarded the Second Class Iron Cross on the 20th of June 1940. By late March 1941 he was commanding the *2. Kompanie* within *Totenkopf's, Panzerjaeger Abteilung*. On the 8th of July 1941 he was awarded the First Class Iron Cross and followed this with the award of the Black Wound Badge. Prior to the end of 1941 he was commanding the entire *Panzerjaeger Abteilung*. He was promoted further to the rank of *SS-Sturmbannführer* on the 20th of April 1942. Just over one week later, on the 28th, he was recommended for the Knight's Cross to the Iron Cross by *Generaloberst* Ernst Busch. This was counter-signed by *Generaloberst* von Kuchler and finally approved and signed by Keitel on the 3rd of May 1942.

A few days prior to the 28th of April he was fighting with his *Kameraden* within the Demjansk Pocket. He had command of a variety of units, at that time known as *Kampfgruppe Bochmann*. With this *Kampgruppe,* he played a successful part in opening the pocket and linking with friendly forces. They began their battle on the 14th of April and for ten days pushed against a determined enemy until they achieved success.

Four days later *Generaloberst* Busch penned the recommendation for Bochmann's Knight's Cross. It is of note that this recommendation mentions Bochmann as an *SS-Hauptsturmführer,* although he had been officially promoted to *SS-Sturmbannführer* on the 20th of April 1942. It is possible that the news of his promotion had not made it through to the front lines by that stage? The recommendation reads as follows:

> '*SS-Hauptsturmführer* Bochmann, at the lead of his *Battalion*, played a significant role in the attack of *Gruppe Eicke*. Under strong leadership and brave personal action of the *Commander*, *KG Bochmann* was successful in

SS-Sturmbannführer Georg Bochmann pictured after his award of the Knight's Cross to the Iron Cross.

carrying out the taking of Nov. Ramuschevo in very hard fighting, which took place on the evening of April 21st.

SS-Hauptsturmführer Bochmann, under his own decision, pushed his *Battalion* forward. In close combat with bayonets, thirteen 2.2-cm cannon and six tractors were taken as booty.

From Nov. Ramuschevo came this first direct contact through visual signals from the leading attacking elements of the *Gruppe von Seydlitz* and also from elements on the west bank of the Lovat River.

It is requested that *SS-Hauptsturmführer* Bochmann, in recognition of his personal excellent action and the value of his success until taking up contact with von Seydlitz be rewarded with the Knight's Cross to the Iron Cross.'

As highlighted above, this recommendation was counter-signed by von Kuchler and Keitel and approved less than one week later on the 3rd of May 1942. It would not be Bochmann's only association with the Knight's Cross and its' various grades. More details of this will follow in future volumes.

Max Seela

Date of Birth: 15.07.1911

SS Number: 257 323

Born in Schoneiche, he served in the *S.A.* from August 1929 until late March 1935. He then moved to the rank of *SS-Untersturmführer* and served on the Staff of the *Reichsführer-SS*. On the 20th of April 1936 he was promoted to *SS-Obersturmführer*. In the pre-war years he moved between the *Reichsführer-SS Haupt Amt* and various *Pioneer* units.

On the 1st of November 1939 he moved to the newly created *SS-Totenkopf Division*. At the end of January 1940 he was promoted to *SS-Hauptsturmführer*. He was awarded the Second Class Iron Cross on the 31st of May 1940, followed by the award of the First Class Iron Cross on the 22nd June 1940, both whilst fighting in the west. He was then awarded the German Cross in Gold on the 26th of December 1941, by that time he was the *Commanding Officer* of the *3. Kompanie* within *Totenkopf's, Pioneer Battalion*. Like their *Kameraden* they were sealed within the Demjansk Pocket from February 1942. Max Seela fought within *Kampfgruppe Ullrich* around Kobylkina. They broke out of that area and joined Eicke in the main pocket area at the end of February.

On the 1st of March 1942 Eicke wrote the recommendation for Seela's Knight's Cross, which contained the following:

An autographed photograph of Max Seela, taken after his award of the Knight's Cross. Some of his other awards, such as the German Cross in Gold, General Assault Badge and Black Wound Badge can also be clearly seen.

'*SS-Hauptsturmführer* Seela, stood after returning from his convalescence beginning in January in Staraja Russa. He assembled a *Kompanie* around Lipowitzy, southeast of Staraja Russa.

After the breakthrough of the Russians over the Lowat River in the fighting at the end of January *SS-Hauptsturmführer* Seela, with the *Kampfgruppe Ullrich* defended the village of Korowtschina on the 24th of February.

Although with the heaviest tanks, violent artillery and numerous aircraft, the Russians uninteruptingly attacked and succeeded in gaining the southern part of the village. *SS-Hauptsturmführer* Seela in heroic and courageous battle prevented them in taking the village and succeeded in taking the bridge over the Lowat.

In spite of the stronger enemy and only partial successful provision from the air by the *Luftwaffe,* Seela again and again led his exhausted men and threw the Russians, although they were on three sides, out and forced them to retreat.

When on the 24th of February 1942 the command for the *Kampfgruppe* to retreat came through, Seela, although injured, made it back to new positions.

I ask that *SS-Hauptsturmführer* Seela, in recognition of his heroic courageous battle, be awarded the Knight's Cross to the Iron Cross.'

Max Seela's award was approved on the 3rd of May, the same day as Bochmann's. Following on from his award of this coveted medal he received a further promotion at the start of September 1942 to *SS-Sturmbannführer.* By mid-January 1944 he was the *Commander* of the *Pioneer Replacement Battalion* in Dresden. Less then three-months later he was serving with the *II SS-Panzer Korps*. He finished the war as a *Regimental Commander* within the *9. SS Panzer Division 'Hohenstaufen'*. He survived the war and died on the 31st of July 1999.

Otto Baum

Date of Birth: 15.11.1911

SS Number: 237 056

Born in Steeten, he joined the *SS* at the start of November 1933 and served initially with the *13. SS Standarte*. He moved to the *SS-VT* on the 6th of March 1934, serving with *Germania*. Towards the end of April 1935 he went to Braunschweig to begin officer training and by November the same year he was holding the rank of *SS-Standartenjunker.* He followed this by attending a *Zugführer's* course in early January 1936 and by the start of April the same year he was serving with the *II Battalion, Germania* and was now holding the rank of *SS-Standartenoberjunker.*

SS-Obersturmbannführer Otto Baum photographed after his award of the Knight's Cross; made for actions whilst serving as an SS-Sturmbannführer in the Demjansk pocket.

On the 20th of April 1936 he was promoted to *SS-Untersturmführer.* His next promotion came on the 12th of September 1937, this time to *SS-Obersturmführer.* At the start of May 1938 he began a spell serving with the newly created *SS-Regiment Der Führer.* Just over one year later, in mid-1939, he had moved to the *LAH.* Whilst with the *LAH* in Poland, he was awarded the Second Class Iron Cross, on the 25th of September 1939. Another promotion, to the rank of *SS-Hauptsturmführer,* came on the 9th of November 1939. He went west with the rest of the *German Army* in 1940 and was awarded the First Class Iron Cross on the 15th of June. In early March of 1941 he moved to the *SS-Totenkopf Division* and he was also promoted higher to the rank of *SS-Sturmbannführer.* He was given command of the *III Battalion, SS-Totenkopf Infantry Regiment 3* and he led this unit eastwards as they entered Russia in mid-1941. On the 26th of December the same year he was awarded the German Cross in Gold.

Whilst with the same *Battalion* he was caught up in the fighting around Demjansk, fighting which resulted in his recommendation for the Knight's Cross to the Iron Cross. This recommendation was written by Theodore Eicke and contained the following:

> '*SS-Sturmbannführer* Baum defended his sector near Salutschje and has actively participated in the fighting against attacks by superior forces since February 23rd, 1942.
>
> On February 7th 1942 at 0020 hours the Russians attacked after barraging the positions of Baum's *Battalion* with heavy artillery and grenade launchers after boxing in Baum's unit along the line connecting the village of Schumilkino and Salutschje. The Russian infantry was also supported by tanks. (This recommendation lists the various enemy units fighting in this area).
>
> Due to heavy casualties of the weakening *Battalion*, the Russians were able to penetrate the northern sector of Schumilkino and the southern area of Salutschje. These penetrations only took place after bitter night fighting.
>
> In response to the situation, *SS-Sturmbannführer* Baum gathered several of his men and part of a *Platoon* sent up to reinforce his units. On his own initiative and without regard for his own life, he accompanied these men in a counter-attack and annihilated the enemy troops that had penetrated his positions in both Schumilkino and Salutschje.
>
> At 0630 on the same day, the main fighting line was secured. All enemy attacks collapsed under heavy defensive fire along the main fighting line. After the conclusion of the fighting, Baum's units counted over 300 dead Russians lying in front of their positions.

> The holding of the position of Baum's *Battalion* was of decisive importance, since a Russian breakthrough would have put our positions in the north and east in danger of being overrun. In addition to that, it would have given the Russians the opportunity to take control of the highway between Kobylkino and Schubina. Control of this highway would have given the enemy the ability to supply materials as well as additional troops to their positions in the northern, western and southern fronts in Bicke. I request that *SS-Sturmbannführer* Baum be awarded the Knight's Cross to the Iron Cross in recognition of his heroic bravery and the resulting decisive success of his actions'.

This recommendation was approved on the 8th of May 1942 and it would not be Otto Baum's only link to the various grades of the Knight's Cross, nor would it be the end of Baum's career in the *Waffen-SS*. More details of those occurrences will follow in later volumes of this work.

Dr Eduard Deisenhofer
Date of Birth: 27.06.1909
SS Number: 3 642
Born in Freising, he entered the *Allgemeine-SS* at the start of October 1930, serving with the *57. SS-Standarte*. By early July 1932 he had achieved the rank of *SS-Scharführer (SS-Unterscharführer)*, followed by *SS-Truppführer (SS-Oberscharführer)* on the 17th of May 1933 and further still on the 21st of August the same year to *SS-Obertruppführer (SS-Hauptscharführer)*. His first officer rank was obtained on the 9th of November 1933 when he became an *SS-Sturmführer (SS-Untersturmführer)*, by this time he was serving with the *2. Kompanie, I Battalion, 56. SS-Standarte*. Less than six-months later, on the 24th of April 1934, he was promoted to *SS-Obersturmführer*, serving within *SS* Area South. Less than two months later he had moved to *SS-Regiment Deutschland* and by late October he had moved again, this time to the *II Battalion, SS-Regiment Germania*. By late February 1935 he was holding the post of *Training Officer* at Dachau. At the start of April he was with the *I Battalion, Totenkopf 'Oberbayern'*. In mid-September 1935 he had been promoted to *SS-Hauptsturmführer*, staying within the *Totenkopfverbande* from then until 1939. He had been promoted to *SS-Sturmbannführer* back at the start of October 1938. By mid-October 1939 he was commanding the *II Battalion, Totenkopf Infantry Regiment 1*. He had already acquired the Austrian and Czech medals by that time.

Moving with *Totenkopf* westwards in May 1940, he was awarded the Black Wound Badge on the 20th of June, for wounds received back in May. This was

A formal portrait of Dr. Eduard Deisenhofer taken after his award of the Knight's Cross.

followed on the 26th of June by the award of both the Second and First Class Iron Crosses. He was away from the front lines recovering from this wound and after that, spent time with *II Battalion 'Nordwest'* and the *Infantry Replacement Battalion 'Ost'*. By the middle of August 1941 he was commanding the *I Battalion, SS-Infantry Regiment 9*. In February 1942 he was back with the *Totenkopf Division,* commanding the *I Battalion, SS-Totenkopf Infantry Regiment 1*. It was with this *Battalion* that he was caught up in the fighting around Demjansk. It was for this fighting that he was awarded the Knight's Cross to the Iron Cross in early May1942. His actions included the following:

> At the beginning of February 1942 five *Divisions* of the *Army* were caught up in the Demjansk Pocket. The enemy had men and material superiority and they were pushing on all sides against the pocket. The enemy felt that the terrible cold, the hunger and poor shelter offered to the Germans would cause their courage to fail. This situation lasted for weeks and the replacement troops did not arrive. Supply to the trapped troops from the air was difficult and the supplies of ammunition and food ran low. The Germans inside this pocket held out for three months. In bitter fighting that raged through the day and night, they stopped the enemy in front of their positions. The more difficult the fighting became, the stronger and more determined the men grew.

SS-Sturmbannführer Deisenhofer had the responsibility on his shoulders and his personal courage and coolness during critical moments and his contempt for his own safety was decisive for the *Battalion*. His men trusted him, they were all *Kameraden*. They knew what was demanded of them and that it was necessary as they were the last reserves.

SS-Sturmbannführer Deisenhofer defended twenty-three enemy attacks around the village of Nish and Ssossnowka over seventeen days and inflicted heavy bloody losses on the enemy. Over one-thousand enemy died in front of their positions. Within the Demjansk Pocket Deisenhofer took two *Kompanies* of the *I Battalion,* the last defenses against the enemy in the west part of the pocket. A Soviet *Battalion* defended Nowosselje, but with fast attacks Deisenhofer took this village in the night. The enemy left uncounted dead, prisoners and large quantities of equipment behind. Later in the night the enemy attacked again and penetrated with three heavy tanks into the southwest of the the village. Despite being outnumbered by the enemy, *SS-Sturmbannführer* Deisenhofer's men pushed against them. In bitter close combat, he was wounded again, but they held the town and threw the enemy out.

It is not known who wrote the recommendation for the Knight's Cross, but it was approved on the 8th of May 1942. Just prior to this, on the 20th of April, he had been promoted to *SS-Obersturmbannführer*. Also, on the 29th of April, he had been awarded the German Cross in Gold.

From September 1942 he spent a one-year stint as an instructor in Bad Tolz, following this with various other teaching posts until March 1944. He then took command of *SS-Regiment 21, 10th SS-Division 'Frundsberg'*. He was promoted to *SS-Standartenführer* on the 20th of April 1944 and by August the same year he was a reserve Officer and he held temporary command of the *SS 'Gotz von Berlichingen' Division*. He then moved to Romania and received a promotion to *SS-Oberführer* at the start of January 1945 and by then was commanding his own *Kampfgruppe*. He was killed at the end of January 1945 in Arnswalde by the Russians.

Besides winning the Knight's Cross to the Iron Cross and other awards listed above, he also was awarded the Infantry Assault Badge, Silver Wound Badge and Russian Front Medal.

Rudolf Pannier

Date of Birth: 10.07.1897

SS Number: 465 891

Born in Gera, he seen military service during the First World War and after the war also fought with the *Freikorps* in 1919 and 1920. He joined the police on the 7th of January 1920 and stayed with them until the end of 1933, serving in the Hamburg area. In that time he was promoted to *Leutnant* at the start of April 1924, *Oberleutnant* at the start of July 1927 and *Hauptmann der Polizei* on the first day of April 1932. He held a variety of posts that included *Battalion Adjutant* and attended many training courses, as well as becoming a training intructor. He then ended his service in the police.

As the Second World War broke out he was once again swept up in the service of his country. By October 1941 he was serving within the *Polizei Division* and by early January 1942 he was holding the rank of *SS-Sturmbannführer* and was in command of the *I Battalion, Polizei-Schutzen Regiment 2*. It was with this unit that he would win the Knight's Cross for actions in late January 1942. An overview of his actions are as follows.

From the 20th of January until the 5th of February 1942 Pannier and his *Battalion* arrived in the area between Ljubino Pole and Motski, where they took on the defense of that area. Strong Russian forces moved towards them and encircled them by the 23rd of January. Strong enemy attacks were launched over the 25th and 26th and included tank, artillery, mortar and aerial attacks, which

An autographed portrait of SS-Sturmbannführer Rudolf Pannier photographed after his award of the Knight's Cross to the Iron Cross. He is seen here wearing his police style uniform.

were launched on all sides. On the 28th and 29th there was a heavy enemy attack in the south that penetrated the German positions, a German counter-attack restored the situation.

Relief attempts towards Pannier's men failed at the end of January. This was then followed by a major attempt to relieve Motski on the 2nd of February. *SS-Sturmbannführer* Pannier could not move forward as no forces were sent as far as Ljubino Pole. Pannier was not prepared to leave his positions for the enemy to take them over. Pannier remained in Ljubino Pole awaiting relief, during this time the Russians made repeated attacks against their positions, but to no avail. Ljubino Pole remained in the hands of Pannier and his men until the end of the first week in February 1942, when a *Heer* unit relieved them. During the battle he cared for the wounded and ensured that they were evacuated on the 2nd of February to the north.

Even this relief was made difficult as the enemy attacked in the middle of the hand-over, but the situation was restored. On the 8th of February Pannier and his survivors from the *I Battalion* moved to Puschkin, at this stage there were only 80 of them left. They were placed into reserve at this point.

At the start of April Wunnenberg wrote the recommendation for Pannier's Knight's Cross, which included:

> 'They had little supplies from the air and *SS-Sturmbannführer* Pannier was constantly active and this time was a heavy test of his resolve. In recognition of his exemplary courage, Pannier encouraged his troops to the highest achievements and they held their positions for fourteen days against strong attacks on all sides. In the most critical hour, he grasped the decision, contrary to orders. Thanks to his decision, the enemy could not expand the area under their control and push north.
>
> On the basis of the achievements detailed I ask that *SS-Sturmbannführer* Pannier be honoured with the award of the Knight's Cross to the Iron Cross'.

General Lindemann also gave a glowing view of Pannier's success: 'Thanks to your hardness and steadfast fighting spirit, you have achieved superhuman results and given the *Army* a shining example of the highest devotion to duty'.

This recommendation was approved on the 11th of May 1942. Pannier had recently won both classes of the Iron Cross, the Second Class Iron Cross towards the end of January and the First Class Iron Cross on the 5th of February – both whilst engaged in the fighting detailed above.

After this award Pannier became the *Chief of Staff Befehlshaber der Waffen-SS* in Holland. By autumn the same year he was *Commander* of a recruit depot for the police in Debica, staying in that role until mid-1943. He had been promoted to *SS-Obersturmbannführer* back at the start of January 1943 and followed this by a further promotion to *SS-Standartenführer* on the 9th of November 1943. After his role with the recruit depot he then moved to the command of a *Jaeger Regiment* fighting against partisans in Estonia and Latvia. He was awarded the German Cross in Gold on the 28th of April 1944. By September 1944 he was commanding *SS-Regiment 31, 14th SS Division 'Galizien'*. He was later heavily wounded and spent a long peiod of convalescence in hospital. During the war he was also awarded the Black Wound Badge and the Silver Wound Badge.

At the end of the war he spent time in Russian, British and American captivity, finally being released in 1948. He died in August 1978 in Hamburg.

Helmut Dorner
Date of Birth: 26.06.1909
SS Number: 422 756
Born in Munchen-Gladbach, he entered the police on the 6th of October 1927 and stayed in the police until the middle of March 1933, he then moved to the *Army*. At the start of November 1934 he was back with the police. From August 1936 until March 1937 he began officer training and by May the same year was commissioned as a *Leutnant*. He rose to the rank of *Oberleutnant* at the end of January 1938 and further still to *Hauptmann* in September 1939.

As the Second World War began, he moved to the *Polizei Division* in late November 1939. He served as a *Battalion Adjutant* and *Kompanie Commander*, fighting in the west during 1940, where he won both classes of the Iron Cross. He was also awarded the Black Wound Badge on the 15th of August 1941, the Infantry Assault Badge on the 2nd of October and the German Cross in Gold on the 24th of December 1941.

On the 5th of January 1942 he was promoted to *Major der Polizei* and by the end of the same month was in command of *Polizei's, II Battalion, Schutzen Regiment 2*.

On the 27th of January 1942 his group was responsible for the destruction of fifty-eight enemy bunkers in the fighting around Leningrad. From the 10th of February until the 4th of March Dorner and his *Battalion* were fighting as a *Kampfgruppe* in the pocket west of the main road used by the Russians, they set about cutting the supply route used by the Russians.

His *Battalion* succeeded thanks to the care, leadership and courage of Dorner. Despite suffering from slight frostbite, they fought through dense forests and deep

Helmut Dorner (centre) photographed on the day of his Knight's Cross presentation.

snow. On the 17th of February they were fighting at Nesterkowo and Glubowo, the following day they were fighting in the forest at Saokino. By the 20th they were two kilometres northeast of Saokino and the following day they were engaging strong enemy forces one kilometre southwards of Konatschki. On the 26th of February his group had fought to block Gorka and the supply route used by the Russians in that area.

A letter was written by the *225 Infantry Division* highlighting his achievements:

> 'In the attack by the *Polizei Division* to close the gap between Spaskaja and Mjassnoj Borwurde, Dorner and his men were in the front line of the fighting. They fought through thick brushwood and knee-deep snow and prepared themselves for the coming attack. On the 15th of March 1942 at 20:30 hours, they took the forest strongpoint at Point 659. An immediate Russian counter-attack came in the early hours of the 16th, but this was successfully beaten off. At 23:00 hours they were able to reach Point 667, where the troops were able to rest and eat for the first time.
>
> On the 17th and 18th of March the *Battalion* engaged in heavy fighting with the Russians in the southeast, then west, then further south and reached Point 692 after non-stop fighting. They blocked the Russian supply route despite the strongest of enemy resistance to the east and west.
>
> Although Dorner and his men had been fighting for five days non-stop they successfully achieved the objectives. Cool decisions and the correct recognition of the situation as it unfolded, fighting at the lead of the *I Battalion* and attacked the supply route of the Russian *305th Infantry Division*. They then constructed a security line to the south, east and west, pushed further south and linked with the advance group of the *58th Infantry Division*, thereby linking with the *XXXVIII Armee Korps*. All of this was as a result of *Major* Dorner's own decisions and courage. For five days he fought in the midst of two Russian *Armies*. Dorner, his decisions resulted in major achievements and caused extraordinary success against the enemy.
>
> I ask that that Dorner be considered for the award of the Knight's Cross to the Iron Cross'.

This overall recommendation was approved on the 15th of May 1942, but would not be his only connection to this award or its' various grades. Details of the further awards will follow in later volumes of this work.

Otto Wilhelm Kron

Date of Birth: 28.02.1911

SS Number: 31 441

Born in Speyer, he served with the *Hitler Youth* from September 1930 for one year. He then moved to the *SS* on the 1st of October 1931 and just over one year later he had achieved the rank of *SS-Scharführer (SS-Unterscharführer)*. Further promotions came with *SS-Oberscharführer (SS-Scharführer)* at the start of December 1933 and *SS-Truppführer (SS-Oberscharführer)* at the start of April 1934. In between then and the start of June 1935 he must have attended one of the *SS* Officer Schools as he was promoted to *SS-Untersturmführer* on that date. He served with the *I Battalion, SS-Totenkopf Standarte 'Oberbayern'* around this time and followed this with service in various *Totenkopf* units pre-war. By the middle of September 1936 he had risen to *SS-Obersturmführer* and further still to *SS-Hauptsturmführer* on the 2nd of October 1938. He took part in the marches into Austria and the Sudetenland.

He advanced westwards in 1940 with the *Totenkopf Division* and on the 22nd of June was awarded the Second Class Iron Cross. He then went eastwards in mid-1941, where his *Flak* unit successfully engaged and destroyed Russian aircraft and tanks. He was awarded the First Class Iron Cross on the 19th of December 1941.

In early 1942 he was trapped inside the Demjansk Pocket along with his *Totenkopf Division Kameraden*. At that time he was *Commander* of a *Kampfgruppe* within the *Flak Abteilung 3*. In late April 1942 he was involved in heavy fighting just after the 'Land Bridge' had been opened. In was for these actions that he was recommended for the Knight's Cross to the Iron Cross by his *Divisional Commander*, Theodore Eicke. It was written on the 26th of June 1942 and contained the following:

> '*SS-Hauptsturmführer* Kron had already proved himself during the hard winter months in defense of Molwatizy. He commanded a *Kampfgruppe* during *Operation Fallreep* in the night of 24th and 25th of April 1942 and they advanced fast over the Wileny Stream and formed a bridgehead, despite heavy enemy resistance. Showing bravery in the course of the attack, *SS-Hauptsturmführer* Kron covered the right flank and constructed a defensive line to the east against the Sutschan Swamp.
>
> In the night of the 25th of April 1942 fresh strong attacks by the enemy from the east in the forest west and southwest of Alexandrowka, the advance of his own troops threatened his own flank. Heavy bloody fighting followed and the enemy succeeded in breaking into their positions.

A formal portrait of Otto-Wilhelm Kron taken after his award of the Knight's Cross.

Another photograph of Otto Kron, taken during a visit to one of his Flak units.

> Recognising the threat to his flank, he swung his attack around and attacked the advancing enemy. In bloody fighting in the swamp, they succeeded in smashing the advance. Displaying personal courage, *SS-Hauptsturmführer* Kron's struggle resulted in a high share of the successful conclusion of *Fallreep,* opening the ring around Demjansk.
>
> I ask that this courageous, brave Officer and the successes connected to his actions be honoured with the award of the Knight's Cross to the Iron Cross.'

This recommendation was counter-signed by Graf von Brockendorff, the *Commander* of the *II Armee Korps* and also *Generaloberst* Busch, the *Commander* of the *16. Armee*. They both agreed to the award of the Knight's Cross to Otto Kron.

This award was approved two days later on the 28th of June 1942. Kron's award was not the last one that came as a result of the actions within the Demjansk Pocket. Otto Kron had been promoted to *SS-Sturmbannführer* on the 21st of April 1942, although his recommendation still referred to him as an *SS-Hauptsturmführer.* After the successes listed above he commanded a *Kampfgruppe* and was involved in heavy fighting during the summer and into the new year of 1943.

He then commanded *Aufklarungs Abteilung 3* and was heavily wounded. In late August 1943 he was commanding the *Training and Replacement Battalion 'Ellwangen'*. On the 20th of April 1944 he was promoted to *SS-Obersturmbannführer.* He survived the war, dying on the 9th of August 1955.

CHAPTER NINE

BARBAROSSA YEAR TWO - JULY 1942 ONWARDS

We have detailed the various *Waffen-SS* actions up to the end of June 1942. This meant that the *German Army* had been fighting the Soviets for one full year. Although none of the soldiers involved knew it then, they would continue this fight for almost three more years. Before detailing that, let us remain to the present situation at the start of July 1942.

Adolf Hitler had stated, 'All that is needed was to kick in the door and the whole rotten edifice would come crashing down'. However, despite one year of difficult fighting, this had not taken place yet. The German surprise attack had caught the Russians off-guard. Hitler's troops stormed into the vast Russian countryside in all directions and succeeded in making some key gains. By the end of 1941 Leningrad, Moscow and Rostov had been reached, with *Waffen-SS* soldiers in the lead in all three areas. Hundreds of thousands of enemy prisoners had been taken, but then the tables turned.

The opening phase of 1942 had seen the initiative pass to the soldiers of Josef Stalin. Massive counter-offensives smashed into the German held positions and the danger of complete destruction loomed for Hitler's men. His troops stood fast and stemmed the flood for the time being. This required a huge effort on their part and produced many acts of bravery and heroism, as already detailed in the preceeding pages. The result from all of this was a stalemate situation by the end of this first year on Russian soil. So what came next?

To re-take the initiative, Hitler's troops needed to push further into Russia and not allow the Soviets to gain strength. To do this effectively required a number of changes. The various *Waffen-SS* units engaged at that time would be affected by these changes in different ways. Some of them would be withdrawn and rebuilt in Germany and the terriroties west of the Soviet Union. Others would remain in situ, whilst others would be pushed deeper into Russia. Let us now highlight these changes, their affects and their results, during the remainder of 1942, covering firstly the period of July, August and September.

Army Group North

SS-Polizei-Division

We last covered the *SS-Polizei-Division* towards the end of June, as they finished their fighting around the Wolchow Pocket. As June drew to a close however, they were put on the move once more.

They were sent to the area around Kolpino, southeast of Leningrad, close to the Newa River. This took them back to the main defensive ring around the city, but brought them within twelve miles of the centre, closer than they had probably been before. Their moves to this area were completed by the middle of July 1942.

In the third week of July the Russians launched an offensive in this area, although it was not until the start of August that the Russian attacks hit the positions of the *SS-Polizei Division* itself. Losses for this unit quickly mounted against the enemy onslaught, which included artillery and tank support. The enemy made inroads from the north and west and the *SS-Polizei Division's* efforts were focused on mounting counter-attacks to regain lost ground or stem the push by the enemy. Replacements arrived in the first half of August and they couldn't have come at a better time. *Polizei* had suffered hundreds of casualties since the start of August alone.

These enemy attacks proceeded on into mid-August, *Regiment 3* and *Regiment 1* were especially hard hit. The main focus of these attacks was in the area where the Tossna River heads south, off the Newa River. This battle unleashed itself on the 19th of August 1942 and it took the whole of this first day and a great exertion of effort to keep the strong enemy penetrations from gaining complete success. It was during this day that *SS-Unterscharführer* Rudolf Seitz excelled himself and played his part in thwarting the enemie's plans. (These actions resulted in the award of the Knight's Cross and will be detailed later on). This difficult situation continued through the rest of August with the Soviets pushing more and more men into this area, whilst the men of the *SS-Polizei Division* attempted to hold and regain positions, as well as defeat these enemy incursions.

After a brief respite at the start of September, the fighting resumed. Back in August, Hitler had ordered for the attack on Leningrad to continue and achieve complete success. It would appear that this coincided with the Russian desire to extend the area under their control. Both sides fed more and more troops into the Leningrad mincing machine. The fighting died down around the 10th of September, after the Russians had suffered thousands of casualties, without achieving their intended targets and objectives. The remainder of September did see some smaller attacks against elements of *Polizei*, but these men successfully held their own.

At the end of September two soldiers of *Polizei* were recognnised for their part in the recent battle. *SS-Standartenführer* Otto Gieseke and *SS-Sturmbannführer* Karl Schumers were both awarded the Knight's Cross to the Iron Cross, details of both of these awards will follow later. Earlier in this month, two of their *Waffen-SS Kameraden* had received this award whilst fighting within Army Group South. Before covering them, we shall briefly cover the other *Waffen-SS* units fighting in the north.

SS-Totenkopf-Division

The situation for *Totenkopf* remained as it was at the end of June. Max Simon was in temporary command and his men were dealing with renewed enemy attacks.

Around the middle of July the situation grew worse. This was due to a new heavy attack by the Russians against all sides of the German held positions. The Russians retook Wassilijewschtschina and despite being ordered to counter-attack *Totenkopf* were in no physical condition to do so, mainly due to further heavy combat losses, but also due to illness. This situation remained as July passed into August. Poor weather provided a short respite from enemy attacks during mid-August, but it was towards the end of August that two significant occurrences took place.

The first of these came on the 28th of August when *SS-Rottenführer* Hans Hirning played a successful part in defeating enemy attempts to halt the supply to the *II Armee Korps*. For these actions he was awarded the Knight's Cross to the Iron Cross, although this would not be approved until the 23rd of October 1942, therefore full details will follow later on.

The second occurrence also came on the 28th of August when *Totenkopf* were ordered to be removed from Army Group North and sent for a refit. However, the final decision for when this would be done was left to the *Army Commanders* on the ground. The result was that *Totenkopf* would remain in this area throughout September 1942.

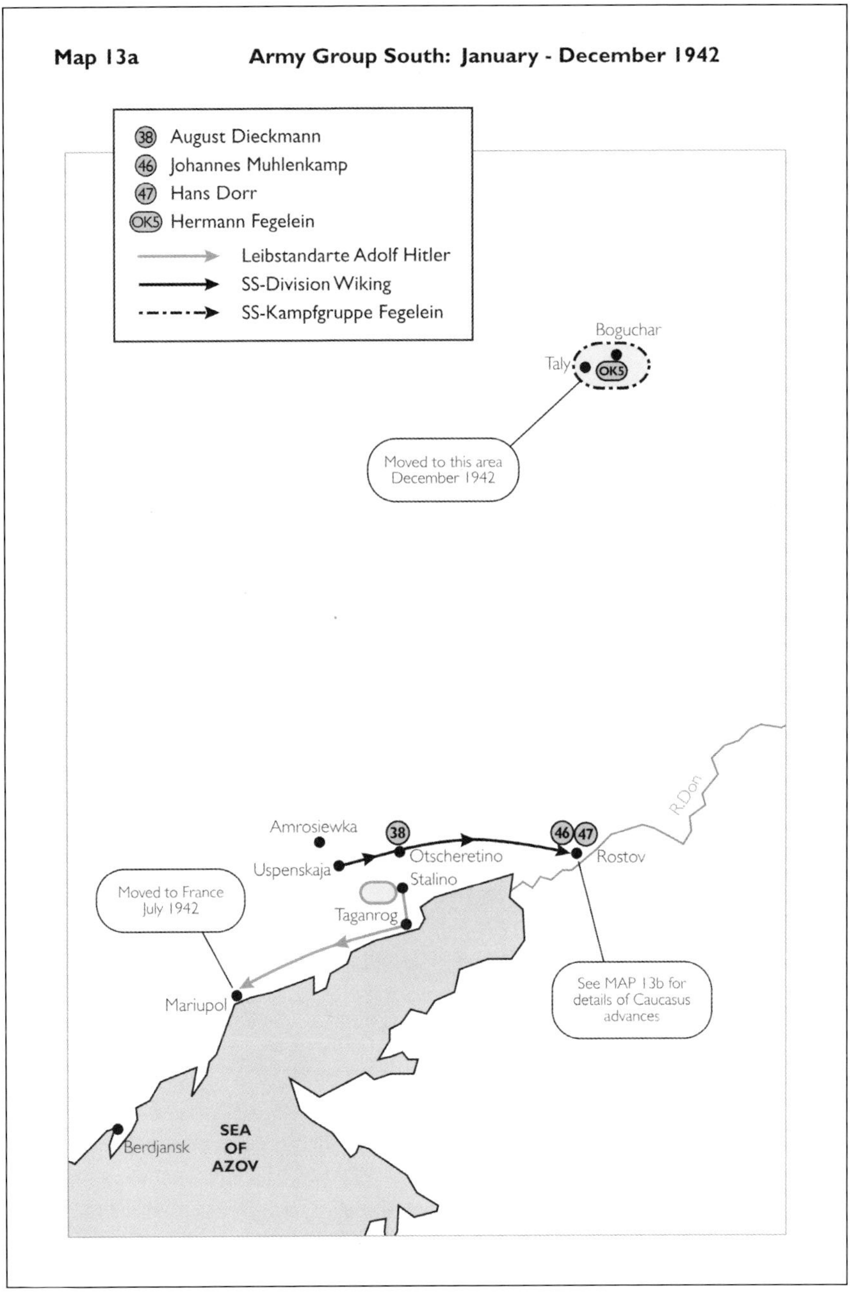

Map 13a
Army Group South: January - December 1942
38 August Dieckmann
46 Johannes Muhlenkamp
47 Hans Dorr
OK5 Hermann Fegelein
Leibstandarte Adolf Hitler
SS-Division Wiking
SS-Kampfgruppe Fegelein
Boguchar
Taly
OK5
Moved to this area December 1942
R.Don
Amrosiewka
38
46
47
Otscheretino
Rostov
Uspenskaja
Stalino
Moved to France July 1942
Taganrog
See MAP 13b for details of Caucasus advances
Mariupol
Berdjansk
SEA OF AZOV

Earlier in September *SS-Unterscharführer* August Zingel was involved in actions that would result in his later award of the Knight's Cross to the Iron Cross, full details will follow later.

2. SS-Infantry Brigade (mot.)

In July they enjoyed a relatively quieter time, but then in August they were moved north, close to Leningrad. Their new area stretched from Krasnoje-Selo through to Mga, south and southeast of Leningrad.

SS-Gebirgs-Division-Nord

We last covered *Nord* over a year earlier in July 1941 when their first action resulted in very heavy losses on the Finnish Border. Afterwards they were sent back to Germany for a major refit. They returned to Finnland in early August 1942 and took up defensive positions. During their time away they had been re-designated *SS-Gebirgs-Division-Nord* during May 1942 and had been given a new *Commander* in the shape of Matthias Kleinheisterkamp, a previous winner of the Knight's Cross with *SS-Division Reich*. Nothing of any great significance happened to *Nord* as summer turned to autumn.

Army Group South

Leibstandarte Adolf Hitler

They were moved to Mariupol in June 1942 and then in early July were ordered to move to France. By late July 1942 they were located in an area around Paris. Like *Das Reich* the *LAH* were to be made into a *Panzergrenadier-Division*. Training of the men and the use of new vehicles became the focus for the *LAH* during the months of August and September. Although the *Allied* landings in Dieppe took place and the *LAH* were placed on alert readiness, nothing came of this for the men. On the same day that *Totenkopf's* Hans Hirning was going through the actions that would result in his award of the Knight's Cross – the 28th of August 1942 – Dietrich joined Albert Speer at the landing site for an overview of what had taken place. There were no real significant changes for the *LAH* during September 1942.

Wiking

In mid-July 1942 *Wiking* were sent into action, or combat ready elements were. Their objective was to assist in the capture of Rostov and then move into the Caucausus – the prize of Rostov was once again a target for the *Waffen-SS*. For

Map 13b **Army Group South: July - December 1942 - Wiking in the Caucausus**

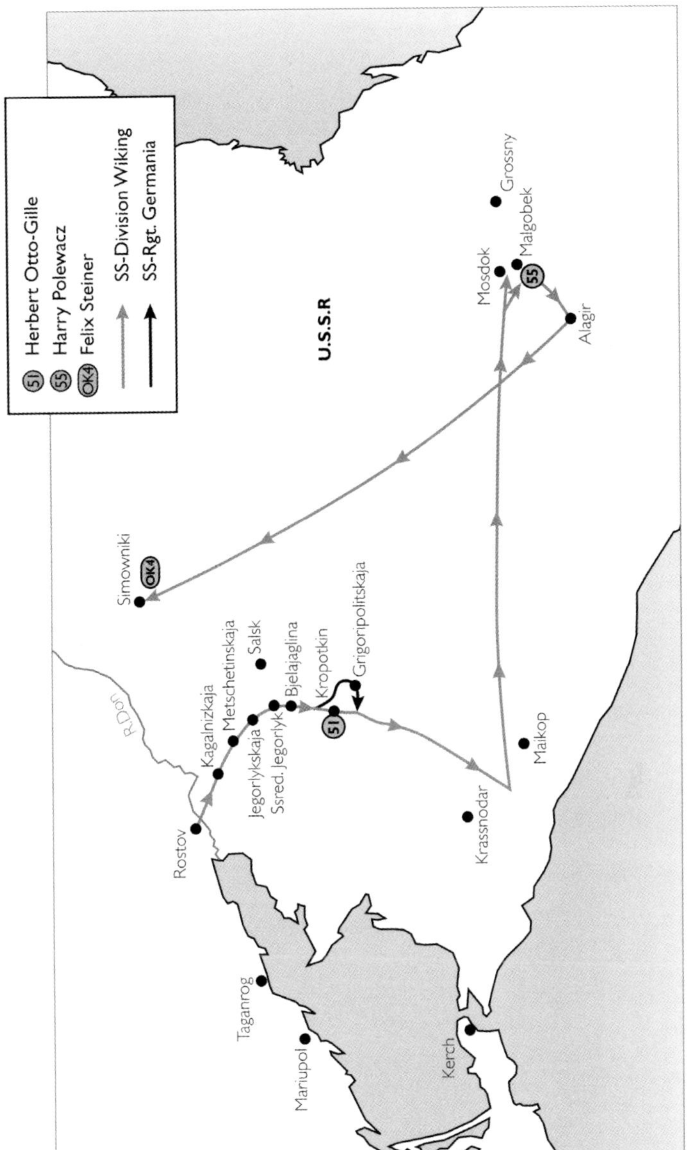

this renewed attack the recently added tanks of *Wiking's, Panzer Abteilung* would fight alongside the infantry and other units.

The men of *Wiking* had to cross three large anti-tank ditches on route to Rostov, but by the 23rd of July, men of the *Waffen-SS* had entered the city confines of Rostov. The lead elements were the *Panzer Abteilung*, under the command of *SS-Sturmbannführer* Johannes Muhlenkamp and a *Kampfgruppe* under *SS-Hauptsturmführer* Hans Dorr. Both men's actions resulted in the later award of the Knight's Cross to the Iron Cross for both of them. The significance of capturing Rostov as the gateway to the Caucausus was not lost on the *German High Command*. For the second time the battle for this key objective had earned a soldier of the *Waffen-SS* the Knight's Cross, full details of both of the two awards mentioned above will be covered later.

As highlighted previously. Army Group North and Army Group Centre's advances had been checked and only by tenacious defense had these positions been held. With the capture of Rostov in the south the advance forwards in Russia became a reality once more and the Germans would waste no time in exploiting their gains. The mighty main bridge across the wide Don River, previously captured by Heinrich Springer in November 1941, and blown up by the Soviets a day later, must have been re-built in the intervening months between then and mid-1942. This same bridge was once again blown up by the Soviets as the Germans reached the river bank. The German advance did continue southwards, but no detail exists as to where the crossing of this very wide river was made, or how!

It was also between the 29th of July and the 3rd of August 1942 that Herbert Gille was engaged in various actions that would result in his later award of the Knight's Cross, with full details following later.

The pursuit southwards and slightly to the south-east continued and by the 5th of August the Kuban River had been crossed by elements of *Wiking*, at Grigoripolitskaja, south-east of Krapotkin. This crossing is located over one-hundred and fifty miles south of Rostov. Krapotkin itself was taken on the 5th and 6th of August. The crossing of the Laben River quickly followed on the 9th of August, made by elements of the *Nordland Regiment*, under Harry Polewacz. By mid-August, elements of *Wiking* were across the Belaja River and thereby sitting within the Maikop oilfields and the Caucausus Mountains. With that, *Wiking* halted and went onto the defense, the priority now was securing this vital area.

This situation did not remain for long as in mid-September 1942 they were ordered eastwards towards Grossny; their skills were required in the eastern Caucausus instead. Earlier in the month, on the 3rd of September, Johannes Muhlenkamp had his Knight's Cross recommendation approved for his earlier successes at Rostov. By the 27th of September the various elements of *Wiking*

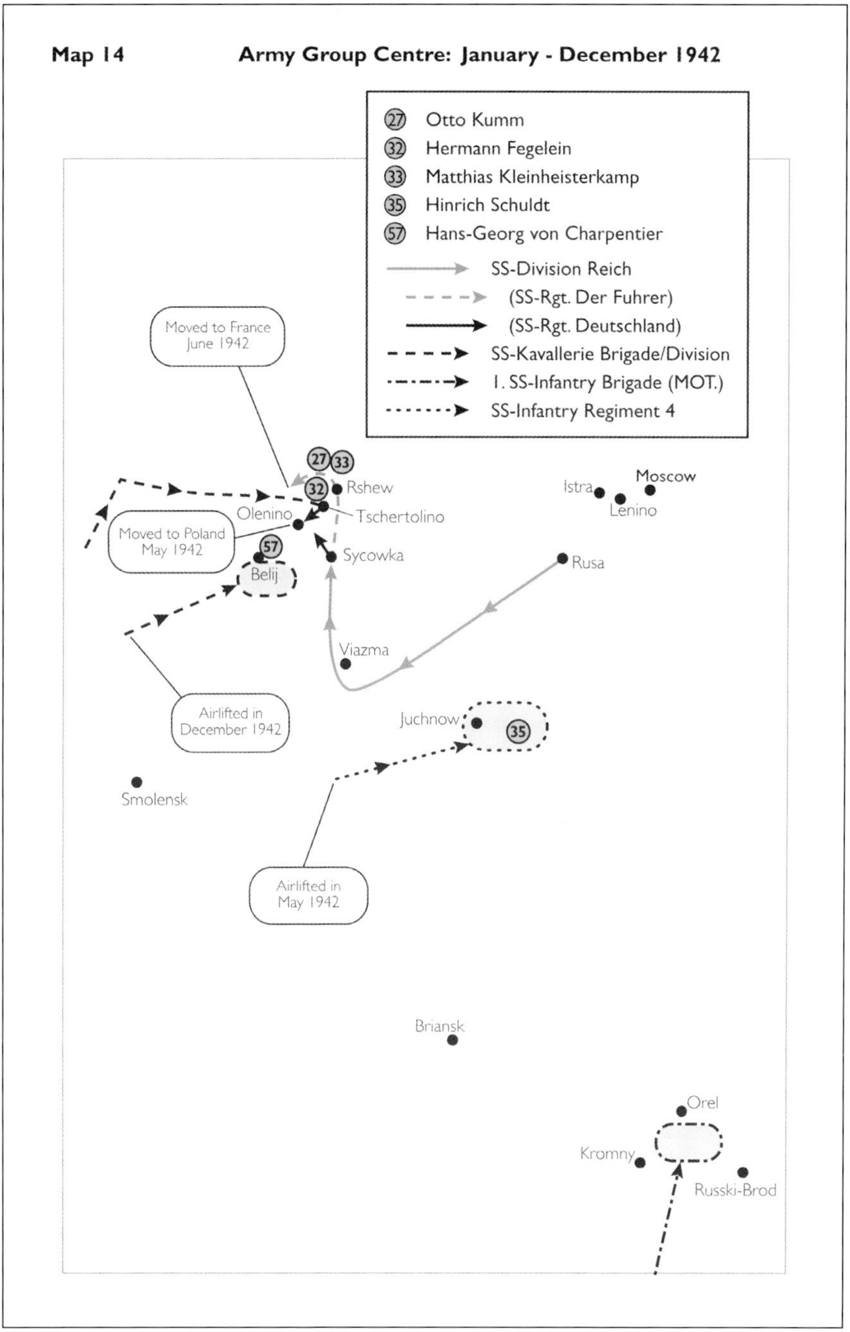
Map 14
Army Group Centre: January - December 1942
27 Otto Kumm
32 Hermann Fegelein
33 Matthias Kleinheisterkamp
35 Hinrich Schuldt
57 Hans-Georg von Charpentier
SS-Division Reich
(SS-Rgt. Der Fuhrer)
(SS-Rgt. Deutschland)
SS-Kavallerie Brigade/Division
1. SS-Infantry Brigade (MOT.)
SS-Infantry Regiment 4
Moved to France June 1942
Moved to Poland May 1942
Airlifted in December 1942
Airlifted in May 1942
Rshew
Olenino
Tschertolino
Sycowka
Belij
Istra
Moscow
Lenino
Rusa
Viazma
Juchnow
Smolensk
Briansk
Orel
Kromny
Russki-Brod

were in position in the eastern part of the Caucausus and ready for their next attack upon the town of Malgobek. This was the same day that Hans Dorr's Knight's Cross was approved.

Over the 25th and 26th of September, Harry Polewacz was involved in actions with his *I Battalion, SS-Regiment Nordland,* that would result in his later award of the Knight's Cross to the Iron Cross – more details of that will follow in the next chapter.

We will now leave the men of the *SS-Wiking Division,* fighting in the far flung Caucausus region and instead briefly cover the *Waffen-SS* formations that were part of Army Group Centre, followed by covering the recent winners of the Knight's Cross to the Iron Cross.

Army Group Centre

As previously covered, both *Waffen-SS* formations that had been employed within the above army group were removed and sent for a re-fit. The *Kavallerie Brigade* went to Poland, where they were re-fitting to become the *SS-Kavallerie-Division*. The remnants of the *SS-Division-Reich* were sent first to Germany and then onto France.

SS-Division 'Das Reich'

By late July 1942 all units of this *Division* had been moved to northern France. They had been part of Himmler's plans to increase the status of the *Waffen-SS* and were earmarked to become a *Panzer-Grenadier-Division*. Some units, such as *SS-Regiment Der Führer* had been in this area since early June, whilst the bulk of the *Division* where in Fallingbostel. Their new position during this time was around Le Mans. In mid-August this unit came under the control of the newly created *SS-Panzer-Korps,* effectively bringing them under the overall command of their former *Divisional Commander*, Paul Hausser. Training continued into September as this *Division* reached full strength once more in both men and equipment.

1st SS-Infantry-Brigade (mot.)

No specific details are available of this unit during this time.

We will now cover recent recipients of the Knight's Cross up to the end of September 1942.

Johannes Muhlenkamp
Date of Birth: 09.10.1910
SS Number: 86 065
Born in Metz, his service in the *SS* began on the first day of October 1934 when he joined the *I Battalion, SS-Regiment Germania*. Six months later he went to the officer's school at Braunschweig. He obtained the rank of *SS-Untersturmführer* on the 20th of April 1936. He moved back to *Germania,* staying with them as World War II began. By that time he had been promoted to *SS-Hauptsturmführer.*

He fought in Poland, earning himself both classes of the Iron Cross, 3rd October and 9th November 1939, respectively. He also fought in the west and the Balkans, before entering Russia in late June 1941. By January 1942 he had been awarded the German Cross in Gold, also during this month he was promoted to *SS-Sturmbannführer.*

He had commanded the *Motorcycle Kompanie* from 1938 unitl late 1940. He moved from that command to take over the *Aufklarungs Abteilung*. He stayed with that unit until he was wounded in mid-October 1941, returning to active service in February 1942. His new command was as head of *SS-Panzer Abteilung 5,* within the *SS-Wiking Division*. It was with this new unit that he led the advance to the south east towards Rostov in July 1942. This quickly culminated, on the 23rd of July, in the capture and securing of this vital objective. Four days later the *Divisional Commander*, Steiner, recommended Muhlenkamp for the Knight's Cross to the Iron Cross. It contained the following overview:

> '*SS-Sturmbannführer* Muhlenkamp, *Commander* of *SS-Panzer Abteilung 5,* as leader of an advanced detachment of the *Division* on July 22/23 1942, overran in a bold and sudden attack after a hard fight, three positions of anti-tank ditches before Rostov. By 14:30 hours on July 23rd, he had broken into the western part of the city of Rostov. He had cleared and occupied it, then has pushed further forward in a wide front until the bank of the River Don. In the course of these battles Muhlenkamp and and his unit has destroyed 19 enemy cannons, 12 anti-tank guns and captured a large number of prisoners.
>
> Through his daring and prudent handling of the unit he has contributed decisively to the breaching of the west and northwest fronts of the deeply set anti-tank ditches positions before Rostov, forcing the opponent to flee in confusion back across the Don. With that he has freed the way to Rostov and to the Don for the *Infantry Division* advancing from the north and the northwest. He has taken a decisive part in the capture of Rostov and provided the conditions for the crossing over the Don of the pursuing *73.* and *125. Infantry Divisions*.'

Johannes Muhlenkamp seen here after his award of the Knight's Cross. His was the first of many Panzer related Knight's Crosses presented to soldiers of the Waffen-SS.

This award of the Knight's Cross to the Iron Cross was approved on the 3rd of September 1942, but it would not be Muhlenkamp's only association with this award or its' higher grades. More details of this will follow in later volumes.

This award was significant for a number of reasons. It was the second time that this award had been presented to a *Waffen-SS* soldier for the fight for Rostov, a city and objective that Adolf Hitler considered essential as part of the wider battle in Russia. Muhlenkamp's *Waffen-SS Kameraden*, Heinrich Springer, had made his assault on foot towards the end of 1941, Muhlenkamp however, had pushed towards Rostov in mid-1942 wrapped in armour plate and this had helped him obtain his objective. With this in mind, this award was also the first '*panzer*' associated Knight's Cross given to a soldier of the *Waffen-SS*. It would however, not be the last as will be seen in later volumes!

Hans Dorr

Date of Birth: 07.04.1912

SS Number: 77 360

Born in Sontheim, he entered the *SS* at the start of May 1933, serving in the *29. Standarte,* spending time with the police the following year. By July 1934 he was serving with *Deutschland*, his first promotion came in October with *SS-Sturmmann*. Two further promotions came in 1935, *SS-Rottenführer* in June and *SS-Unterscharführer* in mid-November. On the 20th of April 1937 he was promoted further to *SS-Scharführer* and in October the same year he went to Bad Tolz. He left there with the rank of *SS-Standartenoberjunker* in mid-August 1938. The following month he was with *Germania* and by November he had obtained *SS-Untersturmführer* rank. He took part in the actions in the Sudetenland before World War II.

He went with *SS-Regiment Germania* into Poland in late 1939, winning the Second Class Iron Cross on the 9th of November. Promoted to *SS-Obersturmführer* at the end of January 1940 he then moved westwards in May of 1940. During that campaign he was awarded the First Class Iron Cross, on the 20th of August 1940, and also the Black Wound Badge at the start of September, for wounds received during May. His next actions were in Russia in mid-1941. By then he had spent time as a *Platoon Leader*, *Battalion Operations Officer* and *Kompanie Commander* for the *10. Kompanie, Germania*.

Towards the end of August 1941 he was awarded the Wound Badge in Silver. By early November he was commanding the *1. Kompanie* and holding the rank of *SS-Hauptsturmführer.* He was awarded the German Cross in Gold on the 19th of December. In April 1942 he was awarded the Infantry Assault Badge and the Gold Wound Badge. In June he was with the *4. Kompanie* and he moved with them towards Rostov in July.

SS-Hauptsturmführer Hans Dorr photographed after his award of the Knight's Cross.

On the 23rd of July he reached the River Don with his men, where they found that the bridges had been blown. Five days later they managed a crossing of this river and headed south. On the 2nd of August he had formed a bridgehead at Grigoripolitskaja and then had to fight in difficult close combat over the next few days in order to hold this bridgehead. On the 8th of August he pushed on further south and reached Tengenskaja. The following day he stood as the lead *Kompanie*, heading up a *Kampfgruppe* that now found itself in the Kuban region of the Soviet Union, reached after two very hard days of fighting.

The advance was made into masses of fleeing enemy who repeatedly threatened the *Kampfgruppe*, but the Germans held fast under Dorr's cool-headed leadership in the most confusing of situations. They had achieved their orders and linked with lead elements of the *16. Infantry Division*. On the 10th of August 1942 they reached Maikop.

By the 14th of August Dorr's men had taken Muk and moved on towards Apscheronskaja. They engaged in four days of bitter combat in a forest between there and Maikop. With help from the *97. Jaeger Division*, they secured this area. They overcame obstacles such as a 15 kilometre long tree barrier, as well as mines. *SS-Hauptsturmführer* Dorr led his men through personal example and achievements were made. The enemy's organized defense continually threatened the advance, but Hans Dorr was always at the focus point, personally using machine pistols and grenades in close combat, which successfully brought the *Kampfgruppe* to the river. This decisive success was due to the unselfishness of Dorr and the pushing of the attack to Chadyshenskaja is due to his leadership and personal actions.

It is not known who recommended Dorr for the Knight's Cross or when it was written. The award itself was approved on the 27th of September 1942. Earlier that same month, he had been awarded the Eastern Front Medal. This would not end Dorr's association with the Knight's Cross or its' higher grades and those further awards will be detailed in later volumes.

Otto Gieseke

Date of Birth: 24.03.1891

SS Number: 357 198

Born in Hohenhameln, his military service began in 1910 and followed on into World War I, where he earned both classes of the Iron Cross. His service during that war began in October 1914 and by December 1915 he had obtained the rank of *Leutnant,* finally ending the war with the rank of *Oberleutnant*.

He fought with the *Freikorps* between 1919 and 1921 in the Baltic region and was involved in very hard fighting with the '*Iron Division*', where he was

An autographed photo of Otto Gieseke after his award of the Knight's Cross. The photo shows him holding the rank of SS-Standartenführer, although it is signed as an SS-Oberführer. His final rank was SS-Brigadeführer und Generalmajor der Waffen-SS.

awarded the Second and First Classes of the Baltic Cross. There is then brief mention of him being in the *Schutzpolizei* in 1935 and holding the rank of *Major.* By 1939 he was *Commander* of the police in Erfurt.

He transferred to the *SS* at the start of June 1940 with the rank of *SS-Sturmbannführer.* He spent time in Fulda with the *Bezirk 67. Regular Battalion.* By the start of March 1941 he was on *Polizei's, Divisional Staff* and holding the rank of *SS-Obersturmbannführer.* On the 20th of April 1942 he moved to *SS-Standartenführer* and was in command of the *1. Polizei-Grenadier-Regiment.* In the early days of Barbarossa he earned the Clasps to both classes of the Iron Cross, 23rd of August 1941 and 7th of September 1941 respectively. He had also won the Infantry Assault Badge in late July 1942. He was then recommended for the German Cross in Gold in early August 1942, which was approved on the 12th of September. By then however, he had been involved in heavy fighting once more and on the 2nd of September Wunnenburg had recommended him for the Knight's Cross to the Iron Cross for actions between the 19th of August and the 26th of August near the Newa River. Contained within that recommendation was the following:

> 'Between the 19th and 26th of August the Russians put in non-stop attacks between the Newa and Tossna Rivers using strong troop landings, tanks, planes, cannonboats, destroyers and fast attack boats. Their objective was to take control of the mouth of the Tossna River. These intense attacks succeeded in establishing a bridgehead on the east bank of the Tossna River. *SS-Standartenführer* Gieseke's *1. Regiment* bore the full weight of the heavy enemy artillery attacks and infantry weapon attacks, especially on the right flank.
>
> This was almost non-stop during the 19/20 August, then again on the 22nd of August. The enemy then attacked with two regiments under the cover of fog towards the Kirow railroad. This attack successfully brought the Russians to both sides of the Tossna and breached our positions.
>
> *SS-Standartenführer* Gieseke, *Commander* of the *1. Regiment,* reads the messages coming in and as quick as lightning recognizes the bigger threat. The losses on his right and the whole eastern sector, he uses the reserve *Kompanie* and all other available men, drivers and other 'rear-line' men. News also arrived from the artillery observers that there were attacks to the north. *SS-Standartenführer* Gieseke now knew that the threat of the *Regiment* being cut-off was there. *SS-Standartenführer* Gieseke personally led the *Kompanie's* in the attack and in bitter fighting *SS-Standartenführer* Gieseke caused heavy, bloody losses on the enemy using weapons and mortars.

> The enemy wasted no time in trying to gain ground, but *SS-Standartenführer* Gieseke destroyed the masses of the enemy troops, the remainder were thrown back.
>
> *SS-Standartenführer* Gieseke produced a decisive outcome and through his personal actions, brought the railroad and road bridge back into our possession. Only this decision is to be thanked for denying the Russians new gains in the fight for the front around Leningrad and to the east towards Mga, where a strong breakthrough to the west resulted.
>
> I recommend *SS-Standartenführer* Otto Gieseke for the award of the Knight's Cross to the Iron Cross in recognition of his personal courage.'

This recommendation was approved on the 30th of September 1942. It was unusual for someone to be awarded the Knight's Cross and German Cross in Gold so close together and the two awards are testament to Gieseke's bravery and courage.

During 1942 he was also awarded the Russian Front Medal. On the 20th of April 1943 he was promoted to *SS-Oberführer.* On the 21st of June 1944 he was promoted higher to the rank of *SS-Brigadeführer und Generalmajor der Waffen-SS* and the following month he was serving in Fulda. He was placed on the Führer reserve list at the end of 1944 due to heavy wounds. By 1945 he was on the personal staff of the *Reichsführer-SS* Heinrich Himmler. He survived the war and died in 1968 in Hannover.

Karl Schumers

Date of Birth: 17.10.1905

SS Number: 422 550

Born in Dusseldorf, he joined the police in 1927. He became a *Leutnant* in 1936, followed by *Oberleutnant* in 1938. By September 1939 he was a *Kompanie Commander* in the *Ordnungspolizei*. Towards the end of November 1939 he moved to the *Polizei Division* as *Commander* of the *7. Kompanie*, within *Regiment 1*.

He moved westwards with *Polizei* in 1940, winning the Second Class Iron Cross on the 19th of June, followed by the First Class Iron Cross on the 1st of July. He was also wounded in June 1940. By early January 1941 he was holding the rank of *Hauptmann*. He moved to the *Aufklarungs Abteilung* in mid-1941, as *Polizei* moved east into Russia, staying with them until mid-September. Just prior to this, on the 26th of August 1941, he received the Wound Badge in Silver for two more wounds received in Russia. In mid-September he became the temporary *Commander* of the *II Battalion, Regiment 1*. He was awarded the Infantry Assault Badge at the start of November 1941. On the 1st of April 1942 he was promoted to *SS-Sturmbannführer* and was given official command of the *II Battalion*. Just

Karl Schumers photographed in 1943 with the rank of SS-Obersturmbannführer, after he received the Knight's Cross. He was presented with this award whilst holding the rank of SS-Sturmbannführer in late 1942.

prior to that, in March 1942, he had been involved in the fighting in the Wolchow Pocket. His actions during the rest of March in that area resulted in the later award of the German Cross in Gold, made on the 12th of August 1942. Around one week later than this award he found himself caught up in the *1. Regiment's* fighting on the Newa River. His actions during the week 19th to the 26th of August 1942 resulted in him being recommended for the Knight's Cross. It contained the following overview:

> (The details of the actions have been covered in Gieseke's recommendation, so there is no need to repeat them here, so instead we will focus on the effect of this fighting upon Schumer's *II Battalion*).
>
> 'On the 19th of August the focal point of the enemy attack was where *SS-Sturmbannführer* Schumer's *II Battalion* sat. The enemy's heavy attacks and multiple landings at the mouth of the Tossna River succeeded in breaking Schumer's right flank and reached the road bridge. *SS-Sturmbannführer* Schumers recognized the threat to the southern sector and the strategically important bridges there. He launched a counterattack into the flank of the enemy thrust, defeating the enemy push and reclaiming the lost ground.
>
> On the 23rd of August he was attacked by between two to three enemy regiments with support from armour, aircraft and heavy artillery; who pushed to the road bridge and pushed *Polizei* back as far as the Kirow railroad. *SS-Sturmbannführer* Schumers led a counterattack with remnants of his men together with some recently arrived replacements from Germany. Close combat followed and *SS-Sturmbannführer* Schumer's personal daring and vigorous actions succeeded in retaking the lost ground, including vital bridges, wiping out the majority of the enemy and causing startled enemy survivors to flee.
>
> Through *SS-Sturmbannführer* Schumers' resolute bravery at decisive moments in this battle, he defeated the enemy attacks and prevented these key areas from becoming enemy held territory. This also prevented the Russians from advancing towards Mga and ultimately Leningrad. He helped defeat two enemy divisions, along with regiments and battalions, tanks and boats also.
>
> For outstanding personal bravery in decisive battle situations, together with an accurate tactical handling, I consider *SS-Sturmbannführer* Schumers especially worthy of being awarded the Knight's Cross to the Iron Cross.'

This recommendation was approved on the 30th of September, the same day as Gieseke's. Schumers was promoted to *SS-Obersturmbannführer* on the 20th of

April 1943, commanding the *7. Regiment* for a time, and *SS-Standartenführer* one year later. He was killed in Greece on the 18th of August 1944 by Communist partisans. He had been given temporary command of the *SS-Polizei Division* two months earlier. On the 1st of August his car went over a landmine with his wounds resulting in his death later the same month. By the time of his death he had also been awarded the Close Combat Badge in Bronze and the Russian Front Medal. He was posthumously promoted to *SS-Oberführer.*

The start of the second twelve-month period in Russia had seen the weight of battle fall upon the *Waffen-SS* troops fighting in the north and south, as their *Kameraden* in the centre were removed for re-fitting. This process would continue with further units being removed in order to be re-built.

The men of the *Waffen-SS* were beginning to learn the tenacity of their Russian enemy and a different approach would have to be taken in order to affect a victory in the Soviet Union. A portent of this new *Waffen-SS* approach had been shown by *Wiking* and their newly incorporated *Panzer* unit. What would the remaining months of 1942 have in store for these men?

CHAPTER TEN

THE SECOND AUTUMN IN RUSSIA - OCTOBER TO DECEMBER 1942

As this first volume draws to a close, we will cover the remaining three months of 1942, October through to the end of December. This was a period of minimal actions for the majority of the existing *Waffen-SS* formations.

LAH

There were no major occurrences during this period for the men of the *Leibstandarte*. The *Allied* landings in North Africa and subsequent occupation of southern France did put the *LAH* on alert, but they were not involved.

In late November 1942, their name changed to *SS-Panzergrenadier-Division Leibstandarte Adolf Hitler*. Then in the closing days of December 1942 orders arrived for the restructured and rebuilt *LAH* to move east for the second time. Details of where they would go and what they did will be covered in Volume 2.

SS-Division 'Das Reich'

At the start of October, *SS-Division 'Das Reich'* moved to various locations in Normandy and continued with their training. A second *Regiment* was also raised from existing units. The *Assault Gun Battalion* was once again raised. In early November 1942 this overall unit's name changed again to the title of *SS-Panzergrenadier-Division 'Das Reich'*.

In late November, *Das Reich* were on the move once more, this time to southern France, around Toulon. This was to counter a possible invasion of southern France by the western *Allies*, who had recently landed in North Africa. This was *Das Reich's* part in the 'friendly' occupation of Vichy France.

December would see them move north once again, this time to Rennes. This stay in France would be short lived as by the end of 1942, the Eastern Front called once more for the men of *Das Reich*.

Army Group North

SS-Polizei-Division

As October began it grew quieter in the sector held by *Polizei*. The recent intense fighting became much smaller in scale and can best be described as tit-for-tat localized fighting. This gave the men of *Polizei* a chance to improve their overall situation. Some replacements arrived from Germany which also helped this relative improvement.

October was also a month for recognition of deeds done during the recent heavy fighting. As covered in the preceding pages, Gieseke and Schumers were awarded the Knight's Cross at the end of September, but news of this did not reach the men at the front until the 14th of October. The following day a recommendation for the Knight's Cross to the Iron Cross was approved for *SS-Hauptsturmführer* Wilhelm Dietrich. There were two other approvals given for *Waffen-SS* soldiers prior to this. Dietrich's award became the third for the recent fighting around the Tossna River. News of his award reached the front on the 20th of October and within a few days, a further award was approved. This time it was Rudolf Seitz who would be the recipient. Inbetween his award, another *Waffen-SS Kameraden* had also been approved. All of these awards will be detailed shortly. Rudolf Seitz became the last Knight's Cross holder for the *Polizei Division* for 1942.

November and December were again quieter months for these men. The temperature dropped noticeably and these *Waffen-SS* soldiers prepared themselves for their second winter on the Russian Front.

Replacement units had been raised during these last remaining months of 1942 in Debica, Poland. Instead of being sent to bulk out the numbers of the *Polizei Division* positioned on the ring around Leningrad, they were sent to the opposite end of the Soviet Union to fight with Army Group South. Like their *LAH* predecessors, men who were officially part of the same *Division* found themselves fighting hundreds of miles apart. This unit's actions will be covered shortly.

We will end coverage of the *SS-Polizei Division* as 1942 draws to a close. Like all soldiers everywhere, the Christmas and New Year was on their minds, but they would spend their second festive period with the 'front-line families', not their real ones.

Map 15 **Army Group North: January - December 1942**

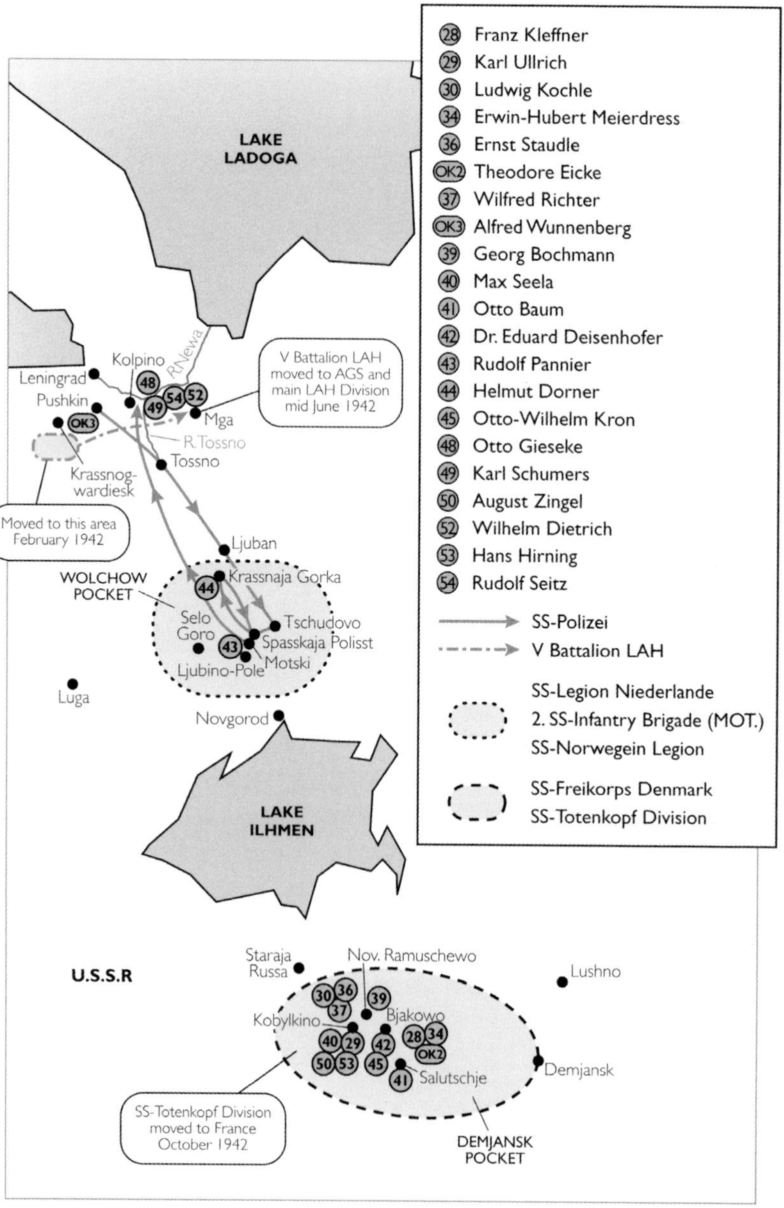

2. SS-Infantry-Brigade (mot.)

There were no major changes to this unit as they remained in their positions around the Leningrad area.

Totenkopf

We last covered *Totenkopf* as they had received official orders to be withdrawn from Army Group North, but still in position. They finally got to leave the Demjansk area on the 16th of October 1942, an area that would forever be associated with *SS-Totenkopf* and their mighty, costly and heroic struggle. Just under two weeks previous to that, on the 4th of October 1942 one of the heroes of Demjansk, August Zingel, had his Knight's Cross recommendation approved. Exactly one week after *Totenkopf's* withdrawal from Russia in 1942, their last Knight's Cross winner for this year was approved. This was Hans Hirning and his approval came on the 23rd of October. Inbetween these two approvals, two further approvals for Knight's Crosses for soldiers of the *Waffen-SS* had been made, full details of all of these will follow at the end of this chapter.

What was left of *Totenkopf* was a virtually non-existant and non-combat capable, not to mention completely burnt out and exhausted shell of a once effective fighting *Division*. These remnants left the Russian Front and slowly made their way to southern France in order to be re-fitted. They therefore joined the *LAH* and *Das Reich Divisions* in this country at that time. *Totenkopf's* stay in this country would be much shorter than their *Waffen-SS* neighbours, as in early January 1943 they would all be sent back to Russia. This gave *Totenkopf* just over two months to fully rebuild itself and reconstitute itself into an effective fighting formation once again. As they were starting to do this in early November 1942, they joined their *Kameraden* in the *LAH* and *Das Reich* units and became a *Panzergrenadier Division*.

We will leave *Totenkopf* as they focused on their rebuild in November and December 1942 and move back to Russia to cover the actions of *Wiking* in the south.

Army Group South

SS-Wiking Division

They were last covered up to the 27th of September 1942 as they prepared to attack Malgobek. The terrain in this area presented natural obstacles that had to be overcome, added to which were the determined Russian troops defending this critical area. *Nordland* led this attack on the southerly portion and ran into immediate difficulties, taking casualties straight away. The following day, the reinforced *Panzer Abteilung* with *Pioneers* and *Westland* joined the attack fighting further north, with the objective of Ssagopschin, south of Malgobek. Like their *Nordland Kameraden*, they suffered high casualties against the determined Russians. As the *Westland Regiment* struggled in their direct attack upon Ssagopschin, Muhlenkamp's *Panzer Abteilung* pushed further eastwards in a flanking attack and pushed against the objective from the northeast. Due to the extreme pressure, *Westland* went onto the defense and the *Panzer Abteilung* had to be pulled back. During this move westwards, the *Panzer Abteilung* ran into a Russian tank advance. What ensued was one of the first of many *Waffen-SS* tank battles, with *Wiking's* tanks coming out of this favourably. Before continuing with this overview, we will take a slight detour.

As highlighted above, the *Panzer Abteilung* and attached *Pioneers* of *Wiking* had advanced to the southeast of Ssagopschin. One of the *Pioneer* Officers in this advance was Eberhard Heder, then holding the rank of *SS-Obersturmführer*. His *Platoon* advanced to a point further southeast than any other German soldier. They had actually advanced to the point furthest southeast from Berlin. After the end of Cold War in the late 1980s, Heder and some of his former *Kameraden* returned to this area. They were treated very well by the local Mayor. As part of this trip they took a bus journey to the Ssagopschin area. They came across a monument that had been erected by the Russians during the Second World War. On this monument was an inscription that read, 'Here the soldiers of the Soviet Union stopped the advance of the Fascist hordes'. So Eberhard Heder had an actual permanent record of the point he and his small group of men had reached. This action was part of the reason why Heder was later awarded the German Cross in Gold. Eberhard Heder would also later be awarded the Knight's Cross to the Iron Cross in 1944, full details of that will follow in the relevant volume. For now, back to October 1942!

After the unexpected tank duel, *Nordland* and *Westland* took up defensive positions west of Ssagopschin. In the first few days of October, the *Germania Regiment* arrived to join in the fight. Starting on the 5th of October they assaulted the target of Malgobek, together with *Heer* units and by the 6th, Malgobek was in German hands. Strong Russian forces were east of Malgobek, so the advance stalled. Finnish *SS* troops captured and held a vital hill in this area during the middle of the month. On the 8th of October 1942, Herbert Gille's Knight's Cross to the Iron Cross was approved.

After staving off this threat, a dangerous situation developed south of their current positions, concerning other units. *Wiking* were moved out and sent south to an area around Alagir and the Caucausus Mountains. They were in position from the 13th of November onwards and the new struggle began.

A few days earlier *Wiking* had become part of the restructure/renaming of the main *SS Divisions* and became known as a *Panzergrenadier-Division*.

For this next battle elements of *Nordland* where on the extreme left, with the rest of *Nordland* in the north, *Westland* where in the central ground, with *Germania* holding the south and southeast.

Throughout the remainder of November and into December the Soviet troops tried to probe weaknesses in the German lines held by *Wiking* and *Heer* units; in most cases they failed. Around the middle of December some changes in the command structure resulted in Felix Steiner taking over the command of the *III Panzer Korps* and Herbert Gille assuming command of *Wiking*.

In the second half of December the overall situation called for a general shortening of the line. This involved *Wiking* being withdrawn and sent north and northeast to Simowniki, reached in the closing days of 1942. We will leave *Wiking* at this point and cover the advances of other *Waffen-SS* units fighting on the Eastern Front at the end of 1942.

Before doing this, it is worth noting that *Wiking* could celebrate the news that Felix Steiner was approved for the award of the Oakleaves to the Knight's Cross, made on the 23rd of December 1942 and also Markus Faulhaber's Knight's Cross approval made on the 25th of December 1942, the last Knight's Cross award for *Wiking* in 1942.

SS-Kampfgruppe Fegelein

Very limited details exist about this particular unit, headed up by the recently promoted *SS-Oberführer* Hermann Fegelein. One component was the *II Battalion, Regiment 3, SS-Polizei Division,* sent down from the north. It is known that they fought in the Taly and Boguchar Valley areas on the Don River, about two hundred miles directly east of Kharkov. These battles took place during December 1942 and involved this *Kampfgruppe* being surrounded, but then managing a breakout to the east. For leading this unit Hermann Fegelein was awarded the Knight's Cross with Oakleaves, some detail of this will follow at the end of this chapter.

SS-Kampfgruppe Schuldt

This formation was raised towards the end of 1942 under the command of Knight's Cross holder, Hinrich Schuldt. Under his command was the *I Battalion, Regiment 1, SS-Polizei Division* (under fellow Knight's Cross holder Wilhelm Dietrich) and the *VII Battalion, Regiment 2, LSSAH*. They were sent further eastwards than *SS Kampfgruppe Fegelein*, further along the Don River at Meschkoff (Meskovskaja). They, like Fegelein's group, came under immediate attacks by strong Russian forces and were forced southwards, east of Kaschary (Kasary) and onwards to

Skassyrkaja (Skosyrskaja). This is where they seen out the last days of 1942, we will of course continue with their exploits in Volume 2, but for now a move to Army Group Centre.

Army Group Centre

SS-Kavallerie Division

This unit re-entered the Russian Front in late October 1942, detraining in the Rudnya area, northwest of Smolensk. They engaged partisans in bitter battles from the outset and continued fighting them into November. At the end of that month they moved northeast to engage Soviet soldiers who had broke through west of Rshew. Fierce fighting erupted and by the 10th of December 1942 the Germans had closed up these enemy troops within a pocket, centered around Belij. They then set about destroying the enemy troops within that pocket, which took around one further week to complete.

Back in the last week of November, Hans-Georg von Charpentier took part in actions that resulted in his award of the Knight's Cross (Details of this will follow at the end of this chapter).

Two other men from this *Division* took part in actions around this time that would result in their later award of the Knight's Cross to the Iron Cross. They were Gustav Lombard, actions on the 25th of November 1942 and August Zehender, actions between the 26th of November and the 2nd of December 1942. They would both receive their Knight's Crosses in March 1943, so they will be detailed in Volume 2 of this project.

Before covering the last group of Knight's Cross recipients for 1942, we will briefly highlight what the newest *Waffen-SS* unit was doing as 1942 drew to a close.

'Prinz Eugen'

As briefly covered in previous pages, this new *Waffen-SS* formation was raised at the start of March 1942 and since that time had been kept busy with training. In October 1942 they became involved in the first of their many military operations. Their first task was a security mission launched in the southern part of Serbia against Serbian Chetnik partisans. No real successes were achieved against these partisans, who knew this area very well and could count on a high degree of support and sympathy from the locals. This situation continued until the end of 1942.

We will now detail various *Waffen-SS* soldiers that were awarded the Knight's Cross to the Iron Cross or the Oakleaves during the remaining few months of 1942.

Wilhelm Dietrich

Date of Birth: 17.11.1912

SS Number: 38 886

Born in Ehringhausen, he served in the *S.A.* from the start of November 1931 until the 10th of March 1932. In April 1935 he is listed as joining the *Landpolizei* with the rank of *Leutnant*. At the same time, however, he is listed as serving within the *Reichsheer* from April 1935 until April 1936. By September 1937 he had obtained the rank of *Oberleutnant*. He took part in the moves into Austria in 1938. At the start of October 1939 he had moved to *Hauptmann* and later the same month he moved to serve with the *8. Kompanie, Polizei Regiment 1*.

He went west with *Polizei* during 1940 and earned the Second Class Iron Cross on the 12th of June, followed by the First Class Iron Cross on the 9th of November 1940. By August 1941 he was the *4. Kompanie Commander*, but two months later he was back with the *8. Kompanie*. He was awarded the Infantry Assualt Badge at the start of November 1941. In early 1942 he took part in a *Battalion Commander's* course in France. In mid-March 1942 he was placed in command of *Polizei's, I Battalion,* within their *1st Regiment*. Throughout the first half of 1942 he spent time commanding both the *II* and *III Battalions,* before moving back to the *II Battalion* in mid-July 1942. On the 1st of August 1942 he was presented with the Russian Front Medal, followed by the German Cross in Gold on the 25th of September 1942. Also around this time he was awarded the Black Wound Badge.

His *Regimental Commander*, Otto Gieseke, had recommended Dietrich for the German Cross in Gold on the 16th of August, but whilst waiting on the outcome of this recommendation, he recommended him for the Knight's Cross to the Iron Cross on the 18th of September 1942. This was for actions that took place between the 30th of August and the 5th of September, by the Newa River. This recommendation highlights the intense attacks by the Soviets in this area using aircraft, tanks, and heavy artillery. It also highlights the infantry attacks that hit the *II Battalion* as the enemy pushed towards the rail and road bridges in their attempts to advance towards Mga and Leningrad.

After several, heavy tank supported attacks, in which the enemy suffered heavy bloody losses, the *II Battalion* halted these attacks. Instead, smaller attacks broke into the positions of the *III Battalion* and close bitter combat ensued, supported by enemy tanks. In the early morning of the 4th of September, these

A formal portrait of SS-Sturmbannführer Wilhelm Dietrich, taken after his award of the Knight's Cross to the Iron Cross.

attacks broke into the western part of the *III Battalion* held area. Simultaneously the enemy penetrated, with strong reserves, deep into the main battle field. Dietrich immediately recognized the emergency if the Russians succeeded. An immediate push against this break-in failed under the heavy enemy tank fire. The Russians successfully pushed forwards. *SS-Hauptsturmführer* Dietrich, despite Stalin's Organs and strong artillery fire, led a handful of men towards the point of the enemy break-in near the Kirow railroad.

In bitter close fighting using grenades and entrenching tools, they fought against the Russians at this point of penetration.

The rolling enemy attacks went further on the 5th of September using tank and artillery fire in the left part of the *III Battalion*. Officers fell and the men became dispersed. Between the *II* and *III Battalions* was a gap of 300 metres. Occupation of this position was not possible. The Russians recognized the possibility of success and pushed harder, elements of the enemy were already in the positions of the *II Battalion* at the Kirow railroad. The Russians sent reserves on the right, but these were held by defensive fire. *SS-Hauptsturmführer* Dietrich's goal in these decisive hours was the neutralizing of these enemy attacks. With the few men left standing, they succeeded in heavy close fighting near the Kirow railroad. The enemy had pushed further and new positions had to be found.

The successful defense in this hostile attack, above all however, the decisive combat situations on the 4th and 5th of September 1942 primarily were mastered through the outstanding bravery and courage of *SS-Hauptsturmführer* Dietrich. Almost all of the heavy machine-guns and other rifles were destroyed by enemy artillery fire. Most of the mortars were lost, so grenades and entrenching tools were the weapons used there.

In ceaseless fighting the enemy lost ten thousand men in bloody battle. Thirteen enemy tanks were also lost. Simultaneously, the last attempts by the enemy to seize the rail bridge over the Tossna River and thereafter use this as a basis to relieve Leningrad was stopped. *SS-Hauptsturmführer* Dietrich tore into this line and his courage and use of his infantry, in spite of the physical exertions needed, set a personal example and thwarted the enemy attempts. Heavy enemy losses in men and material were achieved.

The award of the Knight's Cross to the Iron Cross was requested in recognition of *SS-Hauptsturmführer* Dietrich's personal courage. It was counter-signed by the *Divisional Commander*, Alfred Wunnenburg, who also recommended this award. It was approved on the 15th of October 1942.

Following this award, on the 9th of November 1942, he was promoted to *SS-Sturmbannführer.* He fought within *Kampfgruppe Schuldt* in the south during December 1942 and staying there until February 1943. He was shot in the neck on the 25th of February 1943 and had to leave front line service at that time. From March 1943 until May 1943 he served with the *Replacement Battalion,* he then returned to the *SS-Polizei Division*. At the end of January 1944 he was promoted to *SS-Obersturmbannführer.* He was killed on the 12th of March 1944 whilst serving with his *Regiment*.

Rudolf Seitz

Date of Birth: 11.10.1919

SS Number: 476 141

Born in Charlottenthal, he served in the *Hitler Youth* from the start of October 1936 until the start of August 1939. He then started a three-month spell with the *R.A.D*. On the 1st of March 1940 he moved to *Polizei*.

On the 19th of August 1942 he was holding the rank of *SS-Unterscharführer* within *Polizei's, Assault Gun Abteiling*. He was positioned south of the main railroad on that day, holding a blocking position. His location was on an exposed position on the left flank. He was in this particular location from midday on the 19th through to 8pm the same day. Despite there being only two of them, Seitz and one *SS-Rottenführer,* they stayed there with the *3.7cm Pak* gun, ineffective against the Russian tanks. This gun was still useful against infantry and lighter vehicles.

During their time in this location they endured heavy fighting and they also became surrounded by the enemy. They inflicted losses on the advancing enemy and held their cool despite the increasing threat. They managed to destroy their gun when the enemy was almost on top of their position and then under the cover of darkness they escaped back to their own lines.

For this defensive action during that critical time, Rudolf Seitz was awarded the Knight's Cross to the Iron Cross. It is not known who wrote the recommendation or when, but the approval was given on the 24th of October 1942. As highlighted earlier, this was the last Knight's Cross award to a member of the *SS-Polizei-Division* in 1942 and the fourth awarded for the heavy fighting around the Tossna River in August 1942.

On the 21st of June 1943 he left the front line and began his training to be an officer at the *SS* Officer School in Braunschweig, which lasted until the 18th of December 1943. On the 1st of March 1944 he was promoted to the rank of *SS-Untersturmführer.* By that date he was back with *Polizei,* officially staying with them until the 20th of August the same year. He was however, heavily wounded in late July 1944. He then moved to the *Panzerjaeger Replacement Battalion* and stayed there until the 20th of January 1945.

Rudolf Seitz photographed after his promotion to SS-Untersturmführer in 1944. He was awarded his Knight's Cross in 1942 for actions conducted whilst holding the rank of SS-Unterscharführer.

Besides being awarded the Knight's Cross to the Iron Cross, he was also awarded the Second Class Iron Cross on the 23rd of September 1941, the First Class Iron Cross on the 1st of October 1941, the Infantry Assault Badge, the Russian Front Medal and the Silver Wound Badge; he survived the war.

August Zingel
Date of Birth: 20.01.1921
SS Number: 490 098
Born in Heidmuhle, he entered the *SS* at the start of November 1937. There is very little detail about his service between that date and the start of the war. It can be assumed that he was with *Totenkopf* as they formed in late 1939. What is known is as follows, he was awarded the Second Class Iron Cross on the 10th of October 1941, the Infantry Assault Badge two days later, the First Class Iron Cross on the 27th of Febraury 1942, the Russian Front Medal on the 16th of July 1942 and the Black Wound Badge on the 10th of September 1942. By the early part of 1942 he was holding the rank of *SS-Unterscharführer* and was serving in *Totenkopf's, 15. Kompanie, Regiment 1*. He was with this unit as they fought their life and death struggle throughout 1942 within the Army Group North area of operations.

On the 15th of September 1942 the *Totenkopf Divisional Commander,* Max Simon, wrote a recommendation for the Knight's Cross to the Iron Cross for Zingel. It contained the following:

> 'In the very hard winter fighting, he had developed into a very good leader. Personally brave, he always kept his high spirits. This was noticeable especially during emergencies.
>
> On the Robja front, at Point 58, there were strong Russian positions that could fire upon the route to Nowosellje and on the Robja front, the main road and supply route to Ramuschewo, Omitschkino and Bjakowo. They caused heavy losses to our own men, so it had to be destroyed.
>
> After detailed personal reconnaissance, in the early hours of the 10th of September 1942 the attack began. Using a rubber dingy the men set out for the Robja. In go-getting style they seized the enemy in their field positions. They penetrated further to the main enemy position and destroyed the whole garrison.
>
> In bitter fighting with his men, they took ten heavy bunkers, seven trenches and twenty-two small bunkers. The losses to the enemy were over 150 dead. Zingel's group suffered one dead and one wounded before they returned to their own positions.

August Zingel photographed in a formal portrait, after his award of the Knight's Cross.

> This decisive success is to be owed to the heroism of Zingel alone. He showed cold blooded assessment of the situation, highest personal courage, unusual decisiveness, boldness and high circumspect.
>
> I ask that the Knight's Cross to the Iron Cross is given to this brave leader in recognition of his heroism and the result he achieved.'

This recommendation was approved on the 4th of October 1942. Two days previous to this he was wounded in the right lung and had to be evacuated from the front, being sent to Riga in Latvia for treatment. This wound kept him from front-line service for a number of months. In some of the photographs taken of August Zingel wearing his Knight's Cross, he is seen with the rank of *SS-Oberscharführer.* The exact date of that promotion or any inbetween is not known.

He must have attended Officer School sometime in late 1943 or early 1944, as by the 21st of June 1944 he was holding the rank of *SS-Untersturmführer.* He also spent time in the *Panzergrenadier* School and by November 1944 he was with the *Replacement Battalion*. He was back serving within *SS-Totenkopf* by February 1945 and he survived the war. He died on the 22nd of December 2000.

Herbert Otto Gille

Date of Birth: 08.03.1897

SS Number: 39 854

Born in Gandersheim, Gille's military career began in 1909, when he joined the *Army Cadet Corps*. In 1914 he was in the *LAH's* future home, the senior cadet facility at Lichterfelde in Berlin. At the start of September 1914 he was assigned to *Field Artillery Regiment .30*. Two months later he was moved to *Reserve Artillery Regiment .55*. This was the unit that Gille went to war with before the end of 1914. In late January 1915 he obtained the rank of *Leutnant*. He stayed with the artillery throughout World War One and until the start of April 1919. During World War One he was awarded the Second and First Classes of the Iron Cross as well as other awards.

He joined the fledgling *SS* on the 10th of October 1931, serving within the *49. Standarte*. On the 25th of September 1932 he was holding the rank of *SS-Scharführer.* He was promoted on the 27th of January 1933 to *SS-Truppführer (SS-Oberscharführer)* and again on the 20th of April 1933 to *SS-Sturmführer (SS-Untersturmführer)*. By late May 1934 he was with the *III Battalion, SS-Regiment Deutschland*. Exactly two years after being promoted to *SS-Untersturmführer,* he was promoted to *SS-Obersturmführer.* After spending time at Doberitz, he was promoted to *SS-Hauptsturmführer* on the 9th of November 1935 and was given command of *Deutschland's, 12. Kompanie*. On the first day of October 1936 he

Herbert-Otto Gille photographed in the field, after his award of the Knight's Cross in 1942.

moved to *SS-Regiment Germania,* mainly serving in their *II Battalion*. He was promoted to *SS-Sturmbannführer* on the 20th of April 1937, following this by attending a *Battalion Commander's* course in late 1938. By mid-1939 he was *Commander* of the *SS-Artillery Standarte*.

This *SS-Artillery Standarte* became part of the *SS V Division* and fought in Poland and the west. By that time, Gille had moved to the rank of *SS-Obersturmbannführer,* being promoted in October 1939. He had also received the Clasp to the Second Class Iron Cross, on the 26th of October 1939 and also the Clasp to the First Class Iron Cross, on the 21st of November 1939. In late 1940 he became the *Commander* of the new *SS-Wiking Division's, Artillery Regiment*. By the end of January 1941 he was holding the rank of *SS-Standartenführer.* He went with this *Division* into Russia in mid-1941 and although he was not aware of it then, it was a place he would spend almost the rest of the war in.

On the first day of October 1941 he was promoted to *SS-Oberführer* and then on the 28th of February 1942 he was awarded the German Cross in Gold. He became the *Commander* of *SS-Regiment 'Westland'* in the second half of 1942. It was with this *Regiment* that he advanced towards Rostov. In the last few days of July and first couple of days in August 1942, Gille was involved in actions that resulted in him receiving the Knight's Cross to the Iron Cross. The recommendation was written by his *Divisional Commander*, Felix Steiner, on the 18th of September 1942 and it covered the following:

> 'On the 28th of July 1942 he was moving from the Don towards the Kuban area, when he came across enemy columns in Seljonaja Roschtscha as they were retreating; they smashed the enemy and pushed their attack to the fort at Rakowo Tawritschewski and prevented the enemy from holding that area – pushing them further south. On the 29th of July he was involved in hard fighting south of Rakowo Tawritschewski with strong enemy forces, but Metschetinskaja was taken.
>
> Elements of sixteen different divisions of the *12th Army* were put to flight as a result of this successful attack.
>
> On the 30th of July they were advancing towards Jegorlikskaja, fought against the defending *12th Army* once again and reached Sredny Jegorlyk that evening.
>
> With the help of the *Luftwaffe's, Major* Giesing, they were made aware of the enemy's *17th Army* in the area, moving against the lead elements of the *Division*. In the same night, the Russians attacked the west part of Sredny Jegorlyk and the rear with tanks and infantry, who were fresh units. They also attacked the lead units. Heavy fighting resulted in the halting of these enemy attacks, which included parts of the Soviet *14th Tank Corps*.

With this attack the lead elements of Gille's group moved further west, east of the *17th Army*. The *13th Panzer Division* moved eastwards behind *Kampfgruppe* Gille toward Ssalsk.

On the 1st of August, Gille's group destroyed the Soviet *21st Motorised Infantry Brigade* in their hardest fighting yet near Belaja Glina, they successfully took this village and moved on during the night to Dimitrijewka.

This boldness and heavy losses to the enemy and attack of Gille's lead units, reached the Kuban in the shortest time so far, reached on the 3rd of August. During all of this fighting, *SS-Oberführer* Gille was always at the lead point, providing an example of energy and keeping the momentum going. He demanded the same of himself as that of his men and provided the impulse to achieve success.

It made possible the fast advance of their eastern neighbours, the *17th Army*. Also, the *13th Panzer Division* to the east and lastly, the securing of the Kuban area.

He personally intervened in all of this fighting. Without this we would not have achieved such a meaningful success. I ask for the award of the Knight's Cross to the Iron Cross. All prerequisites for this award have been met.'

Hitler agreed and this recommendation was approved on the 8th of October 1942. It would in no way whatsoever, be Gille's last association with the various grades of this award, nor the last time that Hitler would read of Gille's abilities, but more details of those deeds in later volumes.

Hans Hirning

Date of Birth: 14.11.1922

SS Number: unknown

Born in Ulm, he entered the *SS* on the 30th of November 1939. Little detail is known of what he done in the early years of the Second World War, but by 1941 he was serving with the *Totenkopf Division* in Russia. He was awarded the Second Class Iron Cross on the 23rd of October 1941, followed by the First Class Iron Cross on the 14th of July 1942. He was holding the rank of *SS-Rottenführer* on the 28th of August 1942 when he was involved in actions that resulted in him being awarded the Knight's Cross to the Iron Cross. It is not know who wrote this recommendation or when it was written, but it was approved on the 23rd of October 1942 for the following reasons:

'The main road between Omytschkino and Bjakowo was vital to the German main supply route. The Russians had attempted to cut this route, supplying the entire *II Panzer Korps* in the Demjansk area. The enemy had

Hans Hirning photographed after he was awarded the Knight's Cross. He is seen holding the rank of SS-Unterscharführer. His was an SS-Rottenführer at the time of his Knight's Cross actions.

> moved an anti-tank gun to this road, thereby blocking this life line for the *II Panzer Korps* and the *SS-Totenkopf Division*. Destroying this enemy *PaK* gun with artillery was not possible.
>
> *SS-Rottenführer* Hirning had told his *Kompanie* and *Battalion Commander* of his intentions to advance to the gun and destroy it. They asked what would what happen after he destroyed it, what if he was captured or killed. Hirning replied, 'I do not know of that, the important thing here is that the *PaK* gun is destroyed anything else is insignificant.'
>
> Later on the 28th of August he crept forwards with 6kg explosive charges, through the hollow until he came within 30 metres of the enemy gun. He then ran forwards and attached the explosives to the gun. It did not explode and he had to defensively fight his way back to his own lines. He was shot at with strong enemy fire as well as enemy grenades, but he remained unscathed. He took it upon himself to make a return trip to this enemy gun, one *Kameraden* volunteered to go with him to provide security. They once again perservered and reached the gun. This time, Hirning successfully destroyed this enemy anti-tank gun.
>
> It was through *SS-Rottenführer* Hans Hirning's actions that successfully removed this dangerous threat for the entire *II Panzer Korps*. The supply route was re-opened. An enemy success here would have had unforeseen consequences.'

In recognition of his selfless deeds, Hirning was presented with the Knight's Cross to the Iron Cross. By this stage he was holding the rank of *SS-Unterscharführer.*

No further detail exists of Hirning's actions between that date and April 1945. By this time he was holding the rank of *SS-Oberscharführer* and was a *Platoon Leader*. He was fighting near Dumholz, in Czecheslovakia, where he was killed in action on the 30th of April 1945.

Harry Polewacz

Date of Birth: 31.03.1909

SS Number: 35 952

Born in Berlin, he joined the *SS* before Hitler came to power in 1933, although the exact date of joining is not listed. He was sent as one of the first 117 men, on the 17th of March 1933, who formed what became known as the *LAH*. He was holding the rank of *SS-Truppführer (SS-Oberscharführer)* in June 1933, the same month that he attended a *Platoon Leader's* course at Dobertiz. He joined the *LAH's, 3. Kompanie*, led by Wilhelm Mohnke in October 1933. On the 7th of April 1934 *SS-Sturmführer (SS-Untersturmführer)* Polewacz was with the newly formed *Recruit*

A photograph of Harry Polewacz (right), seen here talking to Hubert Meyer (left) in mid-1941 when the LAH and Wiking briefly fought close to each other, near Shitomir.

Kompanie. When the *LAH's, Training Kompanies* were formed three months later, he was commanding the *8. A Kompanie*, holding the rank of *SS-Obersturmführer*. By August 1939 Polewacz was commanding the *10. Kompanie*, holding the rank of *SS-Hauptsturmführer*.

He went with the *LAH* into Poland where he was awarded the Second Class Iron Cross on the 8th of September 1939, followed by the Black Wound Badge on the 28th of May 1940. The First Class Iron Cross came on the 5th of June 1940. It is not detailed what he done inbetween the western campaign and the start of Barbarossa.

He was serving with the *SS-Regiment Nordland* by the summer of 1941 and went this unit into Russia. He was awarded the German Cross in Gold on the 19th of December 1941, the Infantry Assault Badge on the 11th of January 1942, the Silver Wound Badge on the 30th of January 1942 and the Russian Front Medal on the 10th of September 1942.

By then he was holding the rank of *SS-Sturmbannführer* and commanding the *III Battalion, SS-Regiment Nordland*. Towards the end of September 1942 he took

A formal portrait of Harry Polewacz after his Knight's Cross award.

part in fighting that resulted in his award of the Knight's Cross to the Iron Cross. The details of that fighting are as follows:

> 'At the end of September the *I Panzer Army,* with *Wiking,* were fighting for the Terek bridgehead. The attack point was the *III Battalion, Nordland.* The objective was to attack southeast towards Nishikurp. On the 27th of September the *III Battalion,* under Polewacz, with the *Stug Batterie* reinforcing them, attacked towards this objective in the morning fog.
>
> The enemy put up a strong fight and after the fog lifted, they could observe the movements of the *III Battalion*. Several bitter battles broke out, with the *1. Kompanie Commander* being heavily wounded and the *Commanders* of the *Stug Batterie's, 2. Kompanie* and *3. Kompanie* being killed during heavy fighting on the right flank. The *Ordnance Officer* took over, but he was wounded and then the *Battalion Adjutant* became a temporary *Kompanie Commander*.
>
> The *Battalion* remained in defensive positions against this strong enemy fire. *SS-Sturmbannführer* Polewacz recognized this emergency and rushed through the strong enemy fire, showing the right flank *Kompanie* the ground to attack. He then moved to the left flank and gave further commands to attack the enemy positions. With this, the entire *Battalion* moved forward.
>
> Polewacz was at the head of this attack and was an example of the highest courage. Only his personal actions resulted in the successful breakthrough into the enemy positions. This breakthrough position was used as the start of further attacks to the east.
>
> His *Regimental Commander*, *SS-Oberführer* von Scholz, asked for the award of the Knight's Cross to the Iron Cross as he felt Polewacz was an example of an officer who showed personal outstanding courage, and his decisions led to a success that allowed further advances of the *SS-Wiking Division*.'

This recommendation was signed by von Scholz on the 22nd of November 1942. It was countersigned by Felix Steiner, who offered his warmest recommendations for this award. The recommendation was approved on the 23rd of December 1942.

By the end of 1942, Harry Polewacz was holding the rank of *SS-Obersturmbannführer* and was in command of the entire *Nordland Regiment*. It was whilst leading this *Regiment* on the 12th of January 1943 that he was killed.

Felix Steiner

Date of Birth: 23.05.1896

SS Number: 253 351

We last covered Steiner up to mid-August 1940, when he became one of the first *SS* soldiers to be awarded the Knight's Cross to the Iron Cross. He held the rank of *SS-Oberführer* at that time and was commanding *SS-Regiment Deutschland.*

He was promoted to *SS-Brigadeführer und Generalmajor der Waffen-SS* on the 9th of November 1940, the same day that he was given command of the new *SS-Wiking Division*. He oversaw the raising of this *Division*, containing a high proportion of foreign volunteers. He attended a *Divisional Commander's* course between the 7th of February and the 11th of February 1941. He then led his *Division* into the depths of the Soviet Union in the summer of 1941. As has been detailed in the preceding pages, he was with this *Division* as they advanced southwards during 1941 and also 1942.

On the 23rd of December 1942, the same day as Polewacz, he became the fourth *Waffen-SS* soldier to be awarded the Knight's Cross to the Iron Cross with Oakleaves. The recommendation does not survive on his file, so it cannot be determined who wrote it, when it was written or for exactly what actions he received this high award. Although documents dated later than this do outline some of the reasons:

> 'Under his complete personal leadership, always at the focus and head of the attack, repeated these actions again and again and through his courage and tactics, successes were achieved.'

Around the time of this award being approved, Steiner was wounded and left the command of the *SS-Wiking Division*. He followed this by taking over command of the Army's *III Panzer Korps* briefly, until January 1943.

The award of the Oakleaves would not end Felix Steiner's association with the various grades of the Knight's Cross, but details of that will follow in later volumes.

Markus Faulhaber

Date of Birth: 22.07.1914

SS Number: 113 916

Born in Schomberg, he entered the *SS* in mid-June 1933, after having served a three-month stint with the *S.A.* from March until June 1933. He served with the *16. Kompanie, SS-Regiment Deutschland* in the early days. Between late 1937 and early 1938 he attended the Officers School at Braunschweig. On the 12th of

A formal portrait photograph of Felix Steiner, taken to mark his award of the Knight's Cross to the Iron Cross with Oakleaves.

March 1938 he became an *SS-Untersturmführer* and by April 1938 he was serving with the *9. Kompanie, SS-Regiment Germania*. He served as an *Ordnance Officer* from this time until that start of 1941.

He fought in Poland from the 1st to the 28th of September 1939 and was awarded the Second Class Iron Cross on the 14th of November 1939. He was promoted to *SS-Obersturmführer* on the 30th of January 1940 and fought in the west during May and June 1940. At the start of 1941 he moved to the role of *Platoon Leader* within *Germania's, 3. Kompanie,* staying there until May 1942. It was with this *Kompanie* that he moved eastwards in mid-1941 into Russia. He was awarded the First Class Iron Cross on the 14th of July 1941. Further promotion to *SS-Hauptsturmführer* came on the 9th of November 1941, the same month that he received a wound, being awarded the Black Wound Badge on the 7th of February 1942.

On the 25th of December 1942 he was awarded the Knight's Cross to the Iron Cross for actions that had taken place almost one year earlier.

Back on the 17th of November 1941, *Wiking* were starting their attack north of Rostov as part of the *I Panzer Army*. Faulhaber was serving as an *SS-Obersturmführer* within the *3. Kompanie, SS-Regiment Germania*. They were fighting to secure the Tusloff River sector. The Russian *37th Army* were pushing towards the Sea of Azov and this enemy pressure fell most noticeably upon the *I Battalion, Germania* in the Aleksejewo Tuslowka area.

The reinforced *3. Kompanie* where in Ljubimaja, covering the northeast and northwest directions. Also in Ljubimaja were the *8th & 12th Batteries* of *Artillery Regiment 5*.

In the morning of the 18th of November 1941 the Russians broke into the defensive front of the *Regiment* to the north and began to penetrate the village of Ljubimaja. The *Artillery Battery* was directly threatened – around 1,500 enemy troops were in this area and they penetrated the ground held by Faulhaber's *3. Kompanie*. *SS-Obersturmführer* Faulhaber alerted his *Kompanie*.

With only a few men of his *Kompanie*, Faulhaber burst into the attacking Russians, who were much larger in number. Through this enormous boldness the remaining *Kompanie* leaders went over to the attack.

SS-Obersturmführer Faulhaber used this exemplary example to his men, but there followed very bitter close combat. The artillery staff of the *IV Battalion, Artillery Regiment 5* were pushed out of their positions. *SS-Obersturmführer* Faulhaber reacted and his *3. Kompanie* pushed into these Russian troops. A portion of the *Kompanie* attacked on the flank.

During this fighting the *3. Kompanie* left 300 dead and 620 captured Russian soldiers. Over 1,000 weapons, machine-guns and mortars were captured too. Two

Markus Faulhaber photographed after his award of the Knight's Cross. This award came almost one year after the actions that resulted in that award!

Russian battalions were destroyed through the boldness of Faulhaber. Not only was the Russian attack halted and destroyed, but the enemy was pushed back also. The cold blooded and personal courage of *SS-Obersturmführer* Faulhaber resulted in the rescuing of the *Abteilung Staff* and the penetrating of the expansion of the Russian breakthrough. Faulhaber alone made this happen. If this breakthrough had occurred, it would have been catastrophic for the *XIV Panzer Korps* and would have led onto Rostov. Therefore, *SS-Obersturmführer* Faulhaber's decisive actions helped rescue the threatened *XIV Panzer Korps*.

SS-Obersturmführer Faulhaber was wounded in the face by pistol rounds, he nevertheless stayed with his men. *SS-Obersturmführer* Faulhaber already repeated in the fighting, personal courage in Kuzmin, Smela, in the storm of Krementschug and Dnjeprodserschinsk, as well as in the fighting in the bridgehead of Dnejpropetrowsk.

This recommendation was written by Faulhaber's *Regimental Commander*, *SS-Oberführer* Oberkamp on the 11th of January 1942. It was however, rejected at that stage, as was a recommendation for the German Cross in Gold during early July 1942. It is not known when the successful recommendation was re-submitted or what addendums it had added to it. Markus Faulhaber finally became a holder of the Knight's Cross to the Iron Cross on the 25th of December 1942, making him the last member of the *SS-Wiking Division* to receive this award in 1942.

By the time that Faulhaber received the Knight's Cross, he was performing the role of a *Tactics Officer* to future *Waffen-SS* Officers at Bad Tolz, something he had been doing from May 1942. He was promoted to *SS-Sturmbannführer* on the 9th of November 1943. He stayed in his tactics training role until May 1944, when he took command of the Main Office's, *Amt XI,* staying there until the 10th of June. He next moved to serve with the *SS-Panzergrenadier-Brigade 49,* within the *26th SS Division 'Hunyadi Nr. 2'*. He stayed with that *Division* until mid-September 1944 when he moved to the *17th SS-Panzer Division 'Gotz von Berlichingen'*. He only stayed with them until the end of September, so it can be assumed that he was wounded, as he moved to reserve officer status. It is not detailed what he done between October 1944 and May 1945, but by that time he had also been awarded the Infantry Assault Badge, the Silver Wound Badge and the Panzer Destruction Badge.

SS-Sturmbannführer Markus Faulhaber surrendered to the Americans near Salzburg. They asked him to go into the nearby mountains and persuade his fellow soldiers to surrender. The vehicle in which he was traveling was involved in an accident whilst he was conducting this American request. The accident took place near the Salzach River, close to Salzburg and resulted in Markus Faulhaber drowning.

Hermann Fegelein

Date of Birth: 30.10.1906

SS Number: 66 680

We last covered Fegelein at the start of March 1942 when he received the Knight's Cross to the Iron Cross for actions near Rzhev in northern Russia. Since then he returned to Germany and in May 1942 assumed a role as *Head of Cavalry and Horse Drawn Transportation*. He remained there until the end of November 1942, with some further changes taking place for Hermann Fegelein.

On the 1st of December 1942 he was promoted to *SS-Oberführer* and he was also given command of *SS Kampfgruppe Fegelein*. This *Kampfgruppe* contained the *II Battalion, Regiment 3, SS-Polizei Division* as well as other mixed units. They were sent to the southern part of Russia to engage the enemy.

As highlighted previously, very limited details exist about this particular unit. It is known that they fought in the Taly and Boguchar Valley areas on the Don River, about two hundred miles directly east of Kharkov during late-December 1942. As part of these battles, this *Kampfgruppe* became surrounded, but then managing a breakout to the east.

Fegelein himself was wounded on the 23rd of December 1942 and two days later became the fifth *Waffen-SS* recipient of the Knight's Cross to the Iron Cross with Oakleaves. There is no detail of the recommendation for this high award on Fegelein's file, but a document dating from 1943 provides some insight into what took place.

Two Russian regiments, supported by artillery attacked Golaja from the east and northwest intending to break through. They struck at a time when the Germans were not ready and the subsequent successful defense was attributed to the cold-blooded and personal bravery of Fegelein. He rallied the troops and despite being wounded, stayed with them until midday, after the Russian attack had been halted. In the file is mention of Fegelein capturing an enemy *Corps Commander*, who had valuable maps and orders on his person.

This is the only detail and references to that time. Fegelein left the fighting at that stage and returned to Germany for treatment. It is surprising that so little detail exists for the award of the Knight's Cross with Oakleaves, a rare honour for a member of the *Waffen-SS* at this stage of the war. It would not be Fegelein's last connection to the various grades of this medal, but details of that will follow in later volumes.

Hermann Fegelein shown in a formal photograph to mark his award of the Knight's Cross to the Iron Cross with Oakleaves.

Hans-Georg von Charpentier
Date of Birth: 11.10.1919
SS Number: 258 019
Born in Strassbourg, he spent the first half of 1919 serving in the *Army's, Reiterstandarte 16*. He joined the *SS* at the start of March 1935 and by the 7th of November 1939 had moved to *SS-Totenkopf Reiter Regiment 1*. On the 29th of October 1940 he obtained the rank of *SS-Untersturmführer,* followed by *SS-Obersturmführer* on the 15th of July 1941. He was in Russia by that time and on the 16th of August 1941 he was awarded the Second Class Iron Cross. At this time he became the *Adjutant* to *Kavallerie Regiment 1*. In mid-December 1941 he took command of the *3. Kompanie,* within this *Regiment*. On the 26th of January 1942 he was awarded the First Class Iron Cross. In mid-March 1942 he was promoted to *SS-Hauptsturmführer* and at the start of May he was awarded the General Assault Badge.

On the 11th of December 1942 Wilhelm Bittrich recommended him for the Knight's Cross to the Iron Cross for the following actions:

> 'On the 25th of November 1942 the enemy with strong motorized support, later tank support, broke through the German positions southwest of *Regiment 1* in the area of Beloussewo, the orders went out, everyone to these German positions to prevent the breakthrough.
>
> It was known, that this strong enemy could divide Knjashe and Medwedewo, the battle began. A cornerstone was formed, the furthermost point was at Medwedewo; aim was to halt the enemy there. The *3. Squadron (Kompanie)* under *SS-Hauptsturmführer* von Charpentier set up defense around Medwedewo. The enemy attacked Medwedewo in regimental strength with tank support. *SS-Hauptsturmführer* von Charpentier was cut-off immediately, through his weakly manned left neighbour (a worn down *Kompanie* of *Luftwaffe Field Division 2)* knew this cornerstone and he occupied it to prevent a larger breakthrough by the enemy. They pushed their area to a small area of high ground west of Medwedewo. Through this action, the attack against the main road was prevented near Tschalischtschewo. Higher orders were taken for sending more vehicles. On the 3rd of December 1942 the enemy on the right, cut-off the *Regiment* and cut-off *SS-Hauptsturmführer* von Charpentier and tried to take this vital cornerstone. He gripped the enemy during the day and the night.
>
> In this cornerstone of the defense the enemy lost 500 dead and 6 tanks, 3 of these being T-34s. The *3. Squadron* was down to 20 men at the end of this fighting.

Hans-Georg von Charpentier photographed on the day he was awarded the Knight's Cross to the Iron Cross, the last such award to a soldier of the Waffen-SS in 1942.

Only his readiness and example of courage is to be owed this success. Medwedewo was held in tireless efforts and for 13 days was kept free of the enemy, without any additional cover for this *Squadron*. This cornerstone was formed at the enemy breakthrough point until the countermeasures of the *9th Army* eased the pressure of the enemy on the 7th of December 1942.

Through the recovery of Medwedewo and the occupation of the high ground west of there and through his own decision and that to hold this area, reached a decisive success for the larger battle. Through the enemy breakthrough the German position held due to the courageous deeds of *SS-Hauptsturmführer* von Charpentier.

I hold that *SS-Hauptsturmführer* von Charpentier be rewarded with the Knight's Cross to the Iron Cross.'

This recommendation was approved on the 29th of December 1942 and it therefore became the last *Waffen-SS* Knight's Cross to be awarded in 1942.

On the 1st of December 1943 he was given command of *Regiment 3* (renamed *SS-Kavallerie Regiment 18)*. He was promoted to *SS-Sturmbannführer* on the 11th of October 1944 and remained at the head of *SS-Kavallerie Regiment 18* until the 11th of February 1945, when he was killed in Budapest.

• • •

Summary

This brings to an end the first volume that will cover the *Waffen-SS* recipients of the Knight's Cross to the Iron Cross and the first handful of recipients of the Knight's Cross with Oakleaves.

This first volume has covered the first vital three-and-a-bit years of the Second World War, from September 1939 until December 1942. In 1942 itself, a total of thirty-five Knight's Crosses, together with four awards of the Knight's Cross with Oakleaves had been awarded to soldiers of the *Waffen-SS*. This brought the total to fifty-eight Knight's Crosses and five Knight's Crosses with Oakleaves for *Waffen-SS* men, since the outbreak of the Second World War. The awards had been given to soldiers who ranged in rank from *SS-Rottenführer* to *SS-Obergruppenführer und General der Waffen-SS*. Forty-nine of these Knight's Crosses and all five Oakleaves, or over 85%, had been awarded for actions that had taken place in the Soviet Union, a trend that would continue throughout the rest of the war.

We hope you have found this volume informative and useful. Work is already underway on the subsequent volumes, which will cover 1943, 1944 and the closing months of the war in 1945.

This book was written in order to fully understand how the various *Waffen-SS* Knight's Cross holders connected to one another. Where they right next to one another or 100 miles apart? Did the actions take place on the same day or months apart? To find the answers to these questions, is what has driven this (unfinished) project. It has been a personal quest of mine for a number of years and with this first volume completed, I feel this huge 'jig-saw' is starting to come together. I hope you, the reader, have found this of interest and agree that some of these questions have been answered and that part of my quest has been achieved. This quest continues.

APPENDICES

Appendix 1
List of *Waffen-SS* units raised (including name changes)

1933
Leibstandarte Adolf Hitler
SS-Regiment Deutschland

1934
SS-Regiment Germania

1938
SS-Regiment Der Fuhrer

1939
SS-Heimwehr Danzig
SS-Totenkopf Reiterstandarte
SS-Totenkopf Division
Polizei Division
SS V Division

1940
SS-Division Wiking
SS-Division Reich

1941
SS-Kampfgruppe Nord
1. SS-Infantry Brigade (mot.)
2. SS-Infantry Brigade (mot.)
SS-Legion Flandern

SS-Legion Niederlande
Kommadostab Reichsführer-SS
SS-Kavellerie Brigade
V Battalion LAH
SS-Freikorps Denmark
SS-Legion Norwegian

1942
SS-Polizei Division
SS-Freiwilligen-Division 'Prinz Eugen'
SS-Gebirgs-Division 'Nord'
SS-Division 'Das Reich'
SS-Kampfgruppe Fegelein
SS-Kampfgruppe Schudlt
SS-Kavellerie-Division

Appendix 2
Overview of awards of the *Waffen-SS* Knight's Crosses, plus Oakleaves

Poland 1939
None

The West 1940

SS-Leibstandarte Adolf Hitler	One
SS-Verfungungstruppen	Five

The Balkans 1941

SS-Leibstandarte Adolf Hitler	Two
SS Division Reich	One

Russia 1941

SS-Leibstandarte Adolf Hitler	Two, plus one Oakleaves
SS Division Reich	Five
SS Totenkopf Division	Four
SS-Polizei Division	Three

Russia 1942

SS-Leibstandarte Adolf Hitler	One
SS Division Reich	Two
SS Totenkopf Division	Thirteen plus one award of the Oakleaves
SS-Polizei Division	Six plus one award of the Oakleaves
SS-Wiking Division	Nine plus one award of the Oakleaves
4. SS-Infantry Regiment	One
SS-Kavallerie Brigade/Division	Two
SS-Kampfgruppe Fegelein	One award of the Oakleaves

The total breakdown of all awards made since hostilities began is as follows:

SS-Leibstandarte Adolf Hitler	Six plus one award of the Oakleaves
SS-Division Reich	Thirteen
SS-Totenkopf Division	Seventeen plus one award of the Oakleaves
SS-Polizei Division	Nine plus one award of the Oakleaves
SS-Wiking Division	Nine plus one award of the Oakleaves
4. SS-Totenkopf-Standarte	One
SS-Kavallerie Brigade/Division	Two
SS-Kampfgruppe Fegelein	One award of the Oakleaves

The rest of the *Waffen-SS* units in existence up to the end of 1942 did not have any Knight's Cross recipients.

Knight's Crosses in Russia by Army Group 1941 - 1942

Army Group North	Twenty-six, plus two Oakleaves
Army Group Centre	Ten
Army Group South	Twelve, plus three Oakleaves

Appendix 3
Ranks of *Waffen-SS* Knight's Cross Holders (and Oakleaves)

Knight's Cross:

SS-Obergruppenführer	1
SS-Gruppenführer	2
SS-Brigadeführer	2
SS-Oberführer	5
SS-Standartenführer	6
SS-Obersturmbannführer	3
SS-Sturmbannführer	16
SS-Hauptsturmführer	8
SS-Obersturmführer	4
SS-Untersturmführer	2
SS-Hauptscharführer	1
SS-Oberscharführer	2
SS-Unterscharführer	3
SS-Rottenführer	1
SS-Sturmmann	1

Knight's Cross with Oakleaves:

SS-Obergruppenführer	1
SS-Gruppenführer	1
SS-Brigadeführer	2
SS-Oberführer	1

Appendix 4
Service Arms of *Waffen-SS* Knight's Cross Holders (and Oakleaves)

Knight's Crosses:	
Infantry	37
Aufklarungs	4
Motorcycle Battalion	2
Panzerjäger	3
Flak	2
Pioneer	2
Artillery	3
Cavalry	2
Sturmgeschütze	1
Panzer	1

Knight's Cross with Oakleaves:	
Infantry	4
Cavalry	1

Appendix 5
List of deceased *Waffen-SS* Knight's Cross holders up to the end of 1942

1941

Erich Rossner	30th July 1941
Hans-Christian Schulze	13th September 1941
Gert Pleiss	17th November 1941

1942

Ludwig Kochle	9th June 1942

BIBLIOGRAPHY

Buss, Philip. H. & Mollo, Andrew. *Hitler's Germanic Legions, An illustrated history of the Western European Legions with the SS, 1941-1943*. Macdonald and Jane's Publishers Limited, 1978.

Haupt, Werner. *Army Group North, The Wehrmacht in Russia 1941-1945*. Schiffer Publishing Ltd., 1997.

Haupt, Werner. *Army Group Centre, The Wehrmacht in Russia 1941-1945*. Schiffer Publishing Ltd., 1997.

Haupt, Werner. *Army Group South, The Wehrmacht in Russia 1941-1945*. Schiffer Publishing Ltd., 1998.

Husemann, Friedrich. *In Good Faith, The History of the 4. SS-Polizei-Panzer-Grenadier-Division, Volume 1: 1939-1943*. J.J.Fedorowicz Publishing Ltd., 2003.

Kratschmer, E.G. *Die Ritterkreuztrager der Waffen-SS*. Verlag K.W. Schutz KG, Preussisch Oldendorf, 1982

Kumm, Otto. *Prinz Eugen, The History of the 7 SS Mountain Division "Prinz Eugen"*. J.J.Fedorowicz Publishing Ltd., 1995.

Landwehr, Richard. *Siegrunen No. 40*.

Landwehr, Richard. *Siegrunen No. 41*.

Lehmann, Rudolf. *Die Leibstandarte I*. J.J.Fedorowicz Publishing Ltd., 1987.

Lehmann, Rudolf. *Die Leibstandarte II*. J.J.Fedorowicz Publishing Ltd., 1988.

Lehmann, Rudolf. *Die Leibstandarte III*. J.J.Fedorowicz Publishing Ltd., 1990.

Messenger, Charles. *Hitler's Gladiator: The Life of Sepp Dietrich*. Brassays Defence Publishers,1988.

Meyer, Kurt. *Grenadiers*. J.J.Fedorowicz Publishers Ltd, 2001.

Moore, J.P. *Fuhrerliste Der Waffen-SS, Parts 1 to 4*. J.P.Moore Publishing, 2003.

Scheider, Jost. W. *Their Honor was Loyalty (2nd Edition)*. R. James Bender Publishing, 1993.

Springer, Heinrich. *Stationen eines Lebens in Krieg und Frieden*. Deutsche VerlagsGesellschaft, 1996.

Strassner, Peter. *European Volunteers, 5 SS Panzer Division Wiking*. J.J.Fedorowicz Publishing Ltd., 1998.

Trang, Charles. *The 'Florian Geyer' Division*. Heimdal Publishing, 2000.

Ullrich, Karl. *Like a Cliff in the Ocean, The History of the 3. SS-Panzer-Division "Totenkopf"*. J.J. Fedorowicz Publishing Ltd., 2002.

Weidinger, Otto. *Das Reich I, 2 SS Panzer Division Das Reich*. J.J.Fedorowicz Publishing Ltd., 1990.

Weidinger, Otto. *Das Reich II, 2 SS Panzer Division Das Reich*. J.J.Fedorowicz Publishing Ltd., 1995.

Weidinger, Otto. *Das Reich III, 2 SS Panzer Division Das Reich*. J.J.Fedorowicz Publishing Ltd., 2002.

Yerger, Mark. C. *Riding East, The SS Cavalry Brigade in Poland and Russia 1939-1942*. Schiffer Publishing Ltd., 1996.

Yerger, Mark. C. *Waffen-SS Commanders, Volume 1, Augsberger to Kreutz*. Schiffer Publishing Ltd., 1997.

Yerger, Mark. C. *Waffen-SS Commanders, Volume 2, Kruger to Zimmermann*. Schiffer Publishing Ltd., 1999.

Also: Various letters and face-to-face interviews with surviving *Kameraden* of the various *Divisions* and other units of the *Waffen-SS* from 1998 to 2007.